PRAISE FOR

Dracula

"James Tynion IV and Martin Simmonds have created the *Dracula* comic I've
wanted all my life and you're gonna love it."
– **Robert Kirkman** *(The Walking Dead, Invincible)*

"Tynion & Simmonds craft a what-could-have-been sex-horror nightmare that's
bloodier than Herschel Gordon Lewis but somehow as gorgeous as a
Guillermo del Toro film"
– **Patton Oswalt**

"The writing is as rich and evocative as you'd expect from James, and backed
up by Martin's sumptuous art it makes for a thrilling new take on an age old
character. Highly recommended."
– **Jock** *(Batman: One Dark Knight)*

"Dracula is a tune every horror fan knows. But in the hands of masters, it plays
like a symphony. Tynion's and Simmonds's *Dracula* is masterful in every sense
of the word."
– **Pornsak Pinochete** *(The Good Asian)*

"It's one of my favourite versions I've ever read of that classic tale.
Can't recommend it highly enough."
– **Michael Walsh** *(The Silver Coin)*

"Everything I could want out an adaptation of Bram Stoker's masterpiece.
It's incredibly paced, with a spectacular sense of atmosphere, and amazing
compositions."
– **Riley Rossmo** *(Harley Quinn)*

"...I LOVE the Universal Monsters...needless to say, James Tynion IV and Martin
Simmonds don't miss."
– **Kyle Starks** *(I Hate This Place)*

"Both faithful to the Bram Stoker original, and capable of mining new psychic
terrors, this adaptation will consume you from page one."
– **AIPT Comics**

"Martin Simmonds' depiction of Universal's Dracula is nothing
short of stunning."
– **ComicBook.com**

"*Dracula* pays the ultimate respect to the Universal Monsters version of the story
through this blood-soaked love letter."
– **CBR**

"This is working its way into a top 5 book of the year."
– **Nerd Initiative**

"*Universal Monsters: Dracula* is a grand start to what promises to be a great line
of comics."
– **Screen Rant**

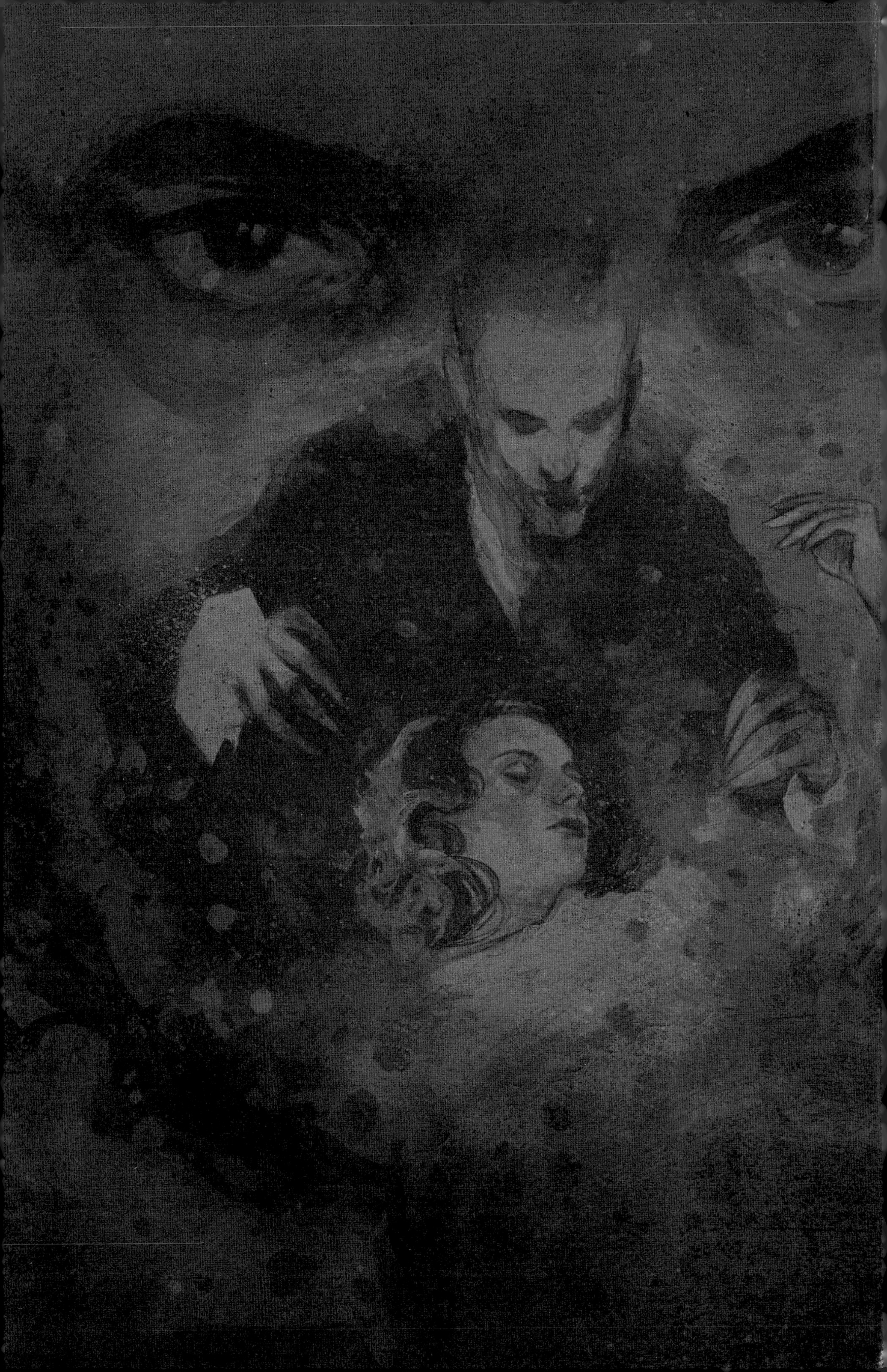

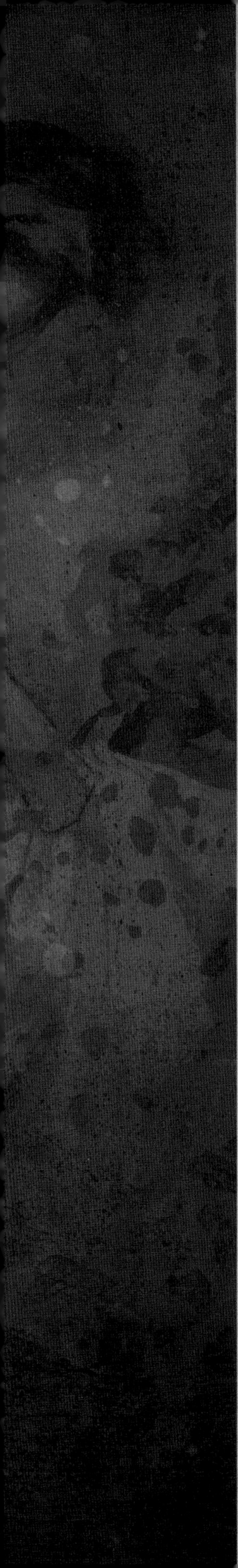

SKYBOUND ENTERTAINMENT AND **IMAGE COMICS** PRESENT

JAMES TYNION IV
WRITER

MARTIN SIMMONDS
ARTIST

RUS WOOTON
LETTERER

UNIVERSAL

MONSTERS

Dracula

MARTIN SIMMONDS • STEPHANIE PEPPER
COVERS

JILLIAN CRAB
DESIGNER

ALEX ANTONE
EDITOR

SPECIAL THANKS TO MIKE SUND, BARB LAYMAN, SUSAN WEBER, KELSEY PARROTTE, MARIANA GALVEZ, MEGAN STARTZ, HOLLY GOLINE, KELLY CANNON, MELISSA RODRIQUEZ, CONNIE SHAO, SHELBY BUTLER-SANTIEL, LAUREN PURNELL AND MADDIE MITCHELL.

FOR SKYBOUND ENTERTAINMENT • **ROBERT KIRKMAN** Chairman • **DAVID ALPERT** CEO • **SEAN MACKIEWICZ** SVP, Publisher • **ANDRES JUAREZ** Creative Director, Editorial • **ARUNE SINGH** VP, Brand, Editorial • **SHANNON MEEHAN** Senior Public Relations Manager • **ALEX ANTONE** Editorial Director **BEN ABERNATHY** Executive Editor • **AMANDA LAFRANCO** Managing Editor • **BLAKE KOBASHIGAWA** Senior Director, Buisness Development, Editorial **JILLIAN CRAB** Graphic Designer • **ASHBY FLORENCE** Production Artist • **RICHARD MERCADO** Production Artist • **ALEX HARGETT** Director of Brand, Editorial • **SARAH CLEMENTS** Brand Coordinator, Editorial • **JOELENA DESPARD** Brand Coordinator, Editorial • **DAN PETERSEN** Senior Director, Operations & Events • Foreign Rights & Licensing Inquiries: foreignlicensing@skybound.com • **SKYBOUND.COM**

FOR IMAGE COMICS, INC. • **ROBERT KIRKMAN** Chief Operating Officer • **ERIK LARSEN** Chief Financial Officer • **TODD MCFARLANE** President **MARC SILVESTRI** Chief Executive Officer • **JIM VALENTINO** Vice President • **ERIC STEPHENSON** Publisher / Chief Creative Officer • **NICOLE LAPALME** Vice President of Finance • **LEANNA CAUNTER** Accounting Analyst • **SUE KORPELA** Accounting & HR Manager • **MARGOT WOOD** Vice President of Book Market Sales • **LORELEI BUNJES** Vice President of Digital Strategy • **DIRK WOOD** Director of International Sales & Licensing • **RYAN BREWER** International Sales & Licensing Manager • **ALEX COX** Director of Direct Market Sales • **CHLOE RAMOS** Book Market & Library Sales Manager **EMILIO BAUTISTA** Digital Sales Coordinator • **JON SCHLAFFMAN** Specialty Sales Coordinator • **KAT SALAZAR** Vice President of PR & Marketing **DEANNA PHELPS** Marketing Design Manager • **DREW FITZGERALD** Marketing Content Associate • **HEATHER DOORNINK** Vice President of Production **DREW GILL** Art Director • **IAN BALDESSARI** Print Manager • **MELISSA GIFFORD** Content Manager • **ERIKA SCHNATZ** Senior Production Artist • **WESLEY GRIFFITH** Production Artist • **RICH FOWLKS** Production Artist • **IMAGECOMICS.COM**

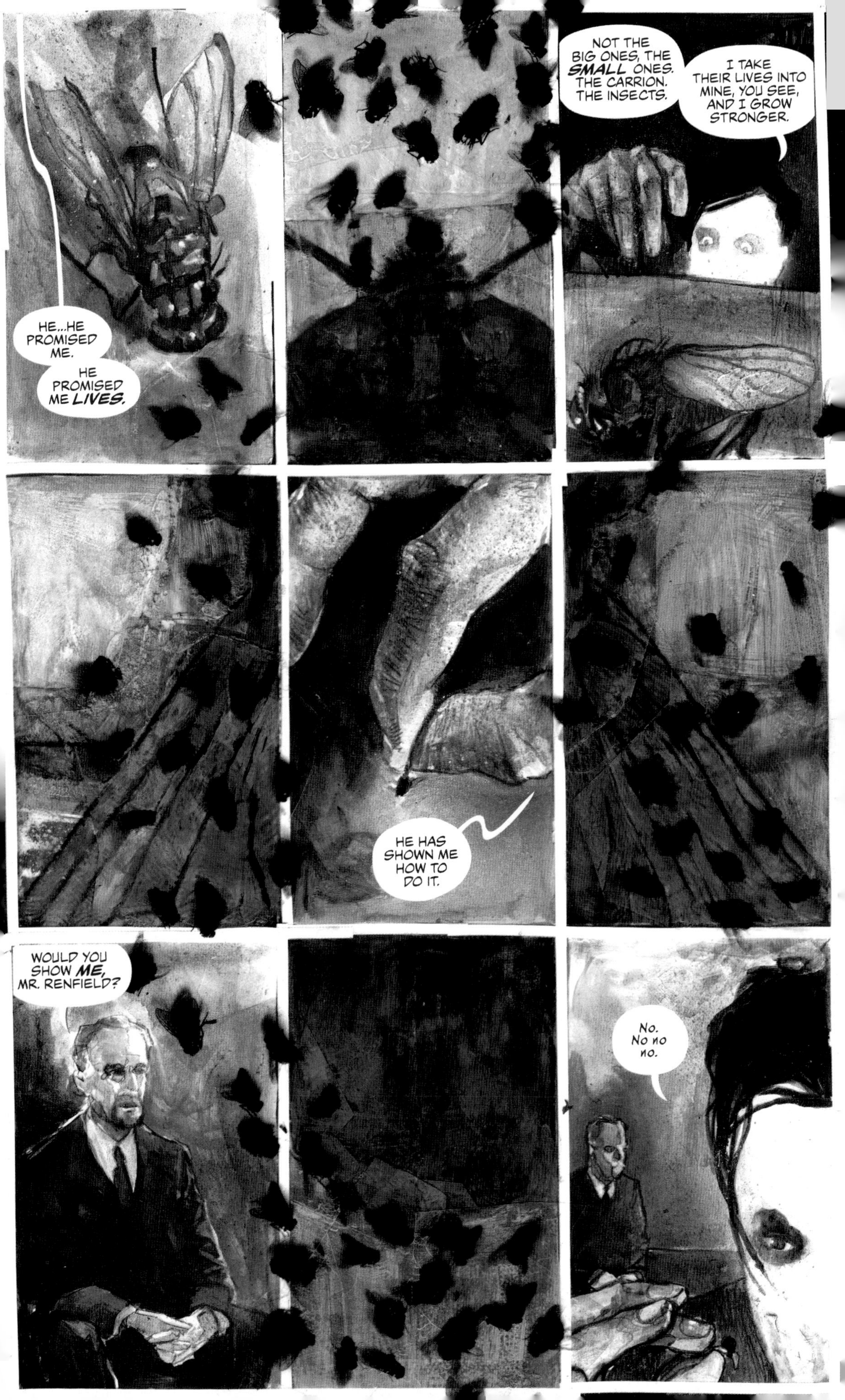
HE...HE PROMISED ME.
HE PROMISED ME LIVES.
NOT THE BIG ONES, THE SMALL ONES. THE CARRION. THE INSECTS.
I TAKE THEIR LIVES INTO MINE, YOU SEE, AND I GROW STRONGER.
HE HAS SHOWN ME HOW TO DO IT.
WOULD YOU SHOW ME, MR. RENFIELD?
No. No no no.

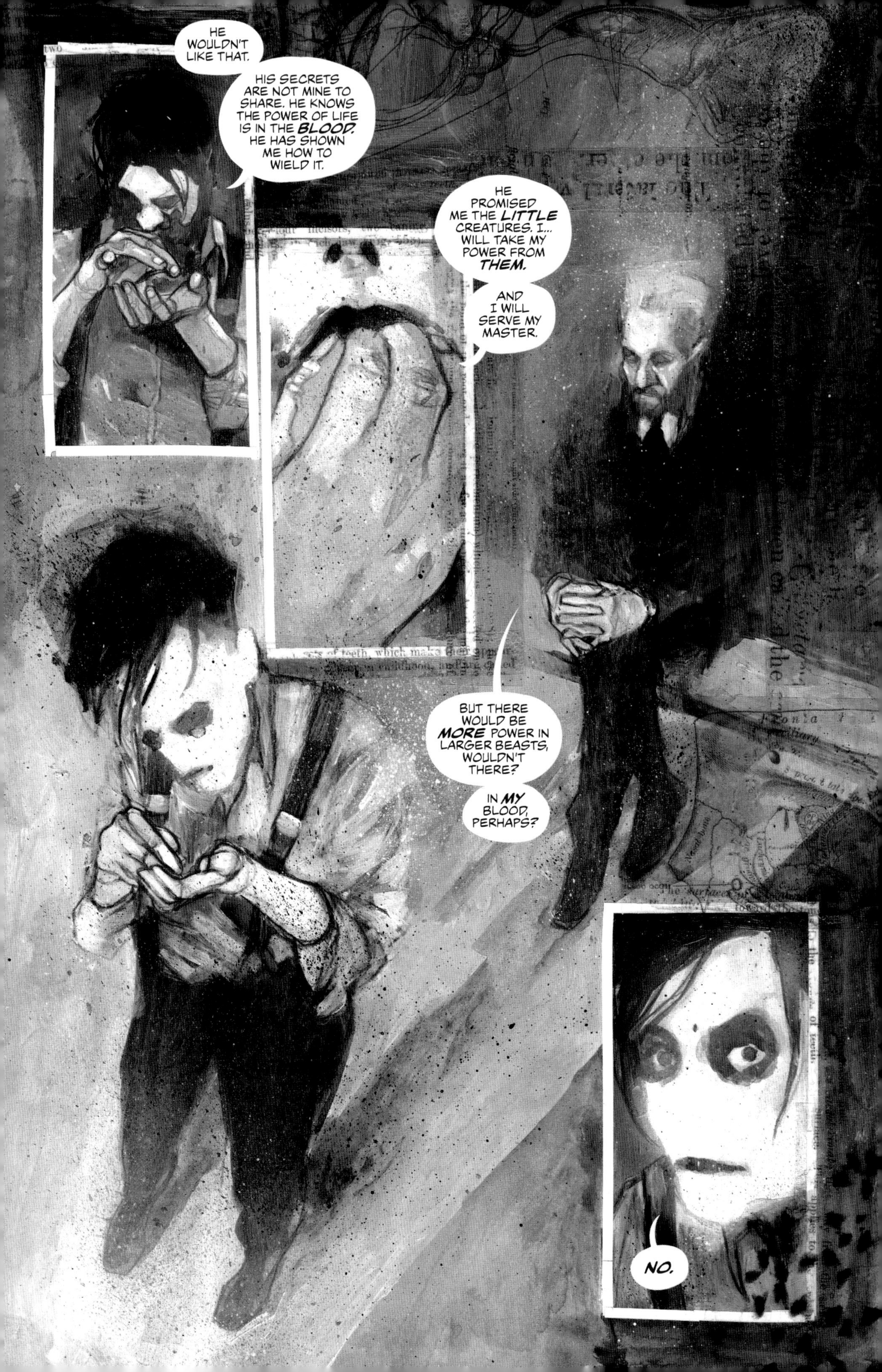
HE WOULDN'T LIKE THAT.
HIS SECRETS ARE NOT MINE TO SHARE. HE KNOWS THE POWER OF LIFE IS IN THE BLOOD. HE HAS SHOWN ME HOW TO WIELD IT.
HE PROMISED ME THE LITTLE CREATURES. I... WILL TAKE MY POWER FROM THEM.
AND I WILL SERVE MY MASTER.
BUT THERE WOULD BE MORE POWER IN LARGER BEASTS, WOULDN'T THERE?
IN MY BLOOD, PERHAPS?
NO.

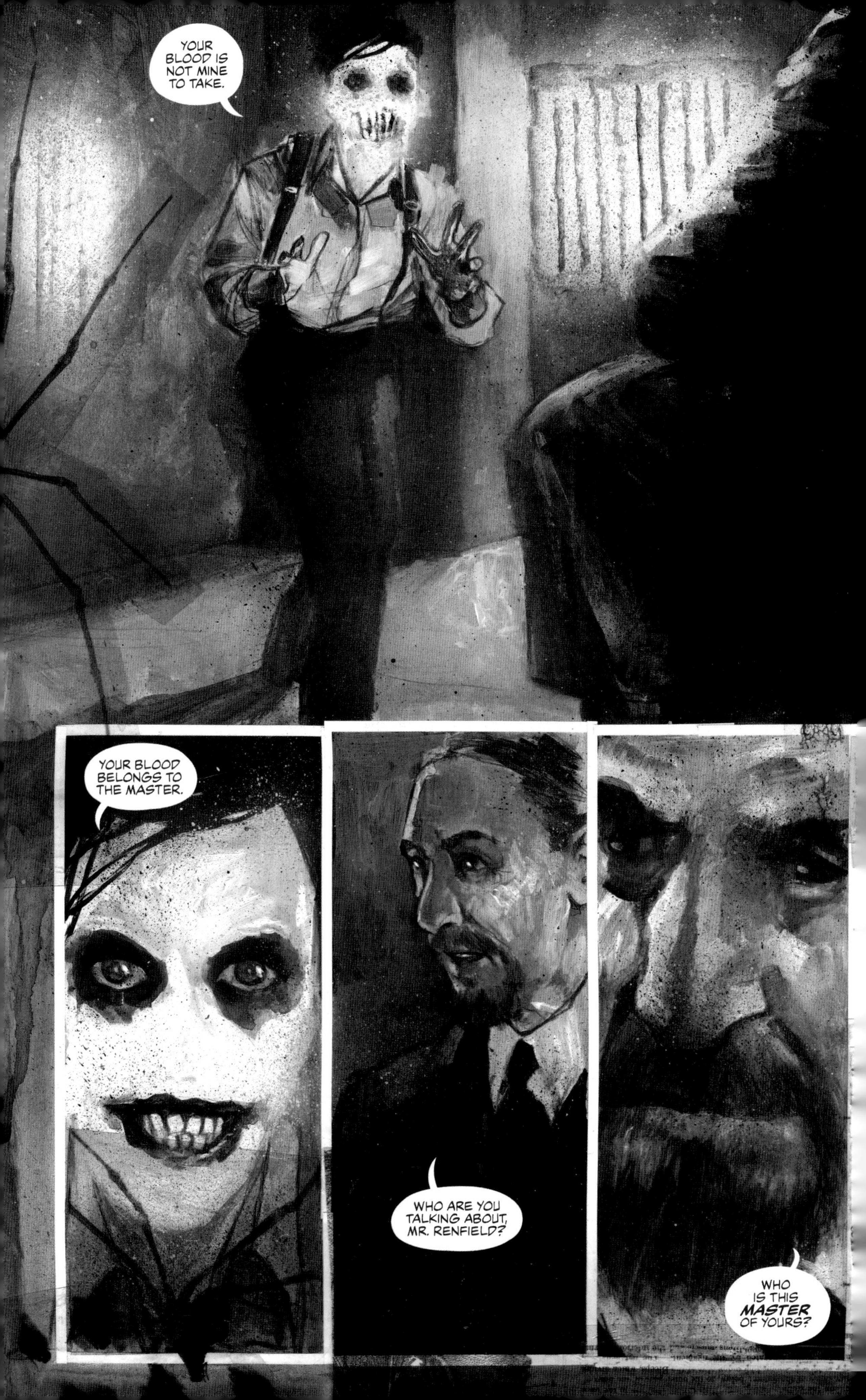
YOUR BLOOD IS NOT MINE TO TAKE.
YOUR BLOOD BELONGS TO THE MASTER.
WHO ARE YOU TALKING ABOUT, MR. RENFIELD?
WHO IS THIS *MASTER* OF YOURS?

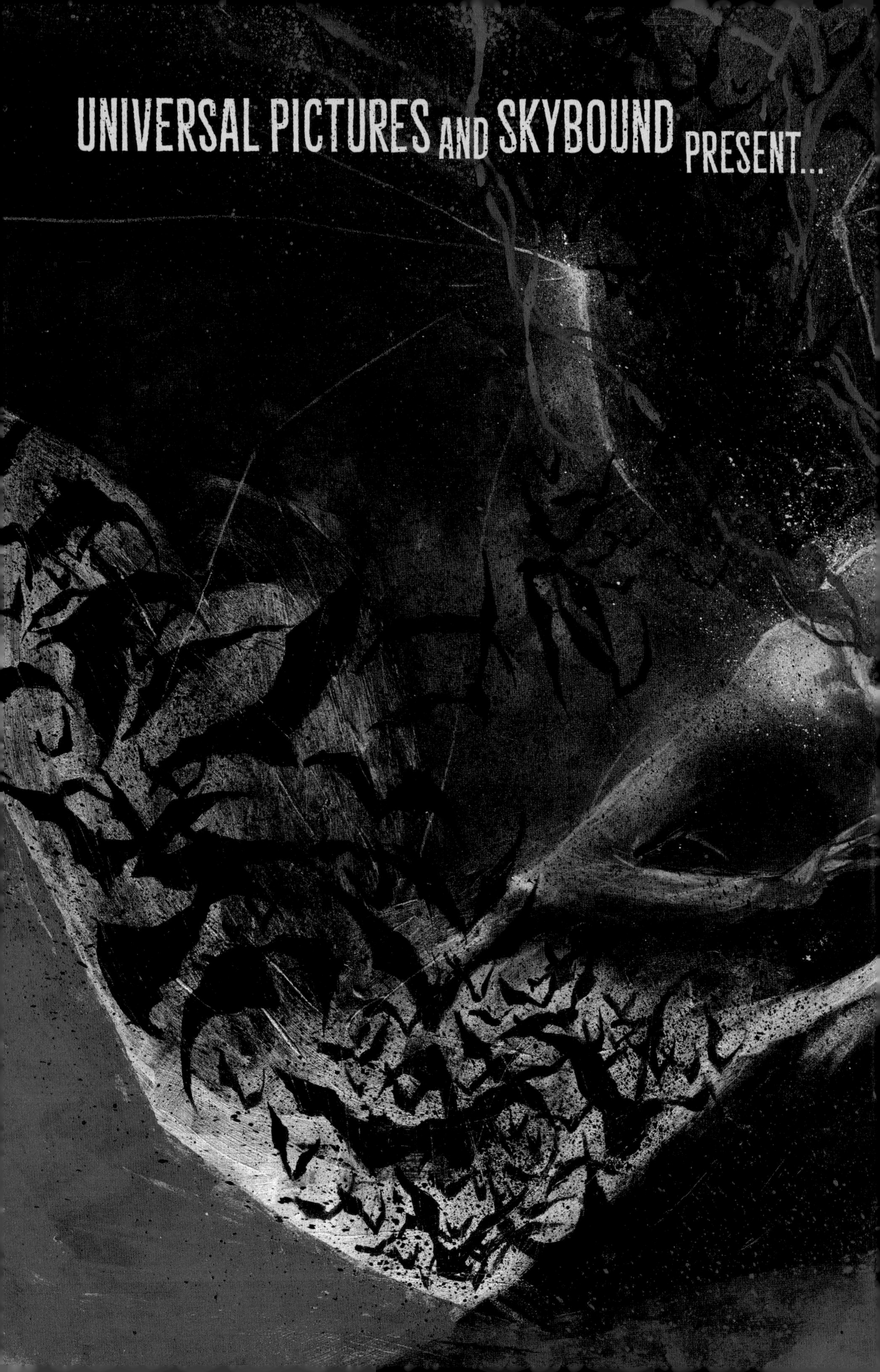
UNIVERSAL PICTURES AND SKYBOUND PRESENT...

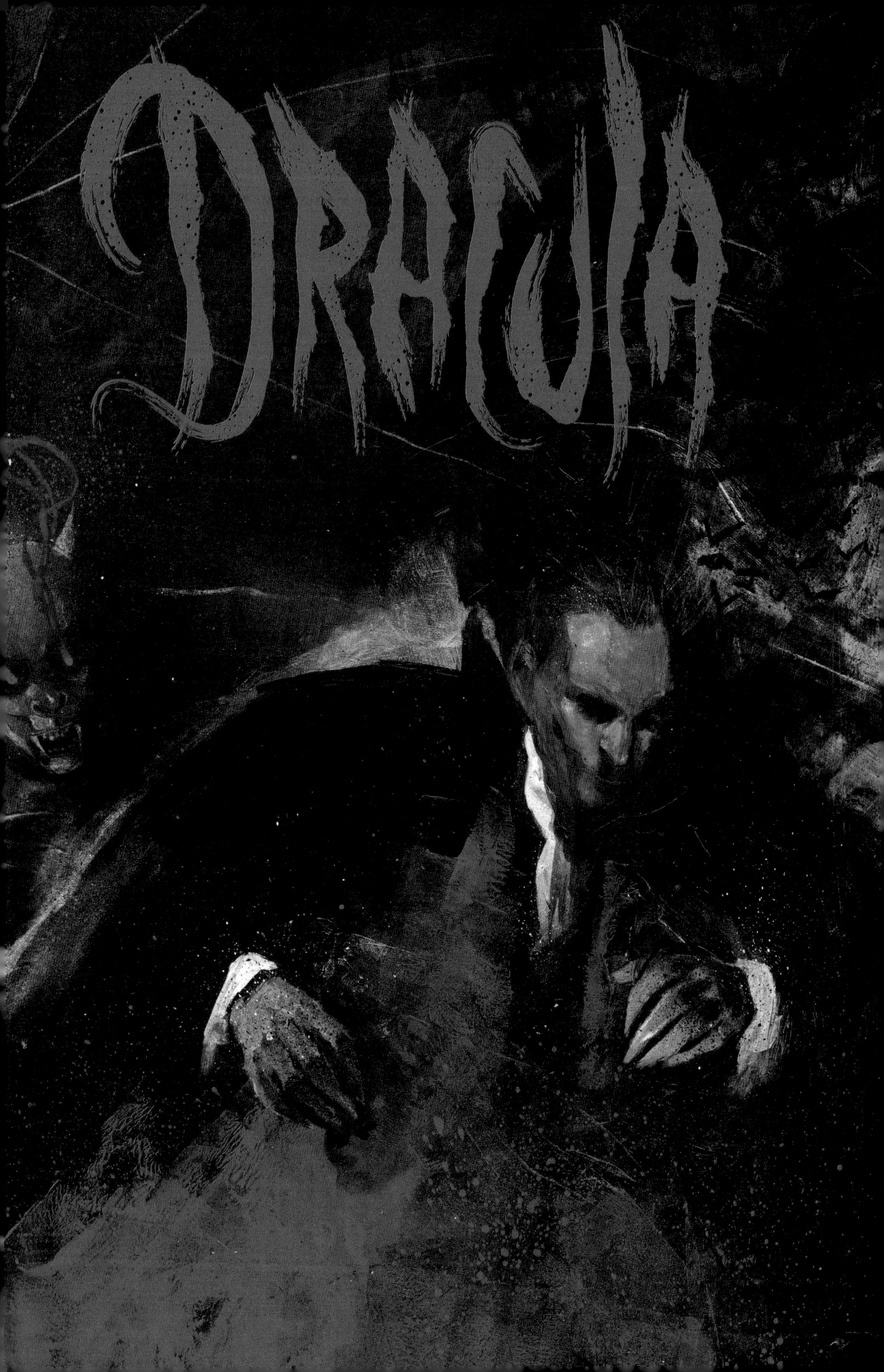
DRACULA

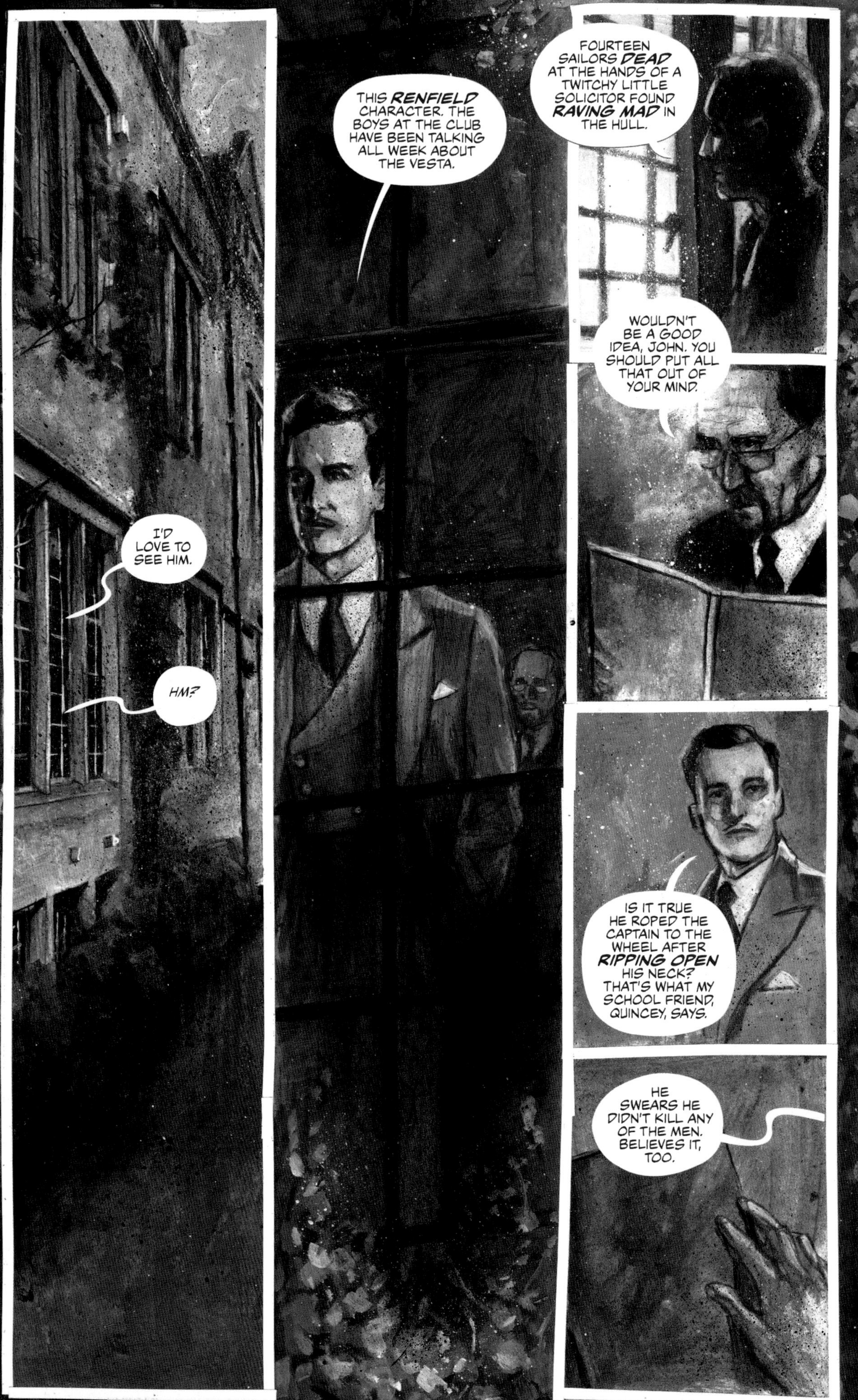
THIS RENFIELD CHARACTER. THE BOYS AT THE CLUB HAVE BEEN TALKING ALL WEEK ABOUT THE VESTA.
FOURTEEN SAILORS DEAD AT THE HANDS OF A TWITCHY LITTLE SOLICITOR FOUND RAVING MAD IN THE HULL.
I'D LOVE TO SEE HIM.
HM?
WOULDN'T BE A GOOD IDEA, JOHN. YOU SHOULD PUT ALL THAT OUT OF YOUR MIND.
IS IT TRUE HE ROPED THE CAPTAIN TO THE WHEEL AFTER RIPPING OPEN HIS NECK? THAT'S WHAT MY SCHOOL FRIEND, QUINCEY, SAYS.
HE SWEARS HE DIDN'T KILL ANY OF THE MEN. BELIEVES IT, TOO.

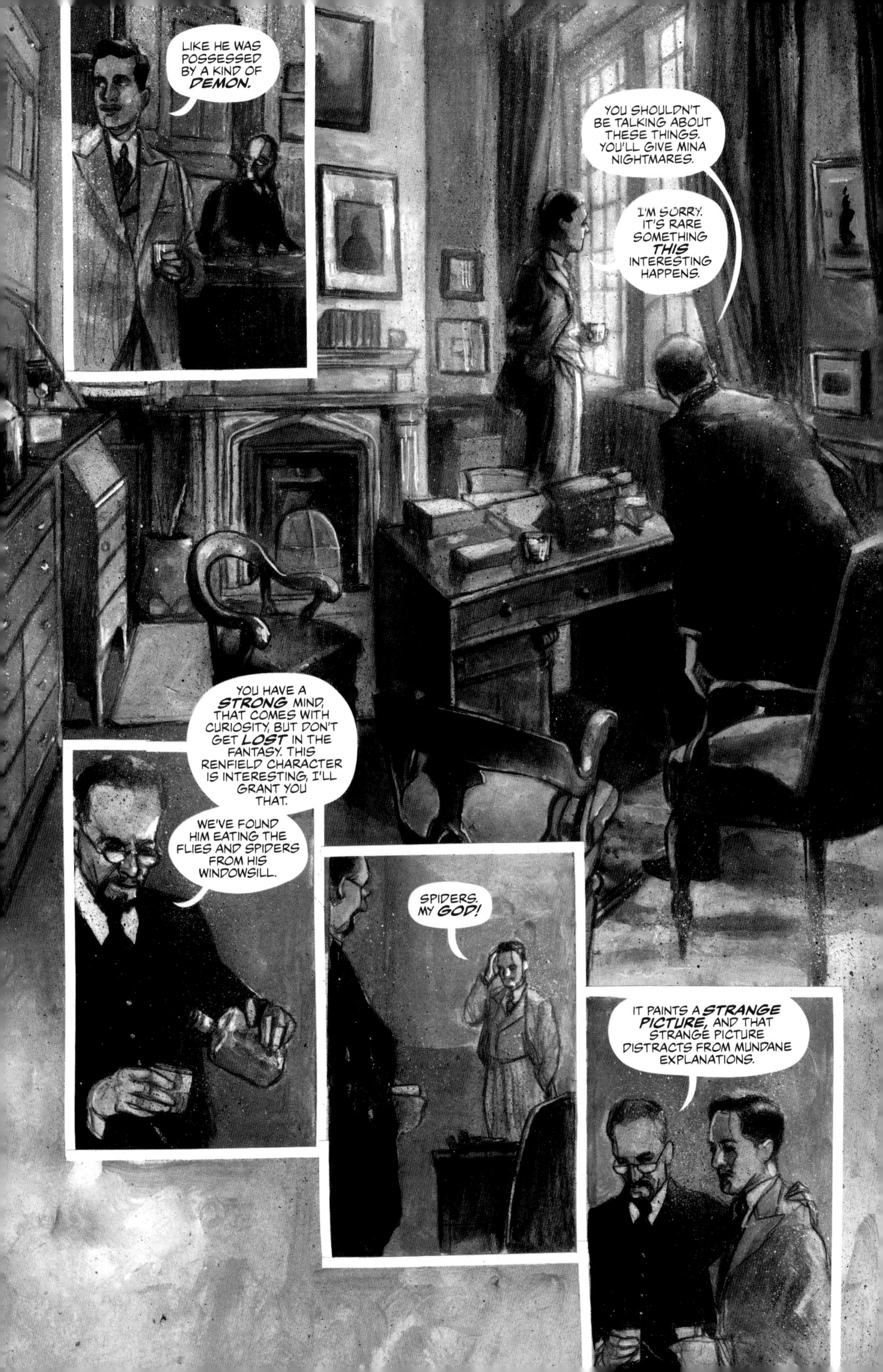
LIKE HE WAS POSSESSED BY A KIND OF DEMON.
YOU SHOULDN'T BE TALKING ABOUT THESE THINGS. YOU'LL GIVE MINA NIGHTMARES.
I'M SORRY. IT'S RARE SOMETHING THIS INTERESTING HAPPENS.
YOU HAVE A STRONG MIND, THAT COMES WITH CURIOSITY, BUT DON'T GET LOST IN THE FANTASY. THIS RENFIELD CHARACTER IS INTERESTING, I'LL GRANT YOU THAT.
WE'VE FOUND HIM EATING THE FLIES AND SPIDERS FROM HIS WINDOWSILL.
SPIDERS. MY GOD!
IT PAINTS A STRANGE PICTURE, AND THAT STRANGE PICTURE DISTRACTS FROM MUNDANE EXPLANATIONS.

I SUSPECT WE'RE NOT EVEN DEALING WITH A SICKNESS OF THE *MIND.*

HIS PALLID SKIN AND STRANGE HUNGER--I THINK HE MAY HAVE SOME KIND OF *BLOOD DISEASE,* CONTRACTED IN HIS JOURNEY TO TRANSYLVANIA.

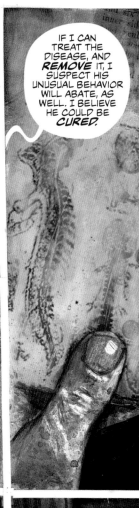

IF I CAN TREAT THE DISEASE, AND *REMOVE* IT, I SUSPECT HIS UNUSUAL BEHAVIOR WILL ABATE, AS WELL. I BELIEVE HE COULD BE *CURED.*

YOU'D WANT A MAN WHO DID *ALL THAT* TO INNOCENT SAILORS TO *WALK FREE?*

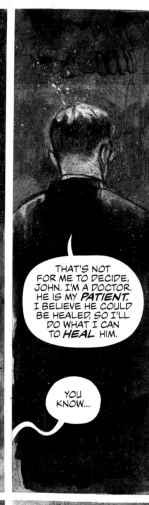

THAT'S NOT FOR ME TO DECIDE, JOHN. I'M A DOCTOR. HE IS MY *PATIENT.* I BELIEVE HE COULD BE HEALED, SO I'LL DO WHAT I CAN TO *HEAL* HIM.

YOU KNOW...

THERE'S THIS *MAD* OLD PROFESSOR WHO COMES DOWN TO THE CLUB. HE SITS AT THE FIRE AND TELLS *GHOST STORIES* ABOUT STRANGE FOLK LEGENDS FROM THE EAST.

ABOUT *GHOULS* AND *WEREWOLVES* AND THE SORT. HE HAD A LOT TO SAY ABOUT THE SAILOR'S NECK. TOLD US ALL TO CARRY A *CRUCIFIX* IN OUR POCKETS.

NOW, JOHN. I'VE ALWAYS RESPECTED YOU FOR HAVING A SERIOUS MIND. DON'T LISTEN TO THAT KIND OF *RUBBISH.*

I *HAVE* A SERIOUS MIND, I SWEAR. BUT I *DO* LOVE A GOOD STORY.

THINK OF MY DAUGHTER. THINK OF *MINA,* AND PUT IT TO REST.

I TOOK THE NOTES FROM MY FATHER'S OFFICE.
FROM WHEN HE SPOKE TO THE CONSTABLE ABOUT THE FOUL CREATURE RENFIELD AND HIS EVIL DEEDS.
I'M CURIOUS. AREN'T YOU, LUCY?
MINA! YOU'RE THE DEVIL IN THE FLESH!
OF COURSE I'M BLOODY CURIOUS. TELL ME THE WORST BIT OF IT. THE MOST HORRIBLE THING.
THEY SAY THE CAPTAIN'S THROAT WAS RIPPED OPEN, NOT WITH A SERRATED EDGE, BUT BY SOMETHING'S TEETH.
ANIMAL OR MAN, THEY COULD NOT SAY.
OH, I COULD USE SOMEBODY RIPPING AT MY THROAT WITH THEIR TEETH.
LUCY!
OH, HUSH. TELL ME MORE.

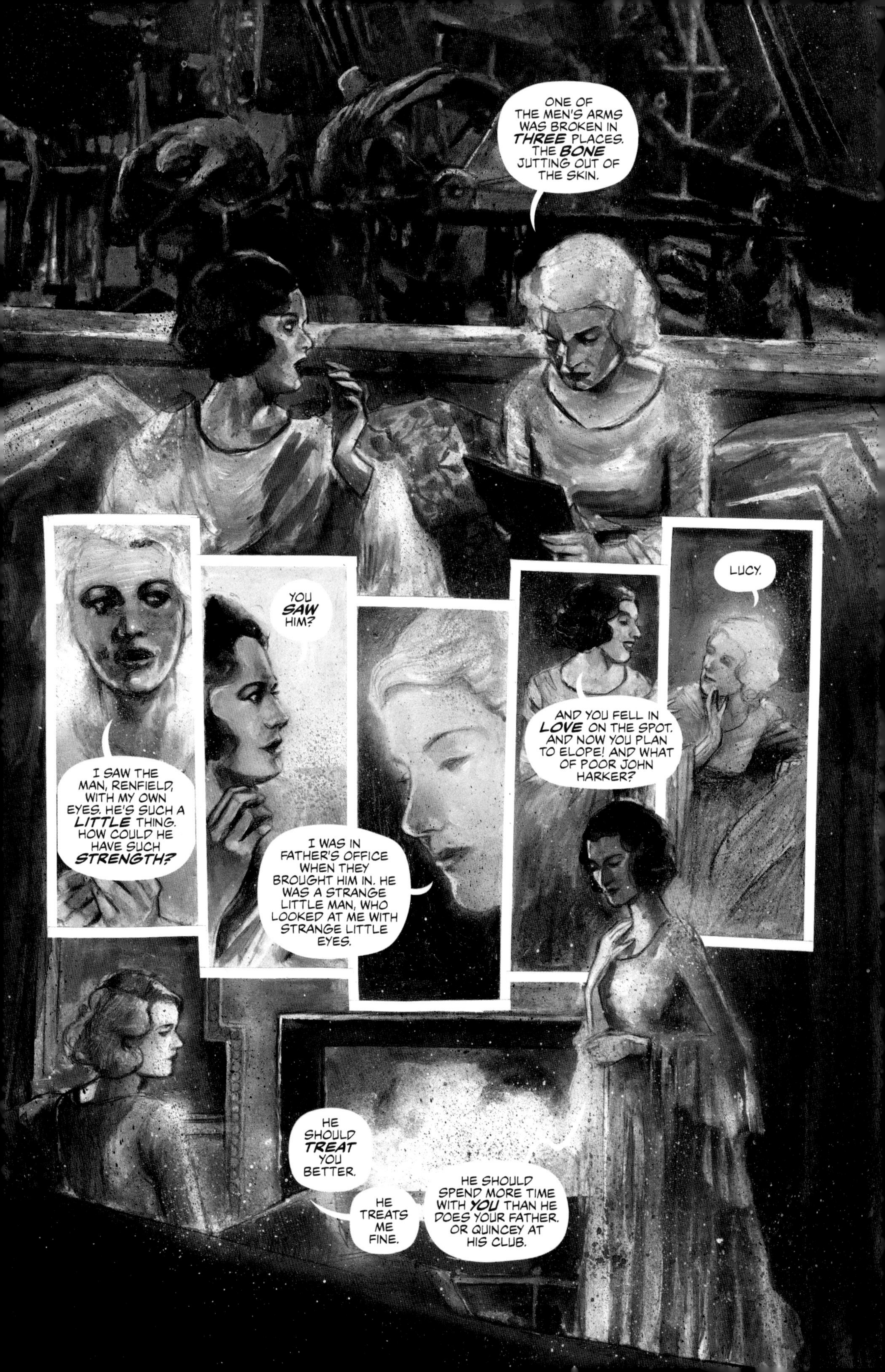
ONE OF THE MEN'S ARMS WAS BROKEN IN THREE PLACES. THE BONE JUTTING OUT OF THE SKIN.
I SAW THE MAN, RENFIELD, WITH MY OWN EYES. HE'S SUCH A LITTLE THING. HOW COULD HE HAVE SUCH STRENGTH?
YOU SAW HIM?
I WAS IN FATHER'S OFFICE WHEN THEY BROUGHT HIM IN. HE WAS A STRANGE LITTLE MAN, WHO LOOKED AT ME WITH STRANGE LITTLE EYES.
AND YOU FELL IN LOVE ON THE SPOT. AND NOW YOU PLAN TO ELOPE! AND WHAT OF POOR JOHN HARKER?
LUCY.
HE SHOULD TREAT YOU BETTER.
HE TREATS ME FINE.
HE SHOULD SPEND MORE TIME WITH YOU THAN HE DOES YOUR FATHER. OR QUINCEY AT HIS CLUB.

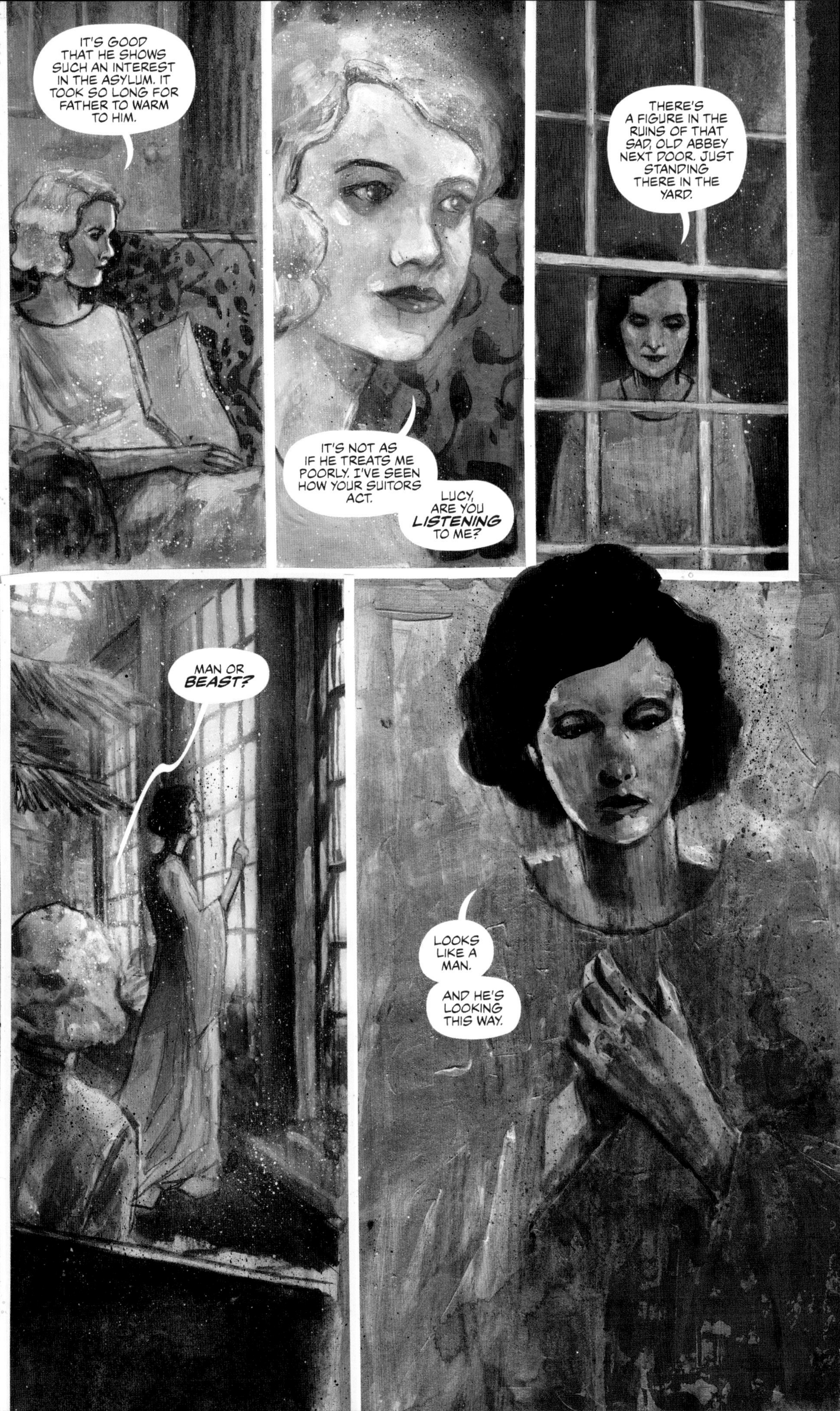
IT'S GOOD THAT HE SHOWS SUCH AN INTEREST IN THE ASYLUM. IT TOOK SO LONG FOR FATHER TO WARM TO HIM.
IT'S NOT AS IF HE TREATS ME POORLY. I'VE SEEN HOW YOUR SUITORS ACT.
LUCY, ARE YOU LISTENING TO ME?
THERE'S A FIGURE IN THE RUINS OF THAT SAD, OLD ABBEY NEXT DOOR. JUST STANDING THERE IN THE YARD.
MAN OR BEAST?
LOOKS LIKE A MAN.
AND HE'S LOOKING THIS WAY.

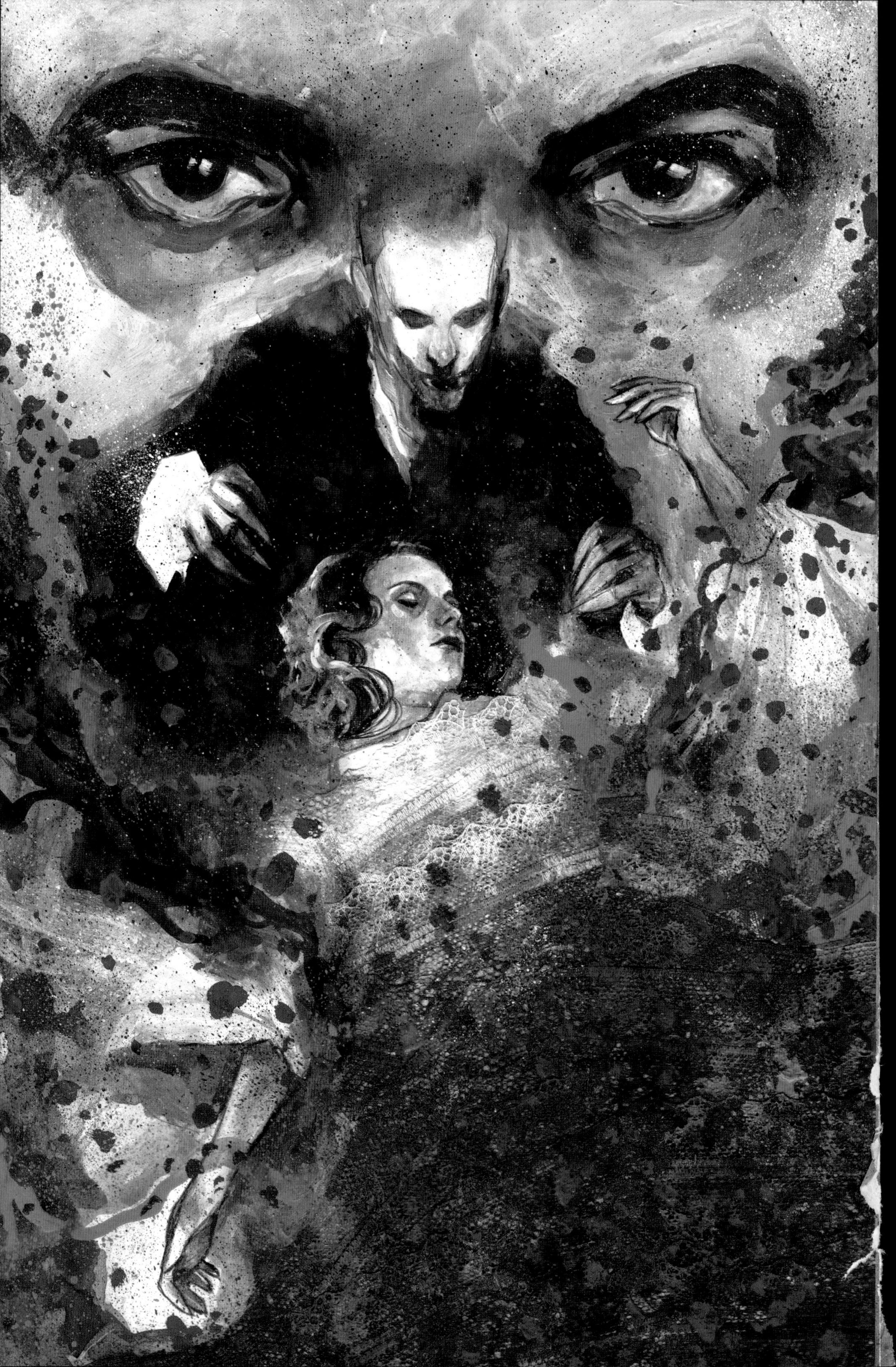

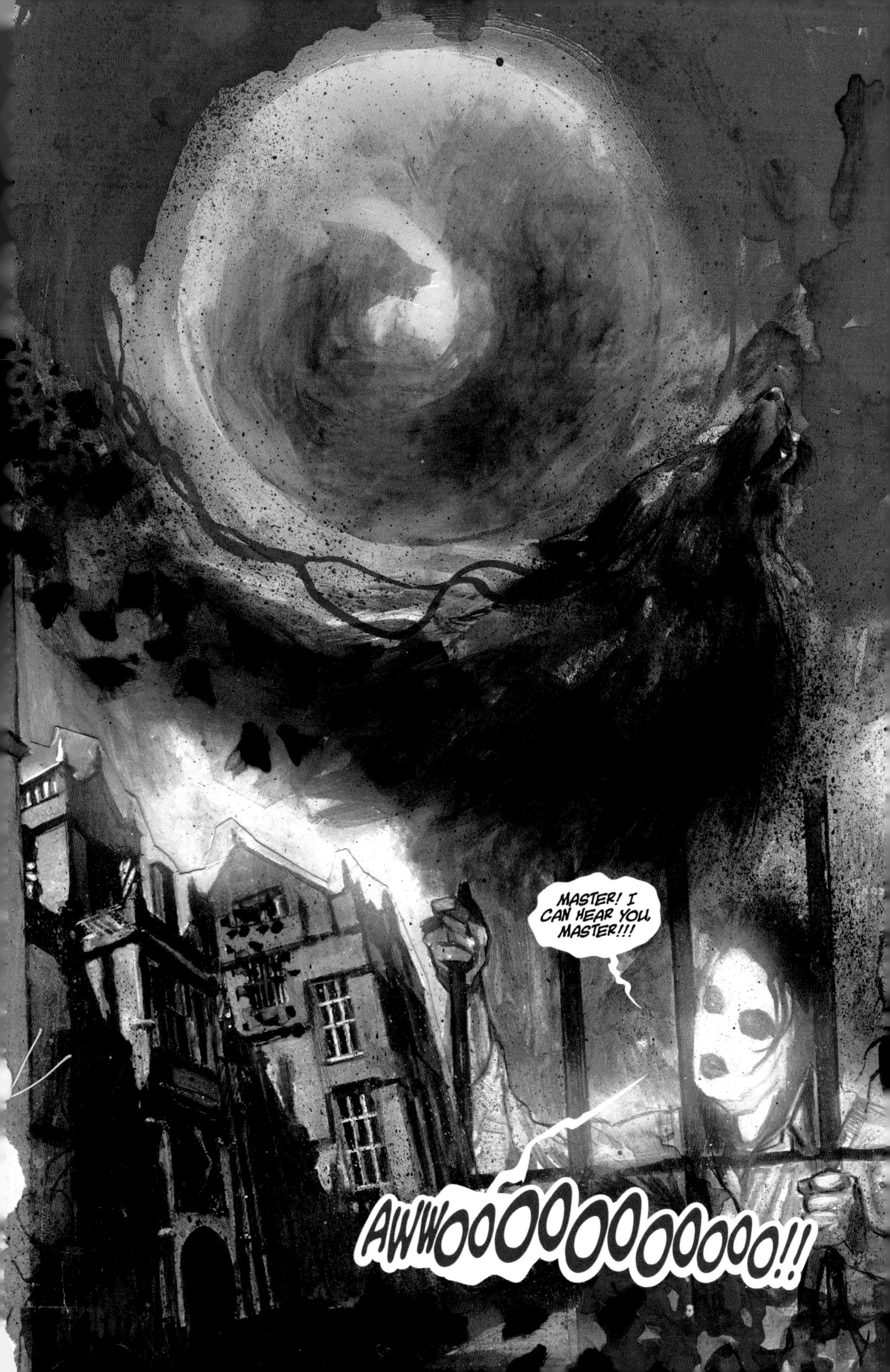
MASTER! I CAN HEAR YOU, MASTER!!!
AWWOOOOOOOOOOOO!!

AWWOOOOOOOOOOO!!
THE HELL ARE YOU ON ABOUT, LITTLE MAN!
IT IS WALPURGIS NIGHT! IT IS THE MASTER'S TIME!
NOW HE'LL FEAST ON THIS DARK CITY.

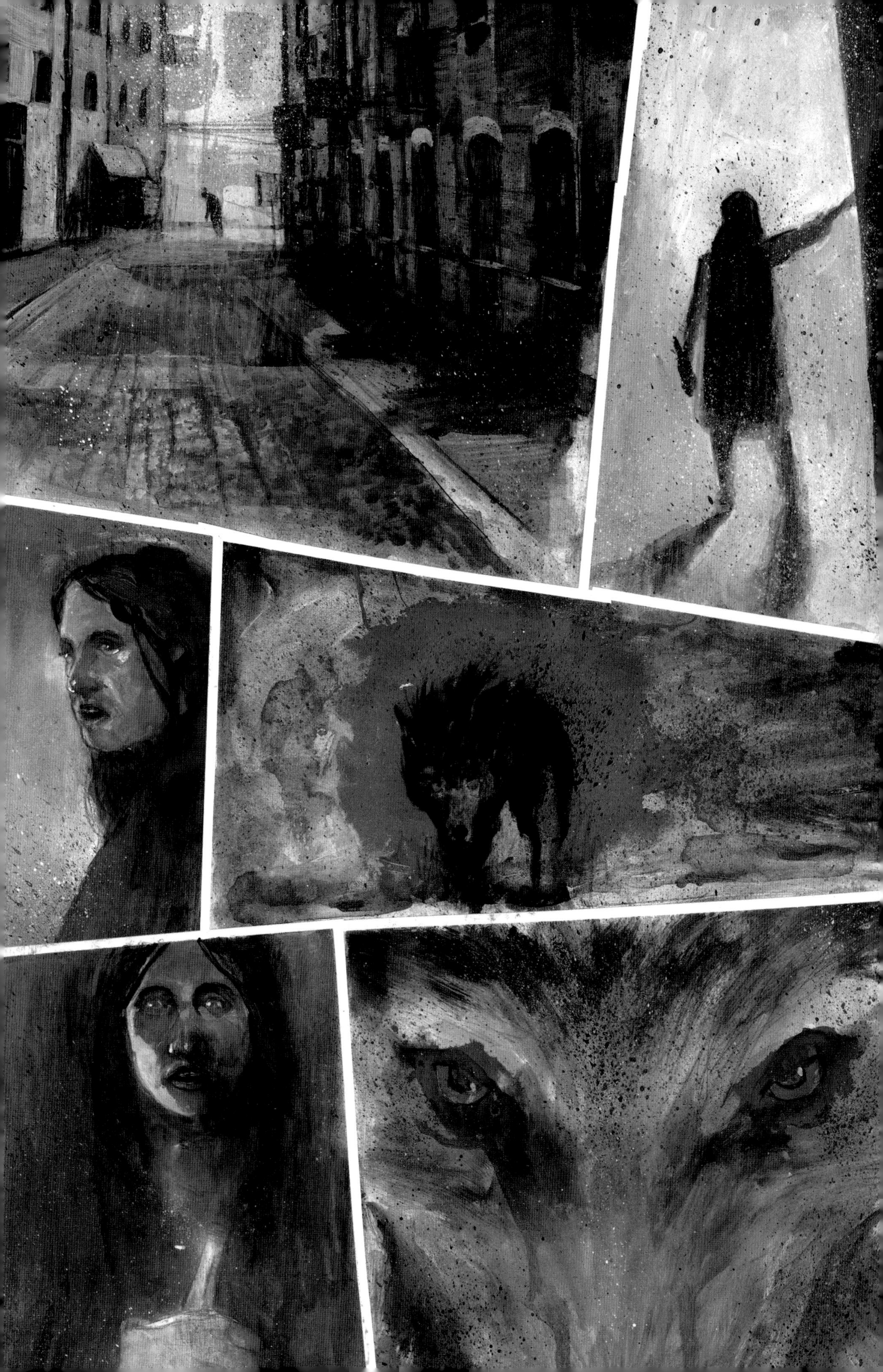

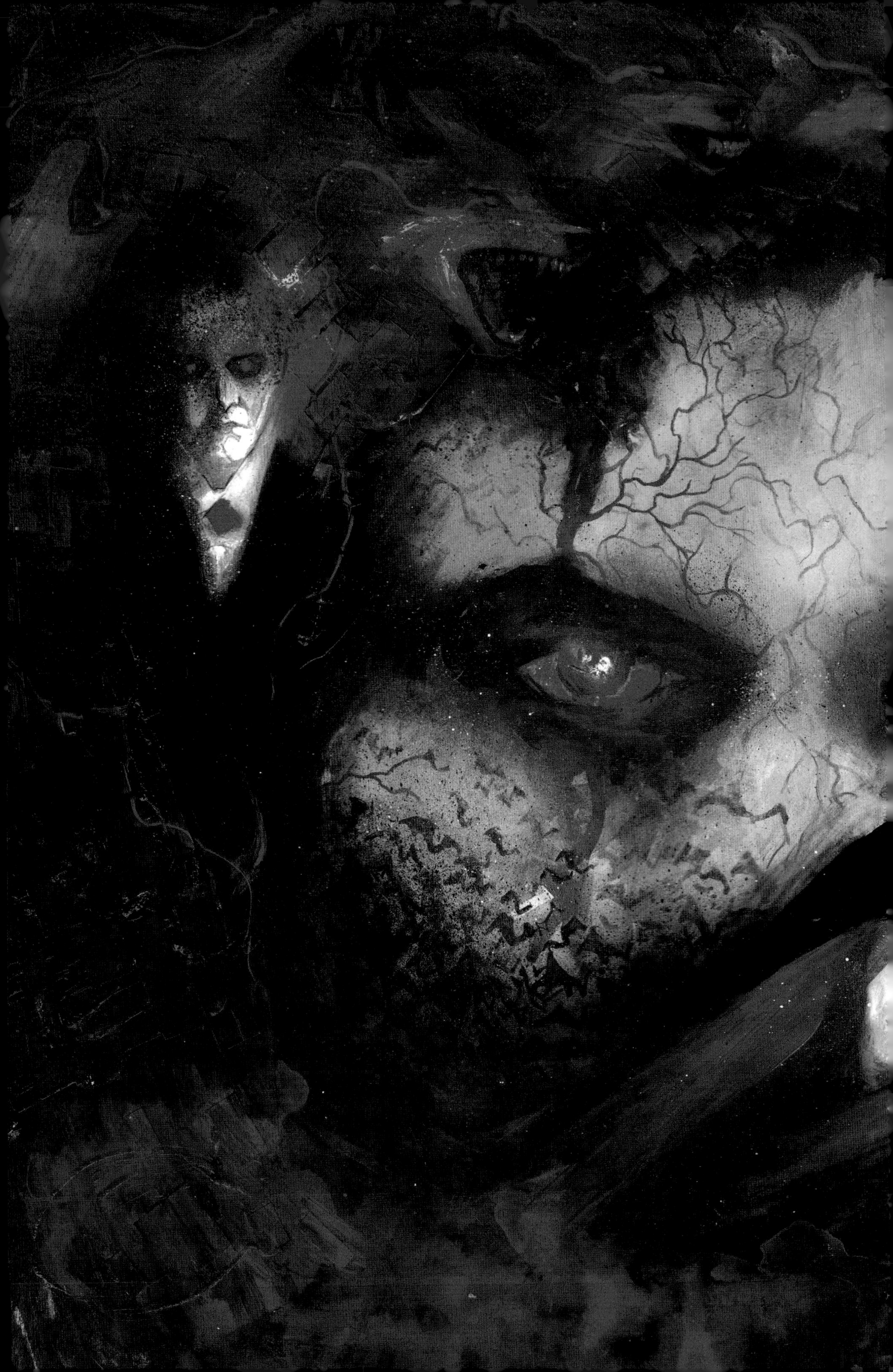

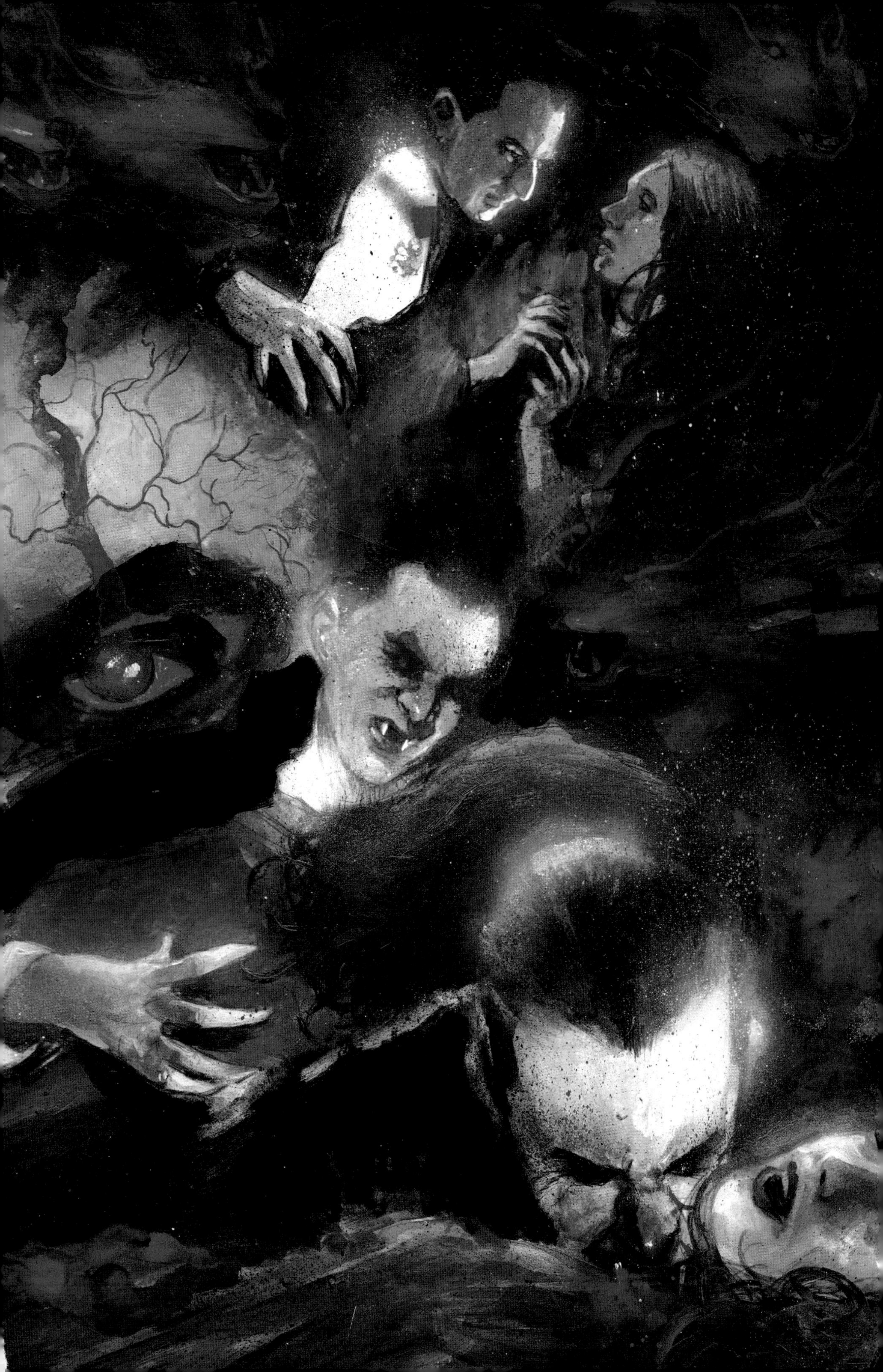

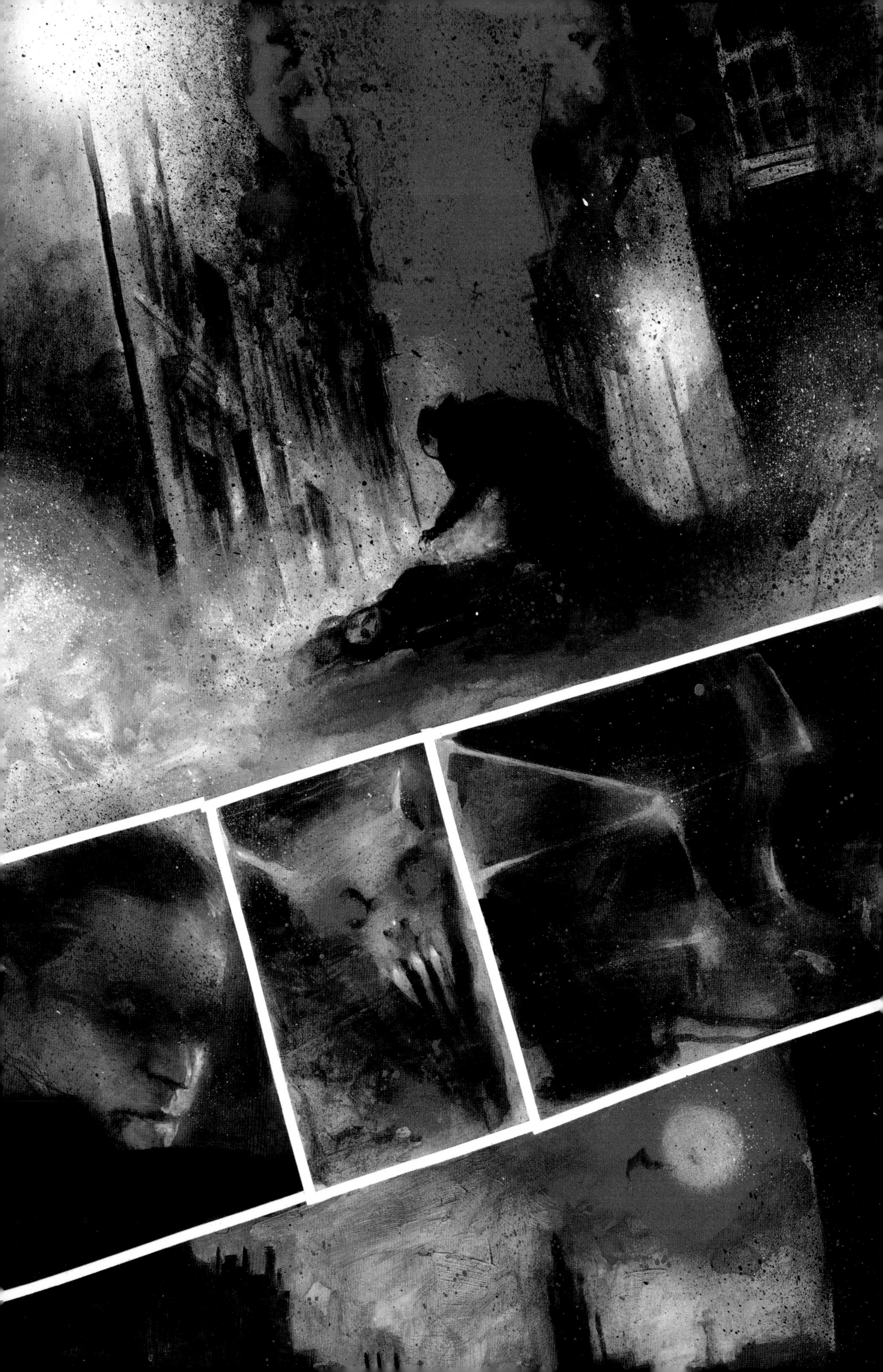

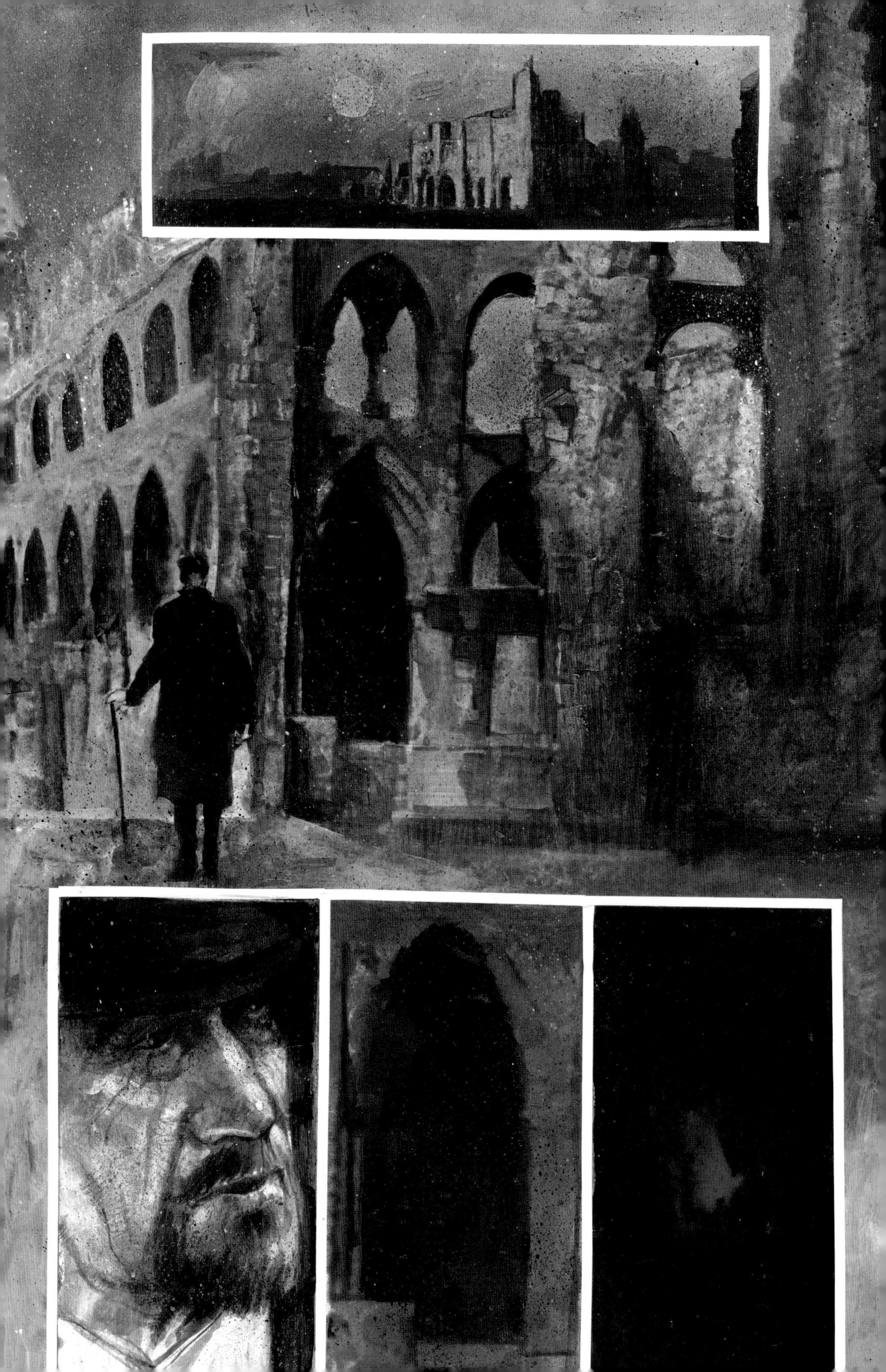

I HEARD WE HAD AN INTERESTING EVENING LAST NIGHT, MR. RENFIELD.

OH, THEY'RE *ALL* A BIT INTERESTING NOW. AND THEY'LL ONLY GET MORE INTERESTING.

THE MASTER GROWS MORE... *POWERFUL.*

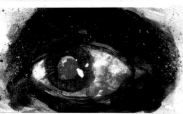

I CAN *FEEL* HIM. IN MY MIND. HIS THOUGHTS.

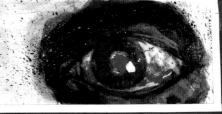

AND WHAT DOES YOUR MASTER THINK?

OH, HE DOESN'T THINK IN WORDS. AND IF THEY WERE WORDS, THEY'D BE...OLD *STRANGE* WORDS...IN A FORGOTTEN TONGUE. OR ONE UNKNOWN TO ME...

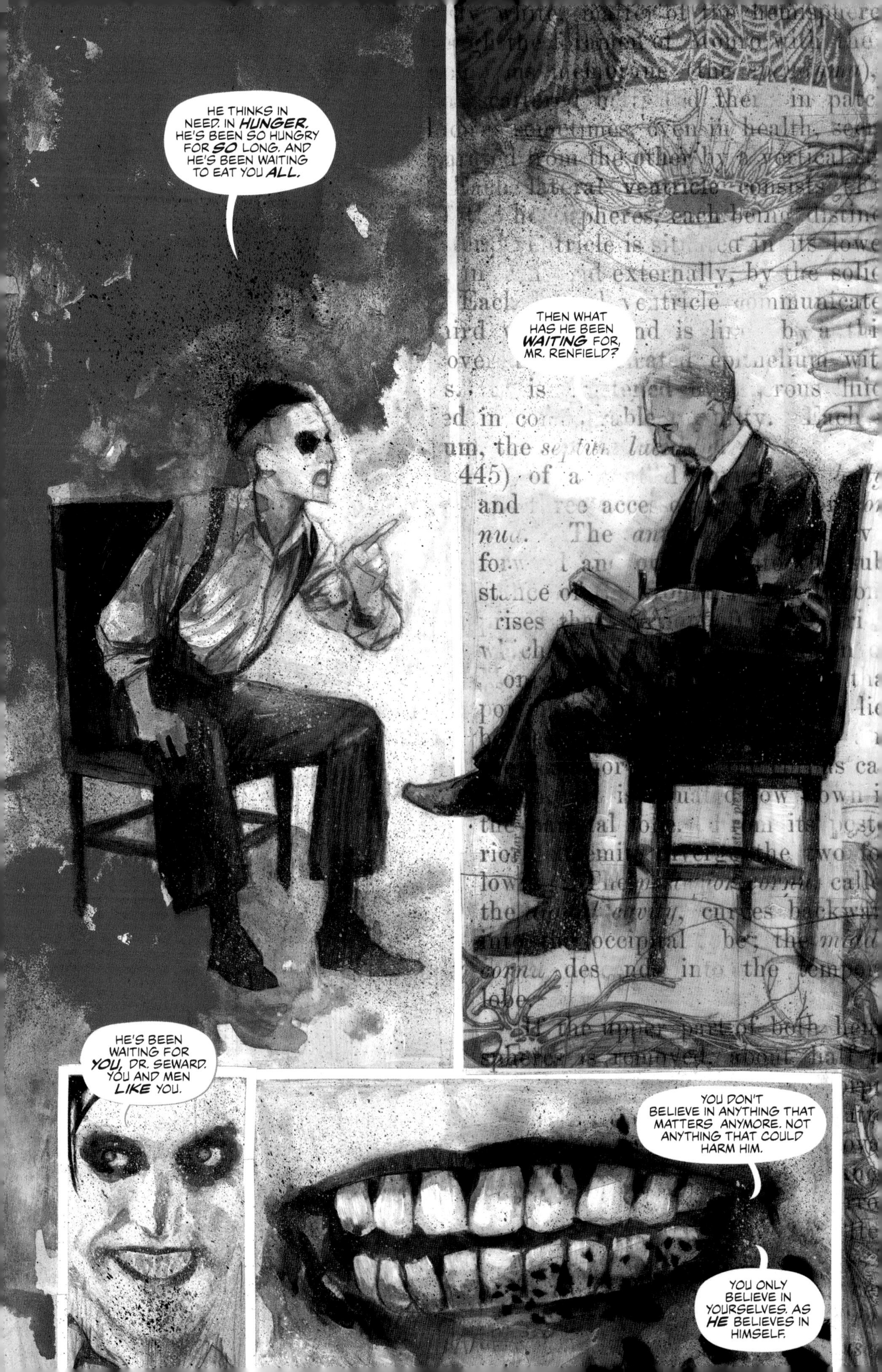
HE THINKS IN NEED. IN HUNGER. HE'S BEEN SO HUNGRY FOR SO LONG. AND HE'S BEEN WAITING TO EAT YOU ALL.
THEN WHAT HAS HE BEEN WAITING FOR, MR. RENFIELD?
HE'S BEEN WAITING FOR YOU, DR. SEWARD. YOU AND MEN LIKE YOU.
YOU DON'T BELIEVE IN ANYTHING THAT MATTERS ANYMORE. NOT ANYTHING THAT COULD HARM HIM.
YOU ONLY BELIEVE IN YOURSELVES. AS HE BELIEVES IN HIMSELF.

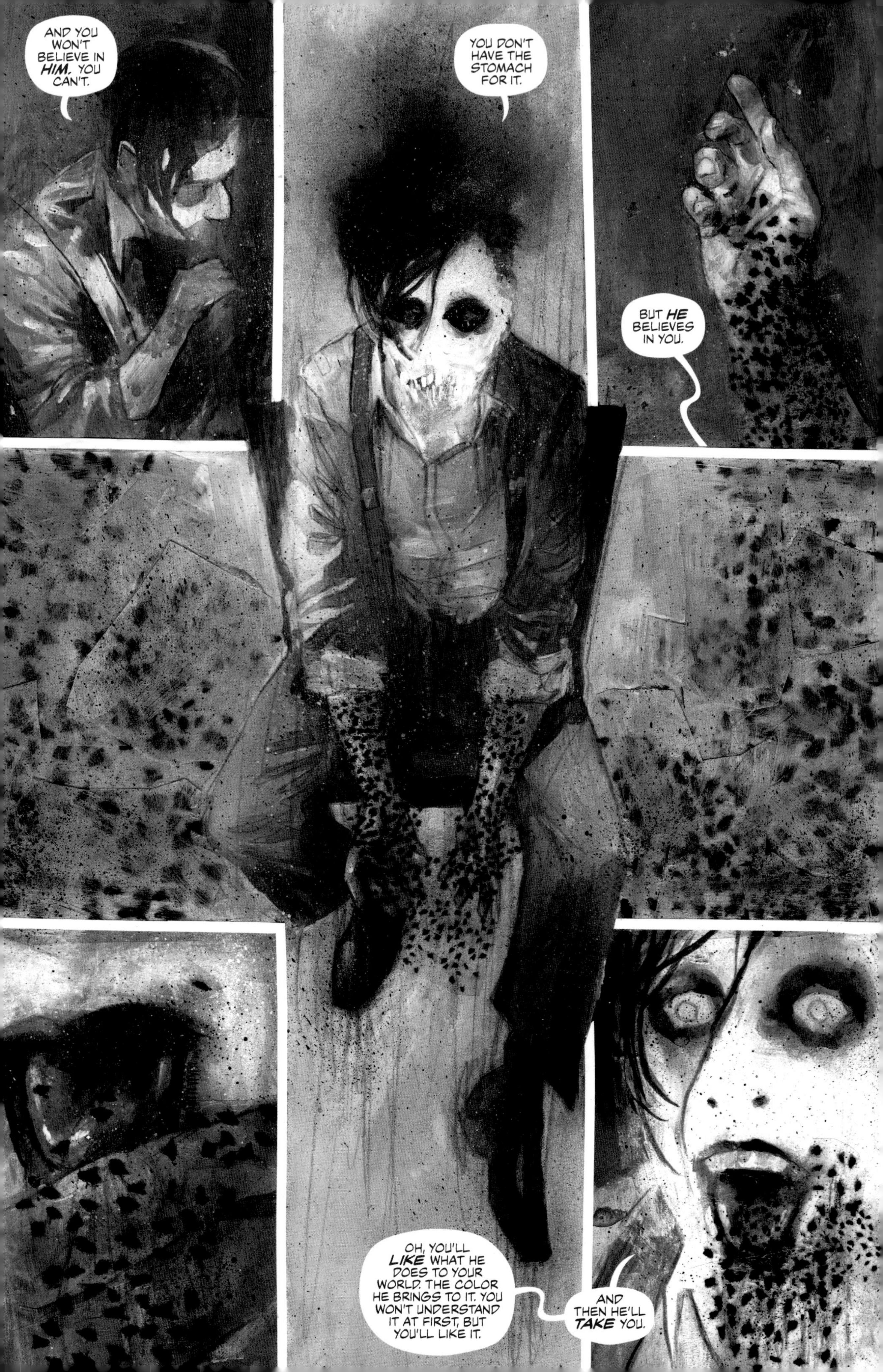
AND YOU WON'T BELIEVE IN HIM. YOU CAN'T.
YOU DON'T HAVE THE STOMACH FOR IT.
BUT HE BELIEVES IN YOU.
OH, YOU'LL LIKE WHAT HE DOES TO YOUR WORLD. THE COLOR HE BRINGS TO IT. YOU WON'T UNDERSTAND IT AT FIRST, BUT YOU'LL LIKE IT.
AND THEN HE'LL TAKE YOU.

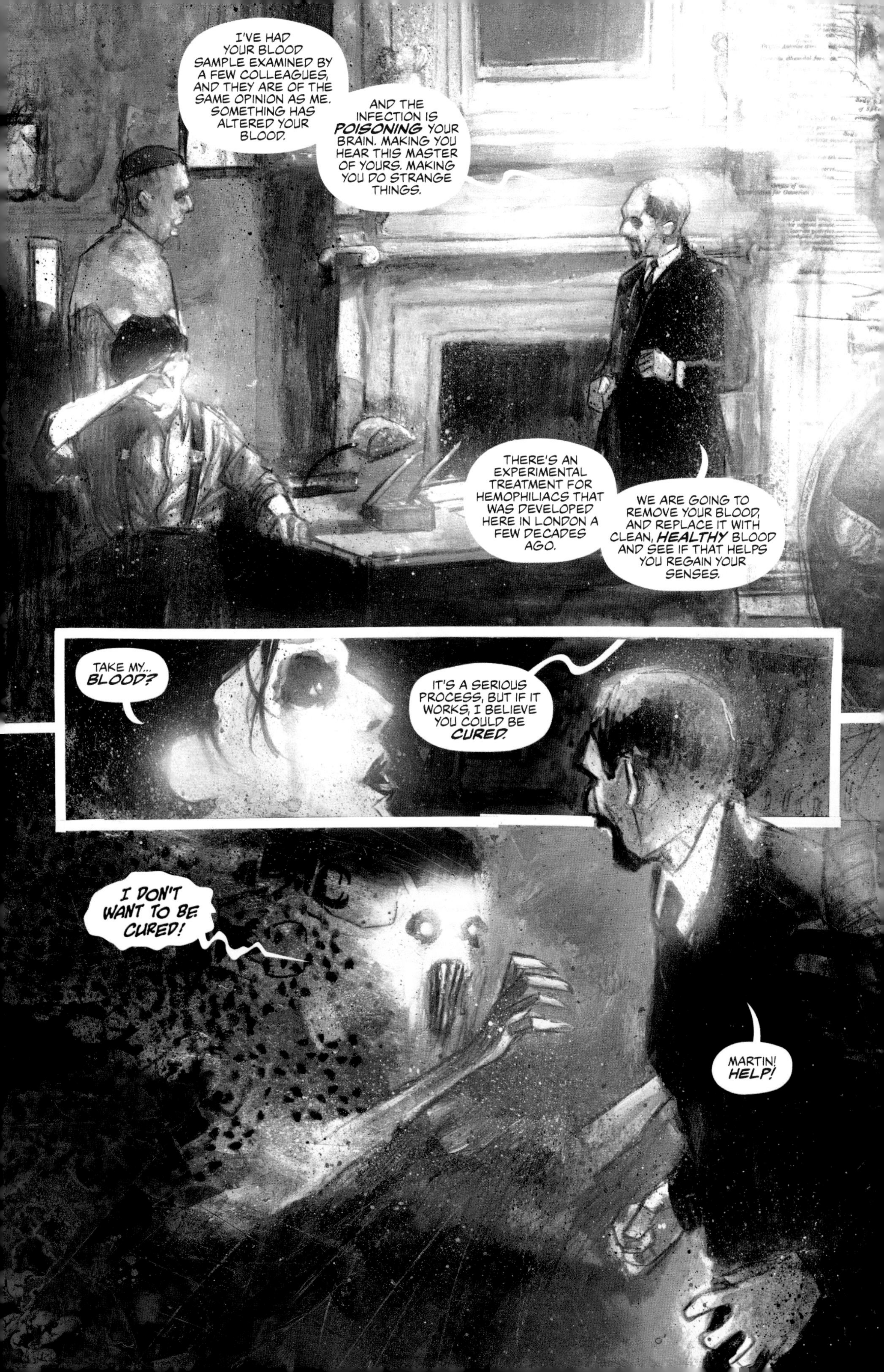
I'VE HAD YOUR BLOOD SAMPLE EXAMINED BY A FEW COLLEAGUES, AND THEY ARE OF THE SAME OPINION AS ME. SOMETHING HAS ALTERED YOUR BLOOD.
AND THE INFECTION IS POISONING YOUR BRAIN. MAKING YOU HEAR THIS MASTER OF YOURS. MAKING YOU DO STRANGE THINGS.
THERE'S AN EXPERIMENTAL TREATMENT FOR HEMOPHILIACS THAT WAS DEVELOPED HERE IN LONDON A FEW DECADES AGO.
WE ARE GOING TO REMOVE YOUR BLOOD, AND REPLACE IT WITH CLEAN, HEALTHY BLOOD AND SEE IF THAT HELPS YOU REGAIN YOUR SENSES.
TAKE MY... BLOOD?
IT'S A SERIOUS PROCESS, BUT IF IT WORKS, I BELIEVE YOU COULD BE CURED.
I DON'T WANT TO BE CURED!
MARTIN! HELP!

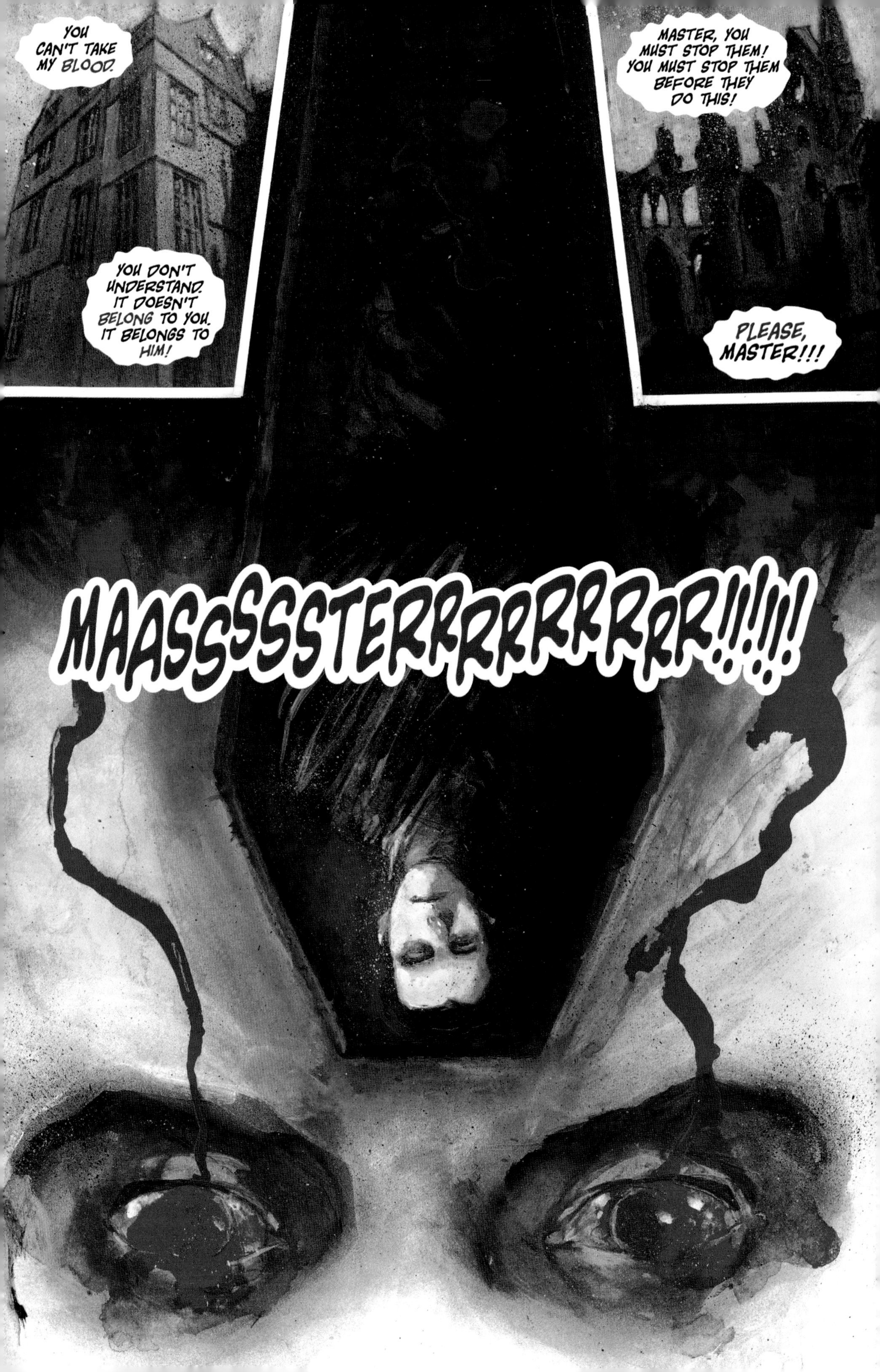
YOU CAN'T TAKE MY BLOOD.
YOU DON'T UNDERSTAND. IT DOESN'T BELONG TO YOU. IT BELONGS TO HIM!
MASTER, YOU MUST STOP THEM! YOU MUST STOP THEM BEFORE THEY DO THIS!
PLEASE, MASTER!!!
MAASSSSSTERRRRRRRRR!!!!!!

WHAT A BIZARRE MAN.

DID HE SAY HE WAS A *COUNT?* WHERE WAS IT HE SAID HE WAS FROM?

TRANSYLVANIA.

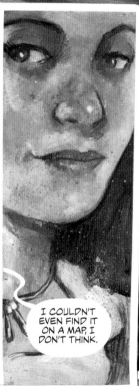

I COULDN'T EVEN FIND IT ON A MAP, I DON'T THINK.

FATHER, WHERE IS TRANSYLVANIA?

VERY FAR FROM HERE. I'M NOT SURE I COULD TELL YOU PRECISELY MYSELF.

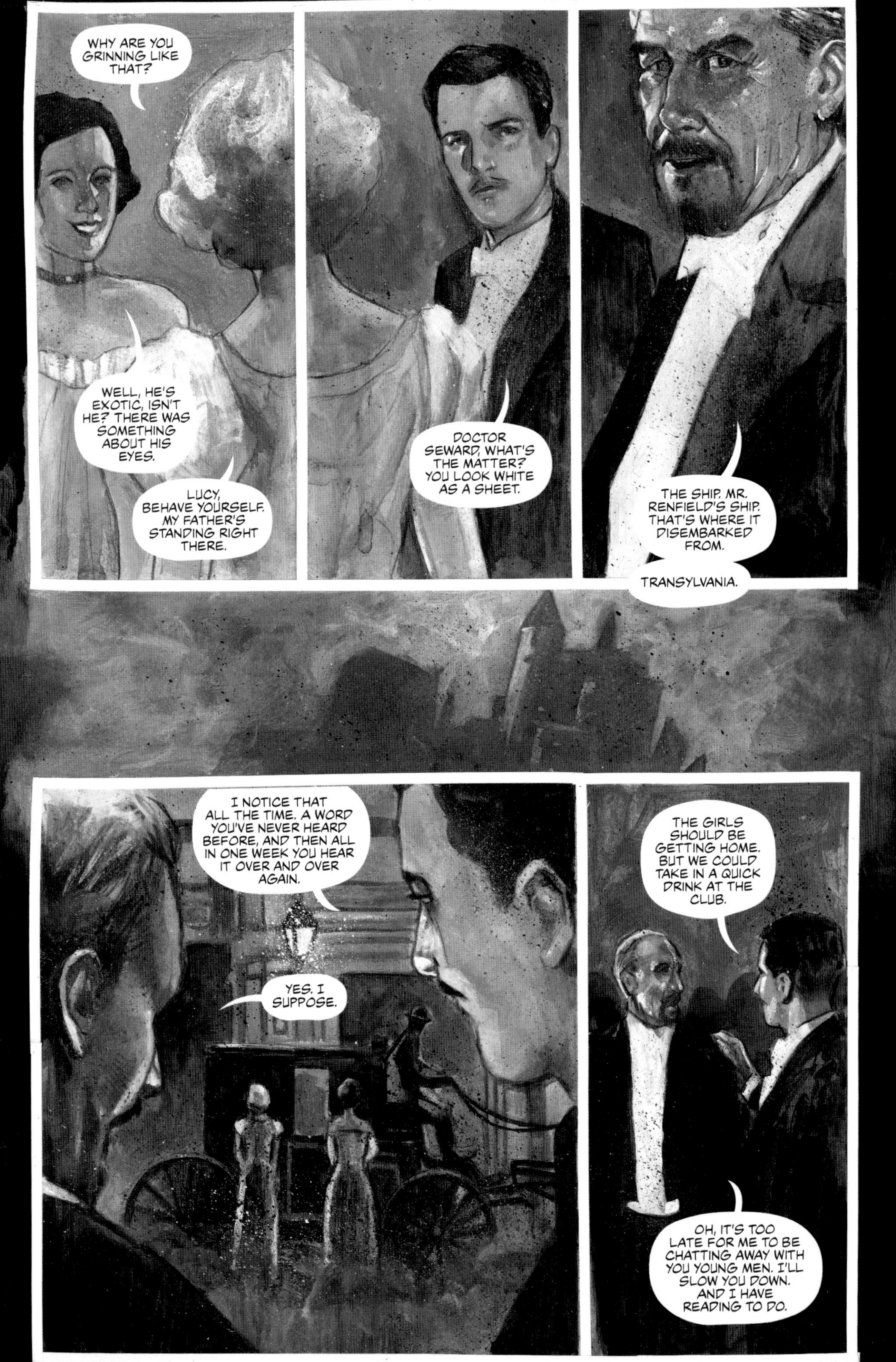

WHY ARE YOU GRINNING LIKE THAT?
WELL, HE'S EXOTIC, ISN'T HE? THERE WAS SOMETHING ABOUT HIS EYES.
LUCY, BEHAVE YOURSELF. MY FATHER'S STANDING RIGHT THERE.
DOCTOR SEWARD, WHAT'S THE MATTER? YOU LOOK WHITE AS A SHEET.
THE SHIP. MR. RENFIELD'S SHIP. THAT'S WHERE IT DISEMBARKED FROM.
TRANSYLVANIA.
I NOTICE THAT ALL THE TIME. A WORD YOU'VE NEVER HEARD BEFORE, AND THEN ALL IN ONE WEEK YOU HEAR IT OVER AND OVER AGAIN.
YES. I SUPPOSE.
THE GIRLS SHOULD BE GETTING HOME. BUT WE COULD TAKE IN A QUICK DRINK AT THE CLUB.
OH, IT'S TOO LATE FOR ME TO BE CHATTING AWAY WITH YOU YOUNG MEN. I'LL SLOW YOU DOWN. AND I HAVE READING TO DO.

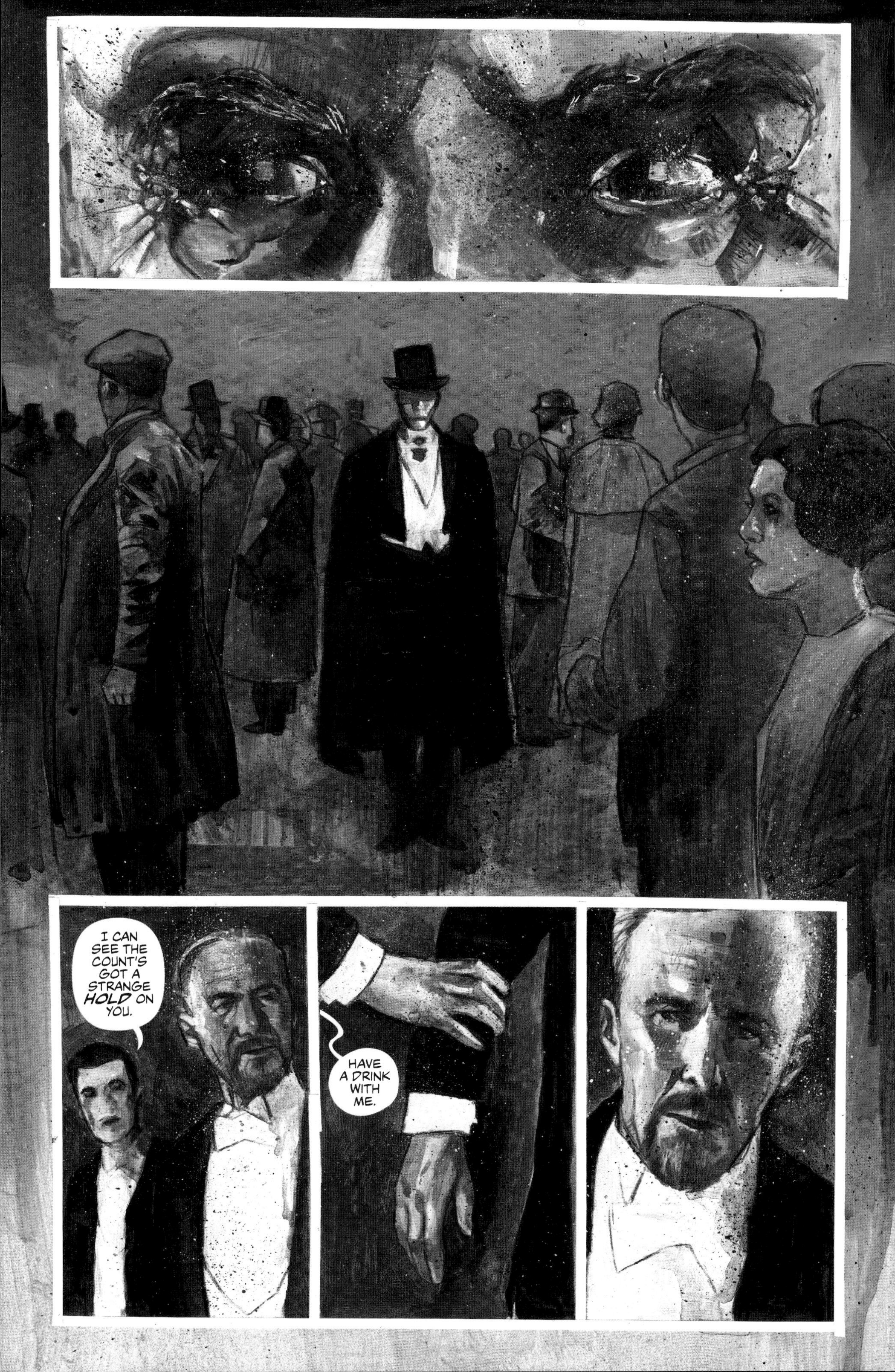
I CAN SEE THE COUNT'S GOT A STRANGE **HOLD** ON YOU.
HAVE A DRINK WITH ME.

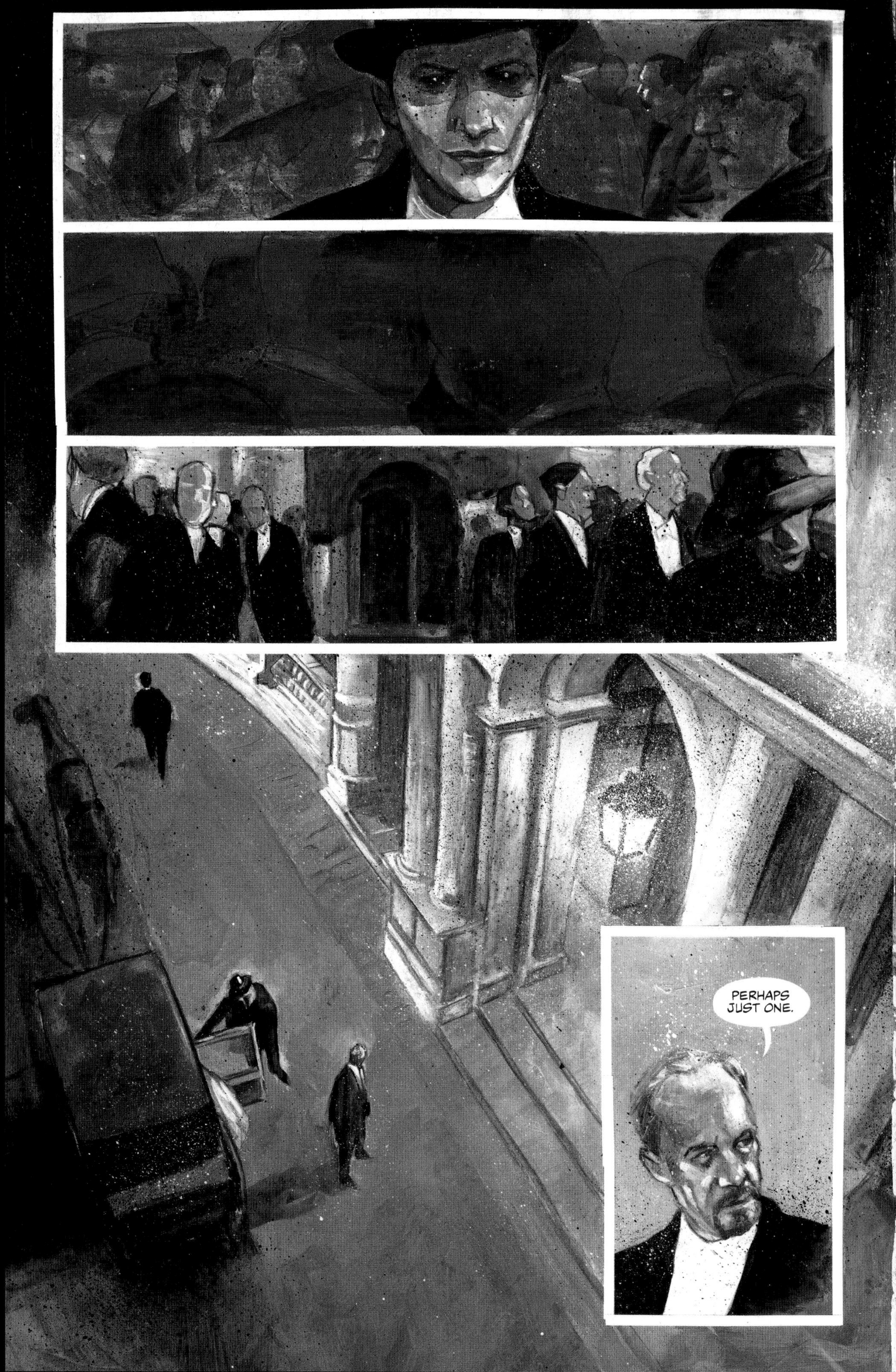
PERHAPS JUST ONE.

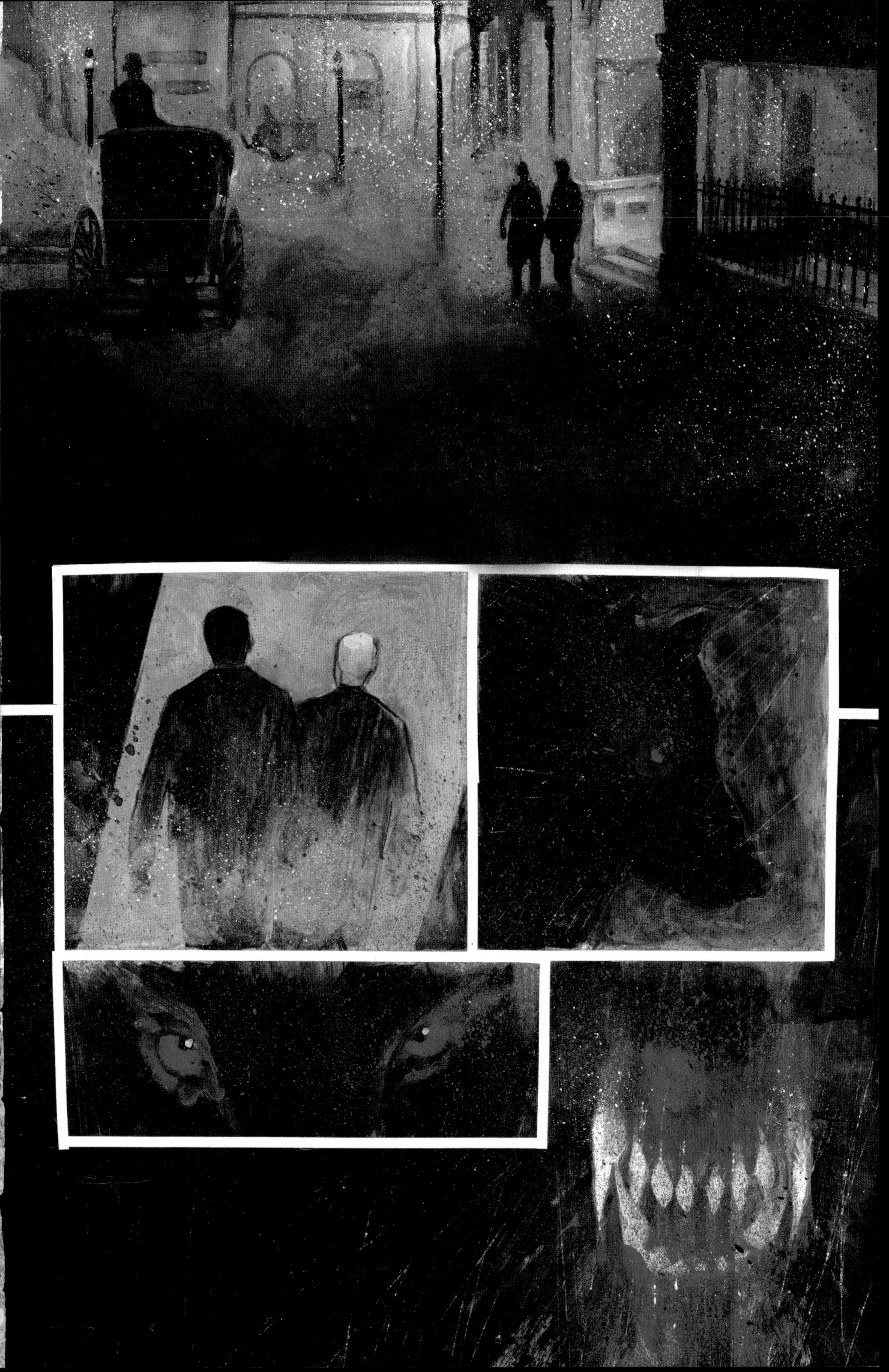

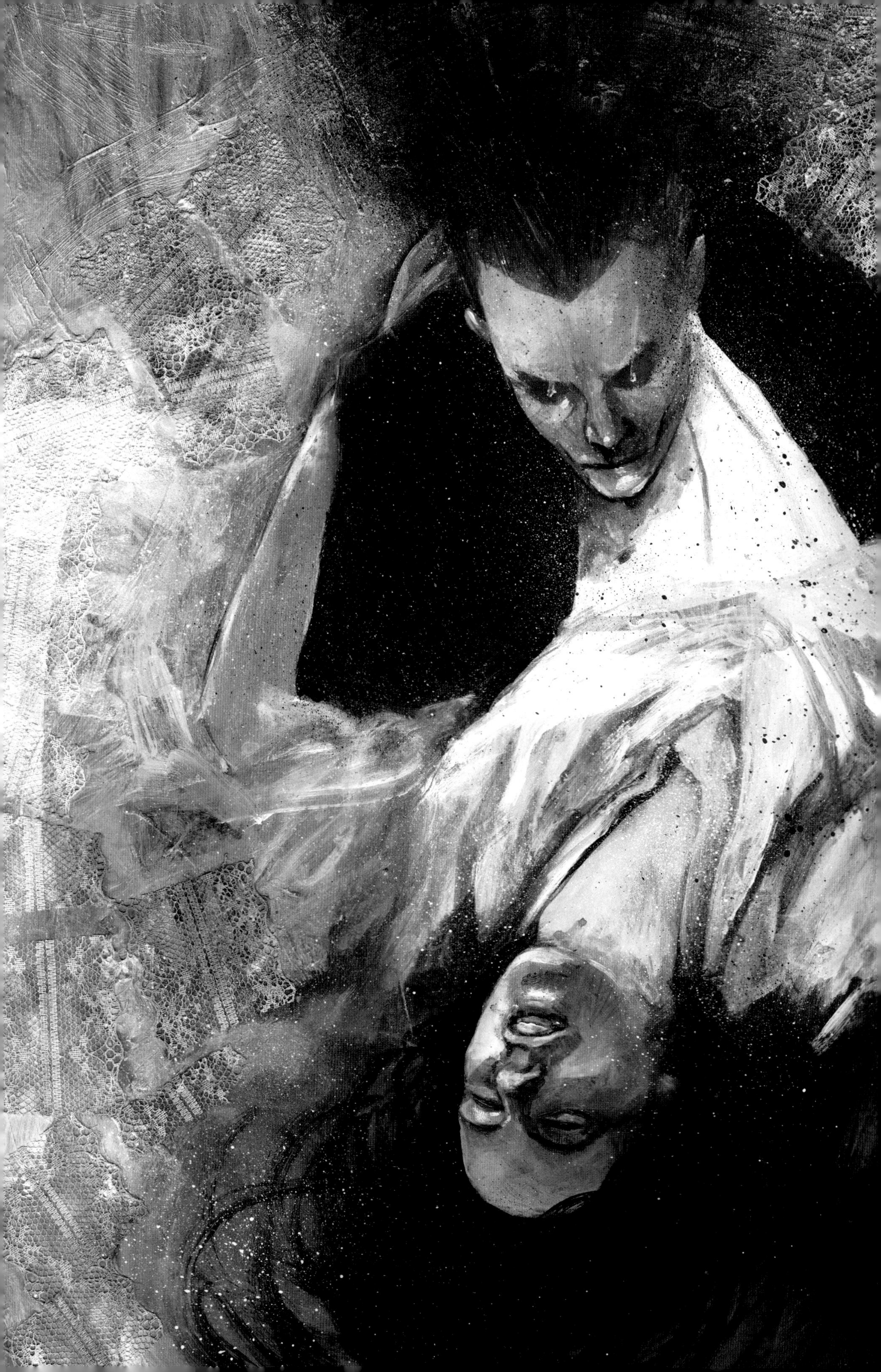

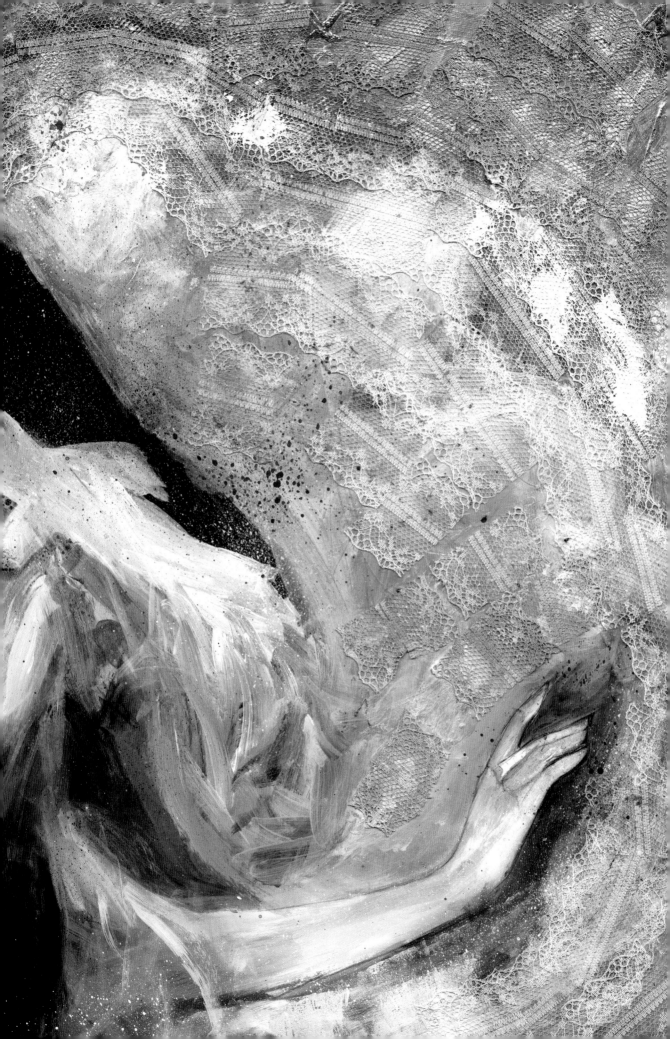

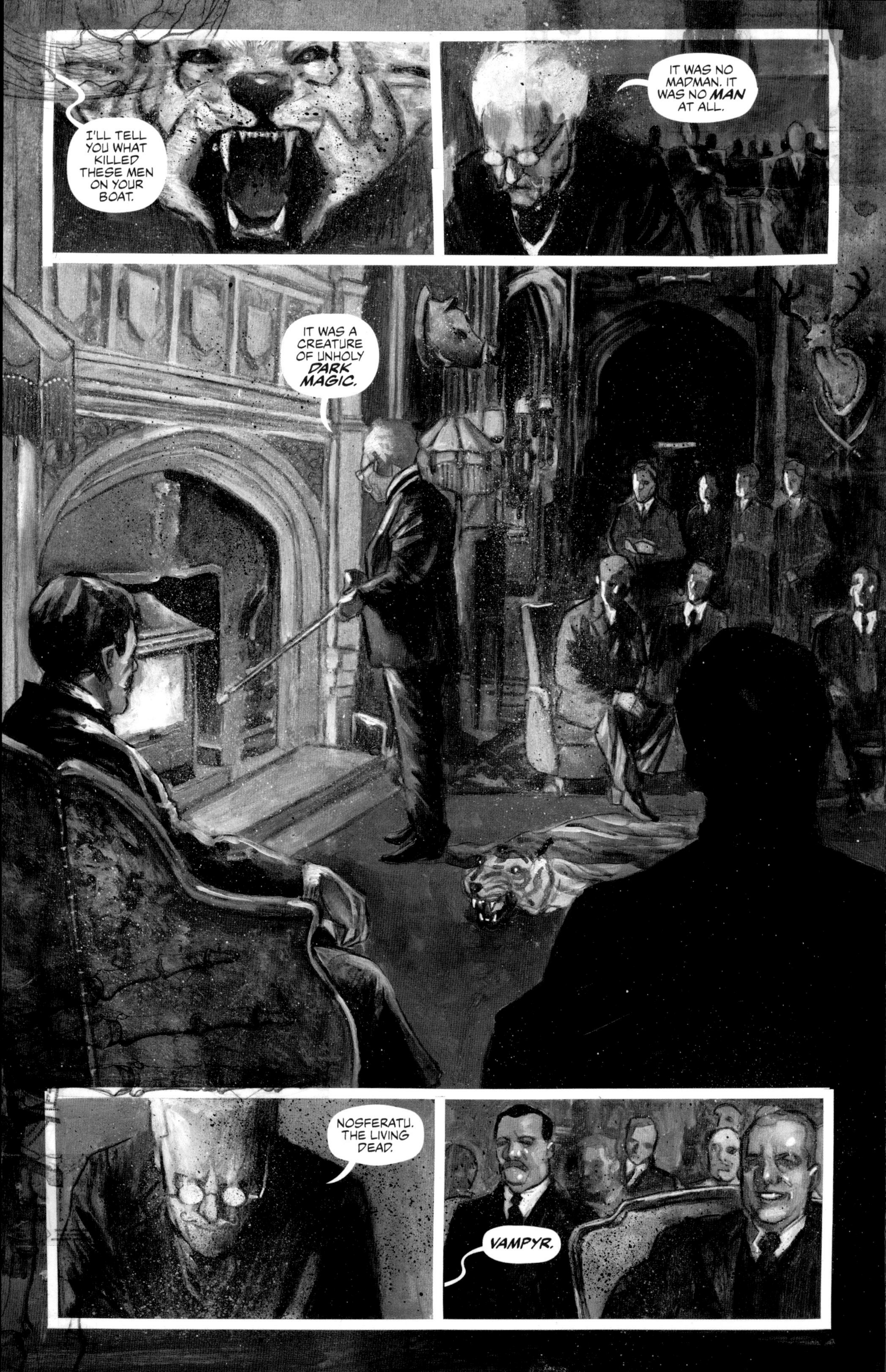
I'LL TELL YOU WHAT KILLED THESE MEN ON YOUR BOAT.
IT WAS NO MADMAN. IT WAS NO MAN AT ALL.
IT WAS A CREATURE OF UNHOLY DARK MAGIC.
NOSFERATU. THE LIVING DEAD.
VAMPYR.

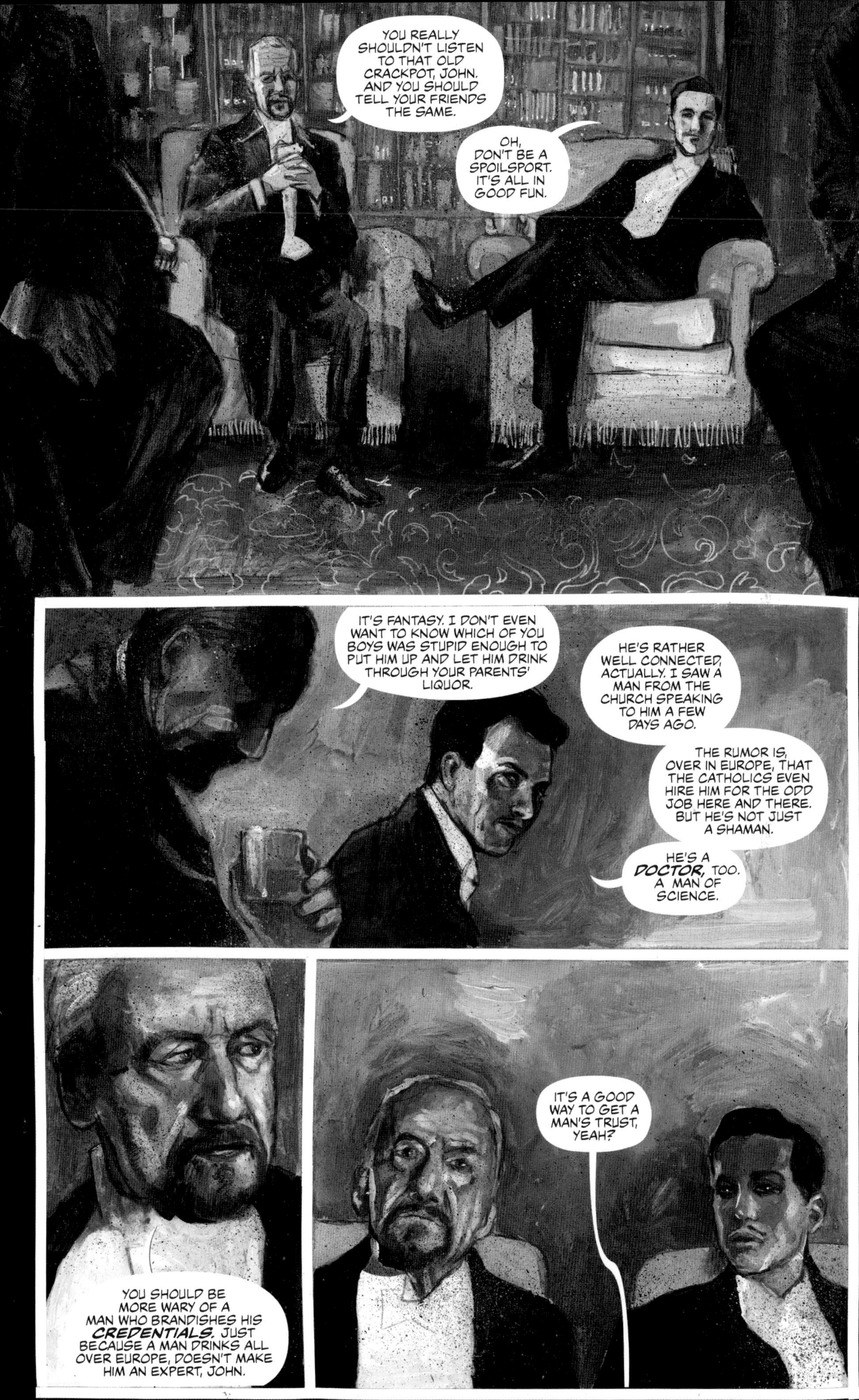
YOU REALLY SHOULDN'T LISTEN TO THAT OLD CRACKPOT, JOHN. AND YOU SHOULD TELL YOUR FRIENDS THE SAME.
OH, DON'T BE A SPOILSPORT. IT'S ALL IN GOOD FUN.
IT'S FANTASY. I DON'T EVEN WANT TO KNOW WHICH OF YOU BOYS WAS STUPID ENOUGH TO PUT HIM UP AND LET HIM DRINK THROUGH YOUR PARENTS' LIQUOR.
HE'S RATHER WELL CONNECTED, ACTUALLY. I SAW A MAN FROM THE CHURCH SPEAKING TO HIM A FEW DAYS AGO.
THE RUMOR IS, OVER IN EUROPE, THAT THE CATHOLICS EVEN HIRE HIM FOR THE ODD JOB HERE AND THERE. BUT HE'S NOT JUST A SHAMAN.
HE'S A DOCTOR, TOO. A MAN OF SCIENCE.
YOU SHOULD BE MORE WARY OF A MAN WHO BRANDISHES HIS CREDENTIALS. JUST BECAUSE A MAN DRINKS ALL OVER EUROPE, DOESN'T MAKE HIM AN EXPERT, JOHN.
IT'S A GOOD WAY TO GET A MAN'S TRUST, YEAH?

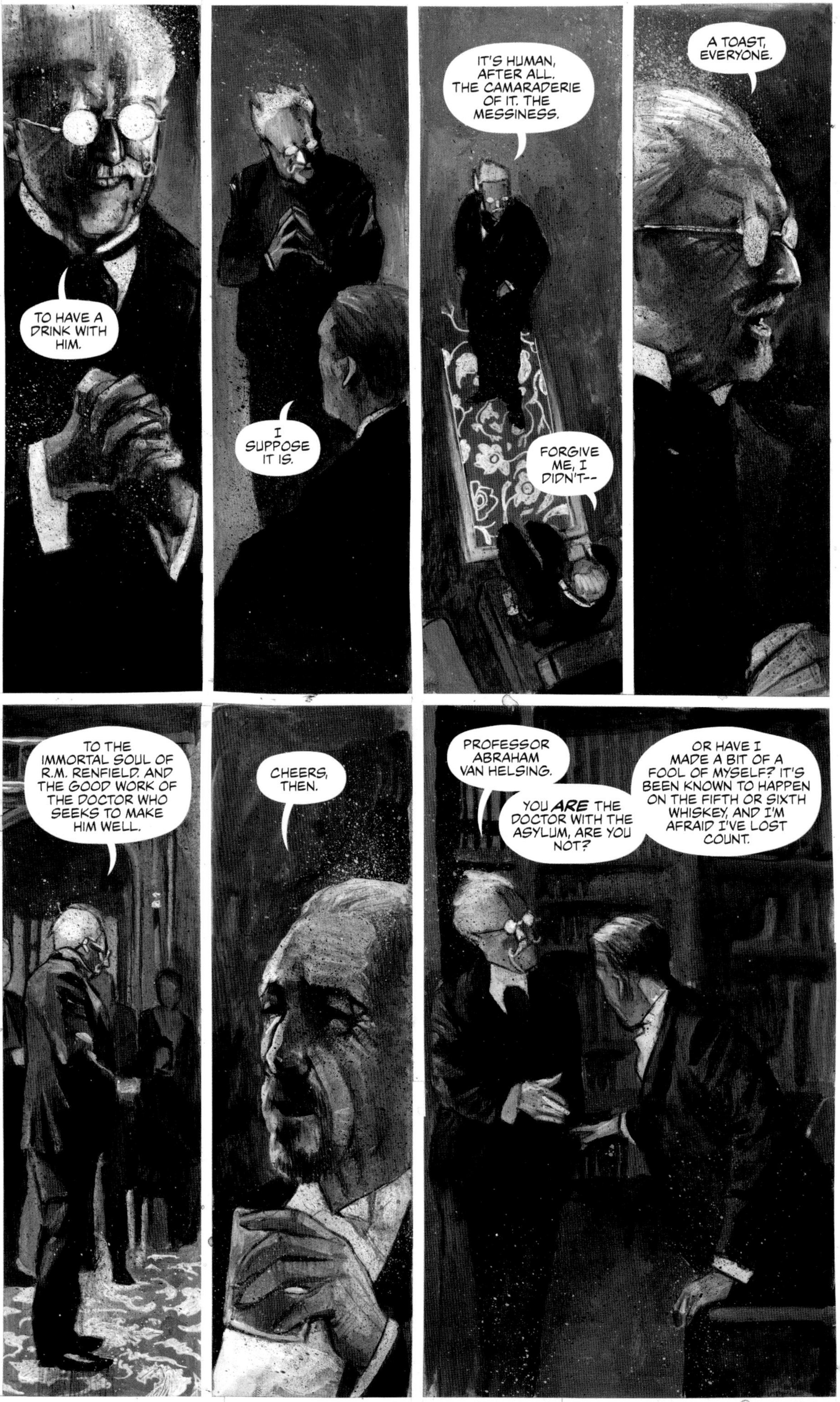
TO HAVE A DRINK WITH HIM.
I SUPPOSE IT IS.
IT'S HUMAN, AFTER ALL. THE CAMARADERIE OF IT. THE MESSINESS.
FORGIVE ME, I DIDN'T--
A TOAST, EVERYONE.
TO THE IMMORTAL SOUL OF R.M. RENFIELD. AND THE GOOD WORK OF THE DOCTOR WHO SEEKS TO MAKE HIM WELL.
CHEERS, THEN.
PROFESSOR ABRAHAM VAN HELSING.
YOU ARE THE DOCTOR WITH THE ASYLUM, ARE YOU NOT?
OR HAVE I MADE A BIT OF A FOOL OF MYSELF? IT'S BEEN KNOWN TO HAPPEN ON THE FIFTH OR SIXTH WHISKEY, AND I'M AFRAID I'VE LOST COUNT.

YOU'VE FOUND ME, PROFESSOR.
GOOD. I WOULD LOVE TO ARRANGE A VISIT AT YOUR ASYLUM. THIS RENFIELD CHARACTER IS OF GREAT INTEREST TO ME AND MY WORK.
I'M AFRAID I WON'T ALLOW IT.
RENFIELD IS IN A FRAGILE ENOUGH STATE AS IT IS.
MY DEAR DOCTOR SEWARD, I FEAR YOU DO NOT KNOW THE ***HALF*** OF IT.
JOHN, I THINK I'LL BE HEADING HOME NOW.
OH, COME NOW. I'M SURE THE PROFESSOR DIDN'T MEAN ANYTHING BY IT.
OH. BUT THE PROFESSOR VERY MUCH ***DID***. AND THE DOCTOR SHOULD HEED A FRIENDLY WARNING.

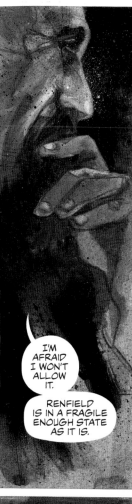

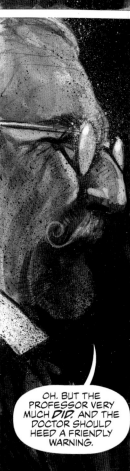

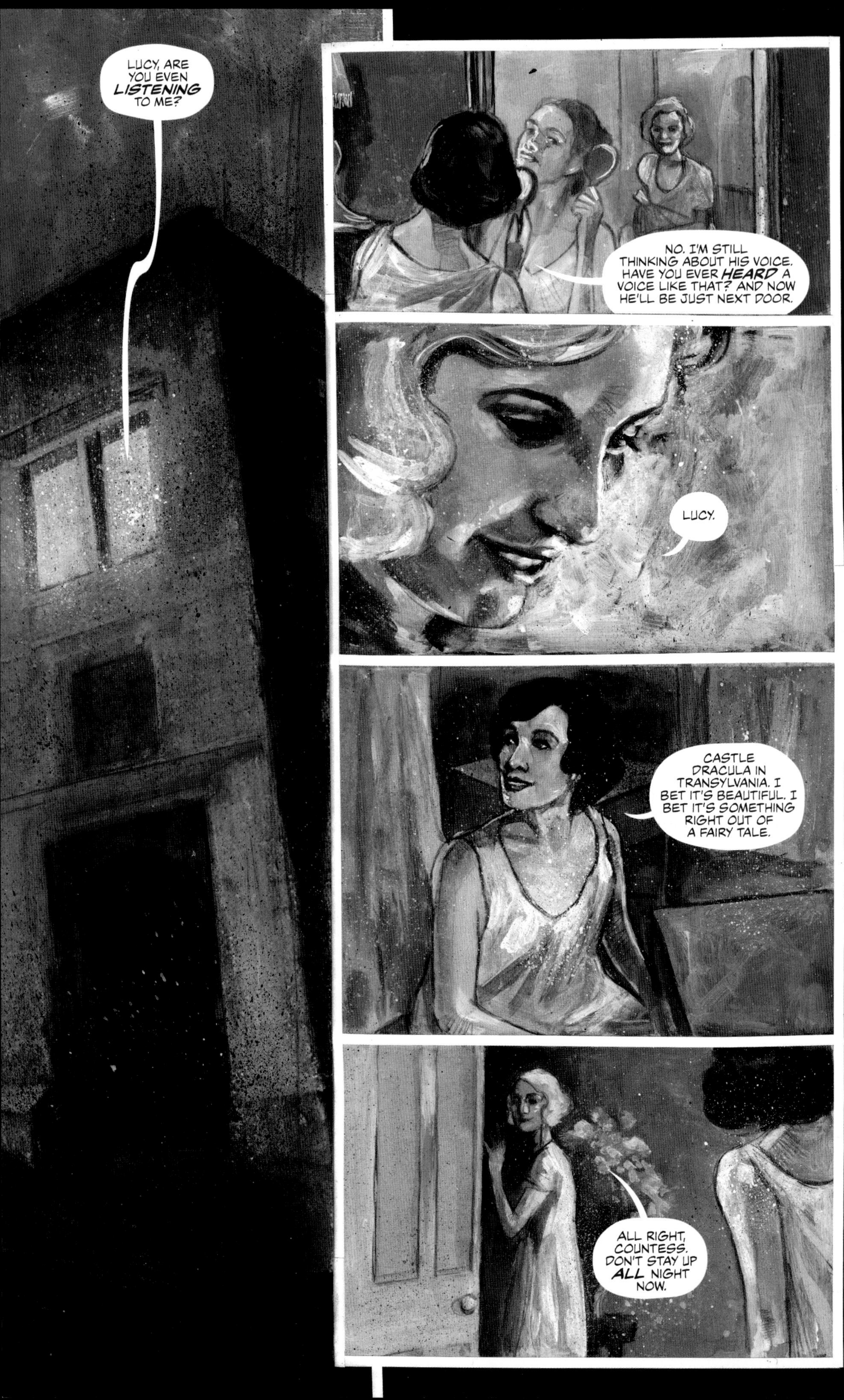
LUCY, ARE YOU EVEN LISTENING TO ME?
NO. I'M STILL THINKING ABOUT HIS VOICE. HAVE YOU EVER HEARD A VOICE LIKE THAT? AND NOW HE'LL BE JUST NEXT DOOR.
LUCY.
CASTLE DRACULA IN TRANSYLVANIA. I BET IT'S BEAUTIFUL. I BET IT'S SOMETHING RIGHT OUT OF A FAIRY TALE.
ALL RIGHT, COUNTESS. DON'T STAY UP ALL NIGHT NOW.

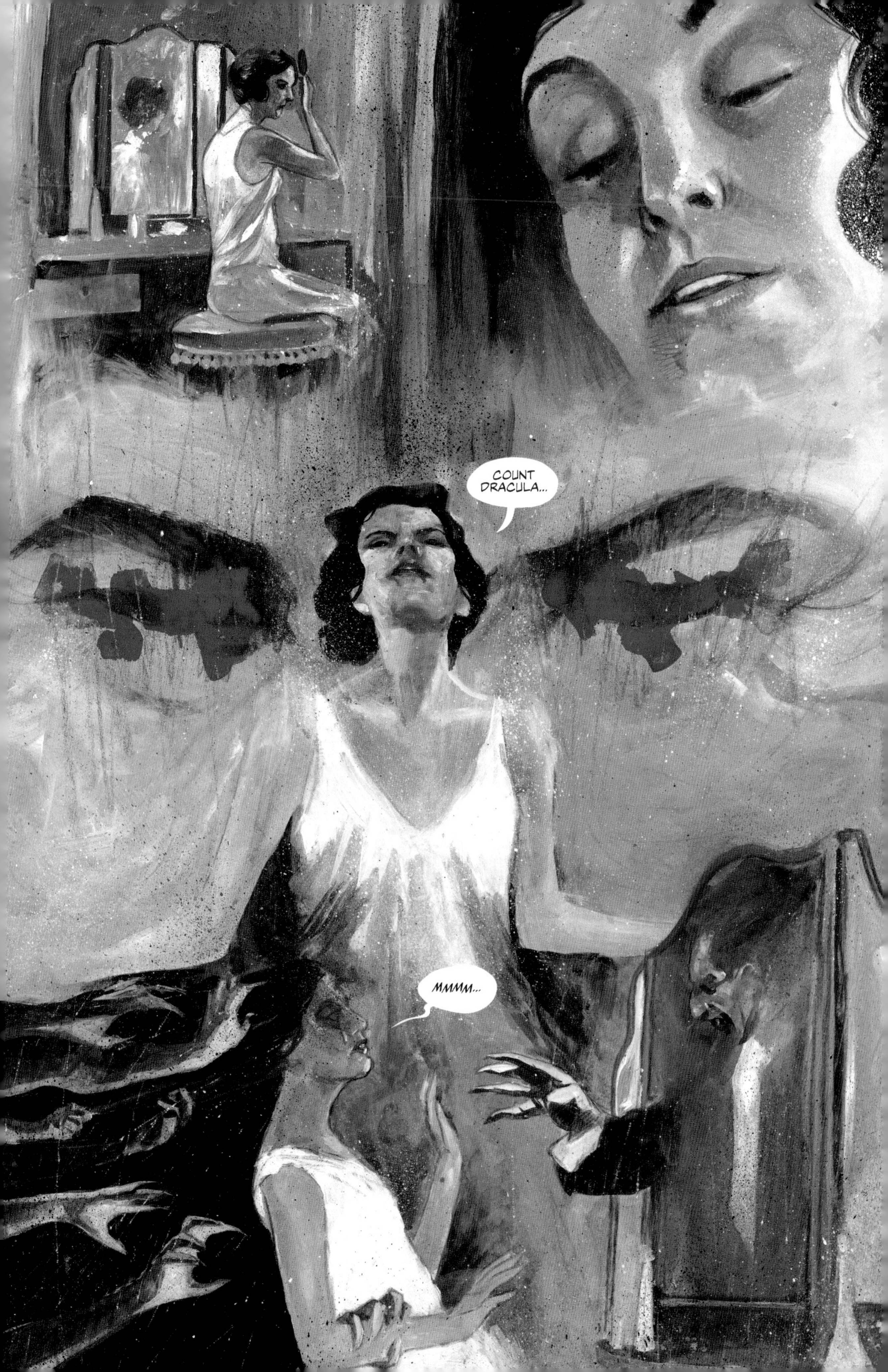
COUNT DRACULA...
MMMM...

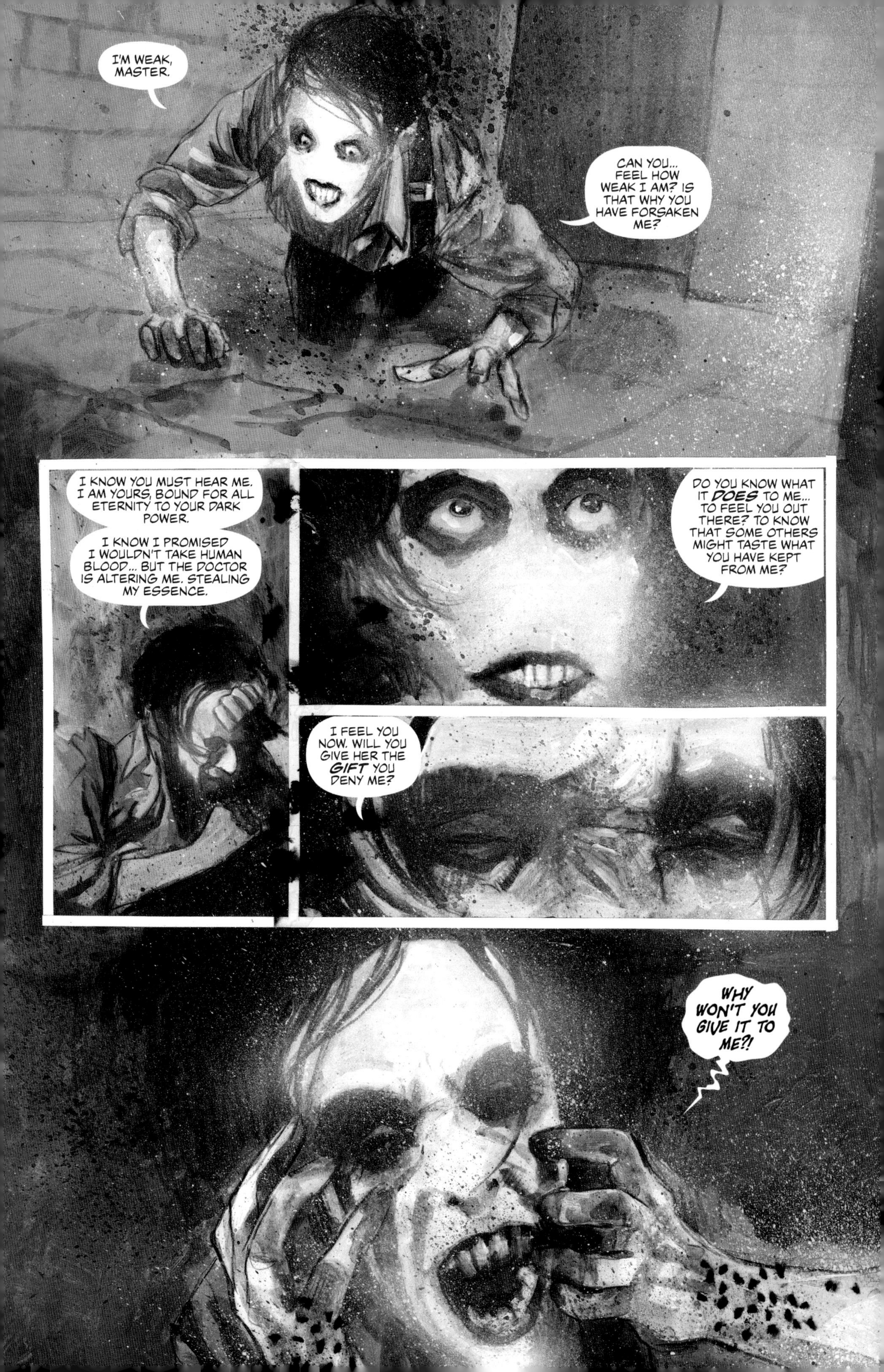
I'M WEAK, MASTER.
CAN YOU... FEEL HOW WEAK I AM? IS THAT WHY YOU HAVE FORSAKEN ME?
I KNOW YOU MUST HEAR ME. I AM YOURS, BOUND FOR ALL ETERNITY TO YOUR DARK POWER.
I KNOW I PROMISED I WOULDN'T TAKE HUMAN BLOOD... BUT THE DOCTOR IS ALTERING ME. STEALING MY ESSENCE.
DO YOU KNOW WHAT IT DOES TO ME... TO FEEL YOU OUT THERE? TO KNOW THAT SOME OTHERS MIGHT TASTE WHAT YOU HAVE KEPT FROM ME?
I FEEL YOU NOW. WILL YOU GIVE HER THE GIFT YOU DENY ME?
WHY WON'T YOU GIVE IT TO ME?!

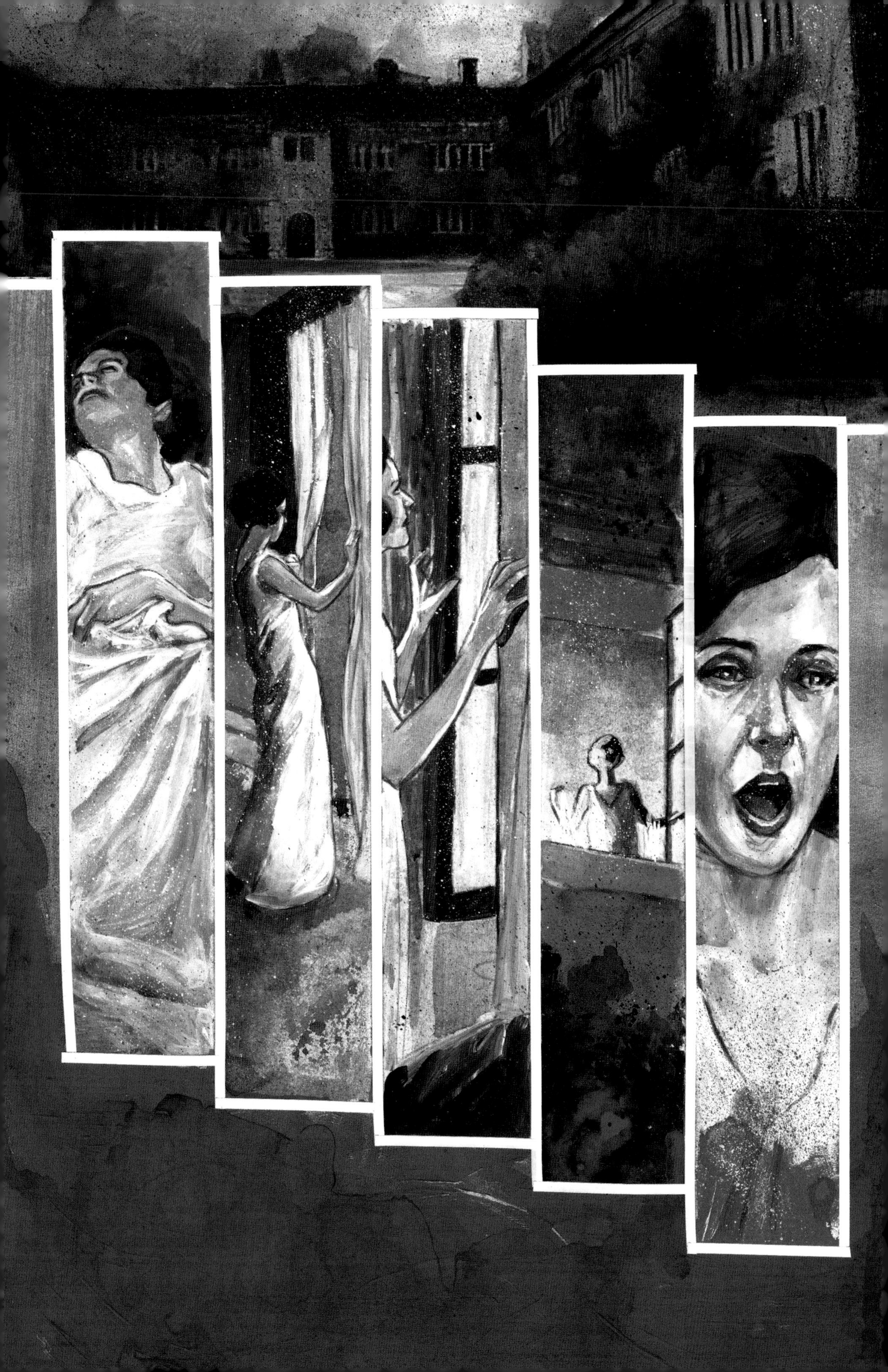

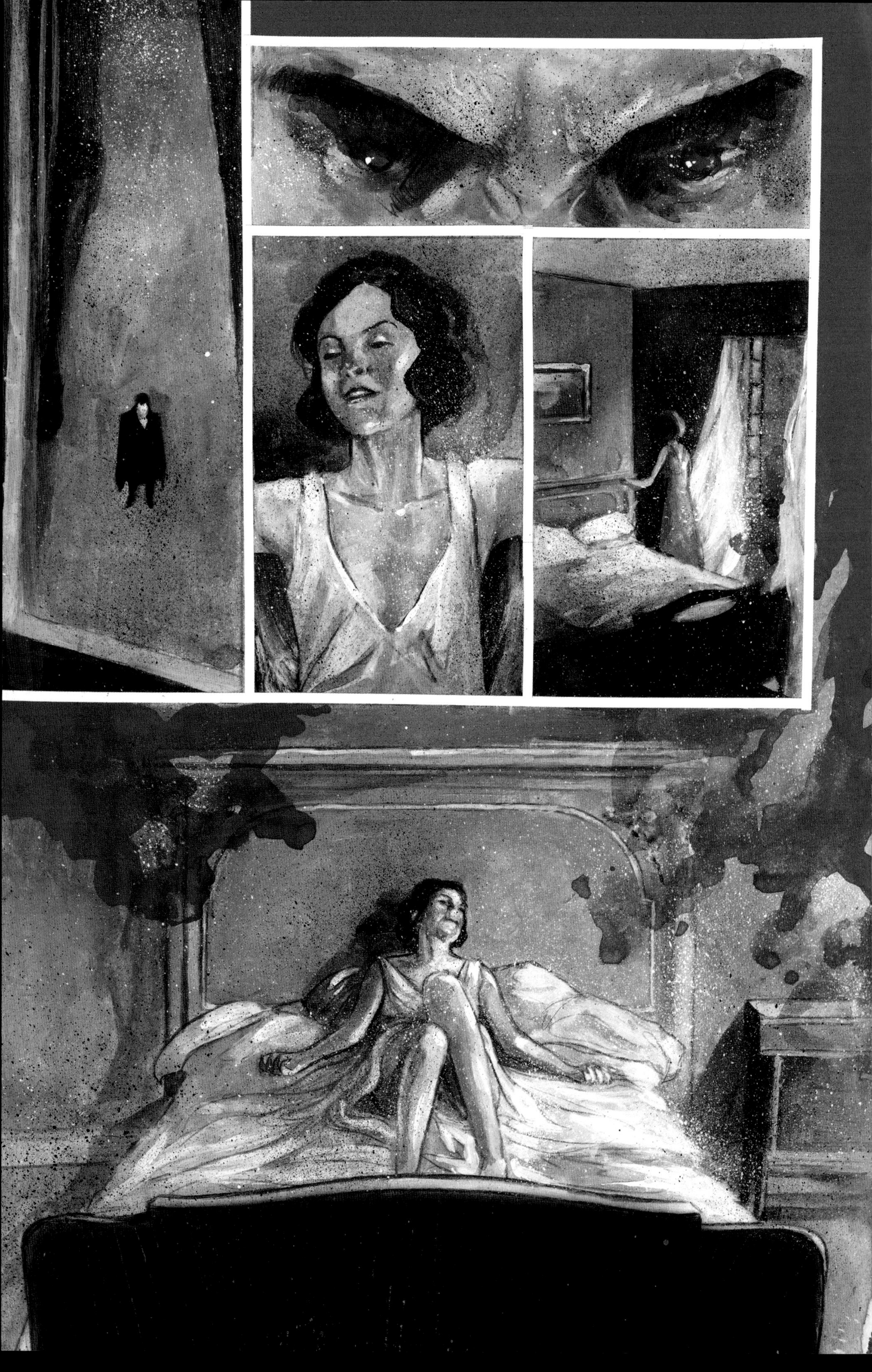

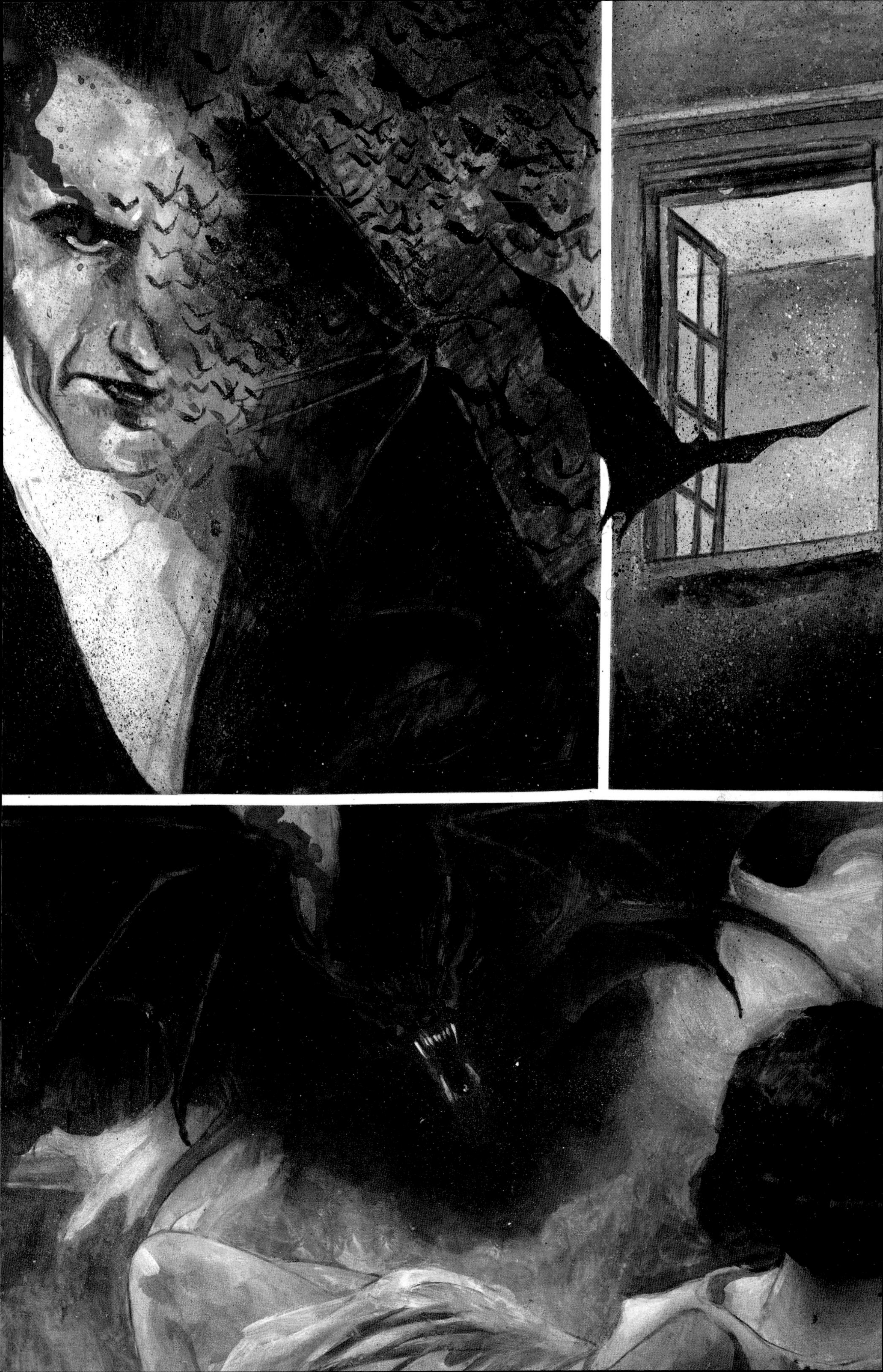

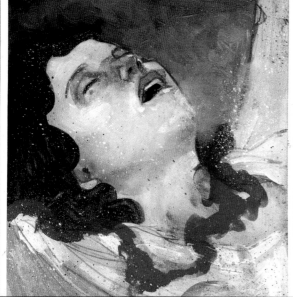
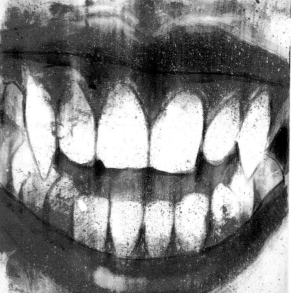

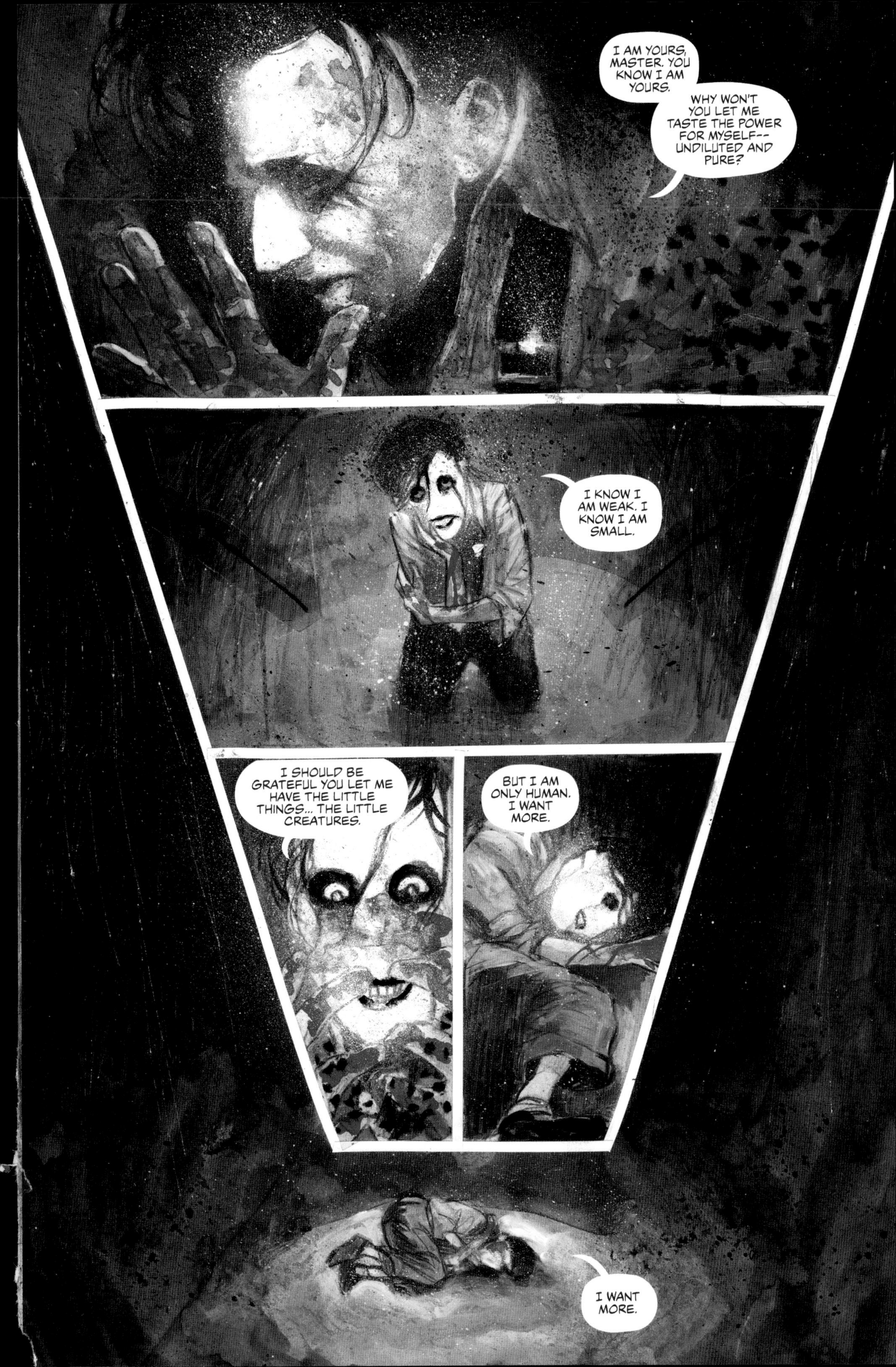
I AM YOURS, MASTER. YOU KNOW I AM YOURS.
WHY WON'T YOU LET ME TASTE THE POWER FOR MYSELF-- UNDILUTED AND PURE?
I KNOW I AM WEAK. I KNOW I AM SMALL.
I SHOULD BE GRATEFUL YOU LET ME HAVE THE LITTLE THINGS... THE LITTLE CREATURES.
BUT I AM ONLY HUMAN. I WANT MORE.
I WANT MORE.

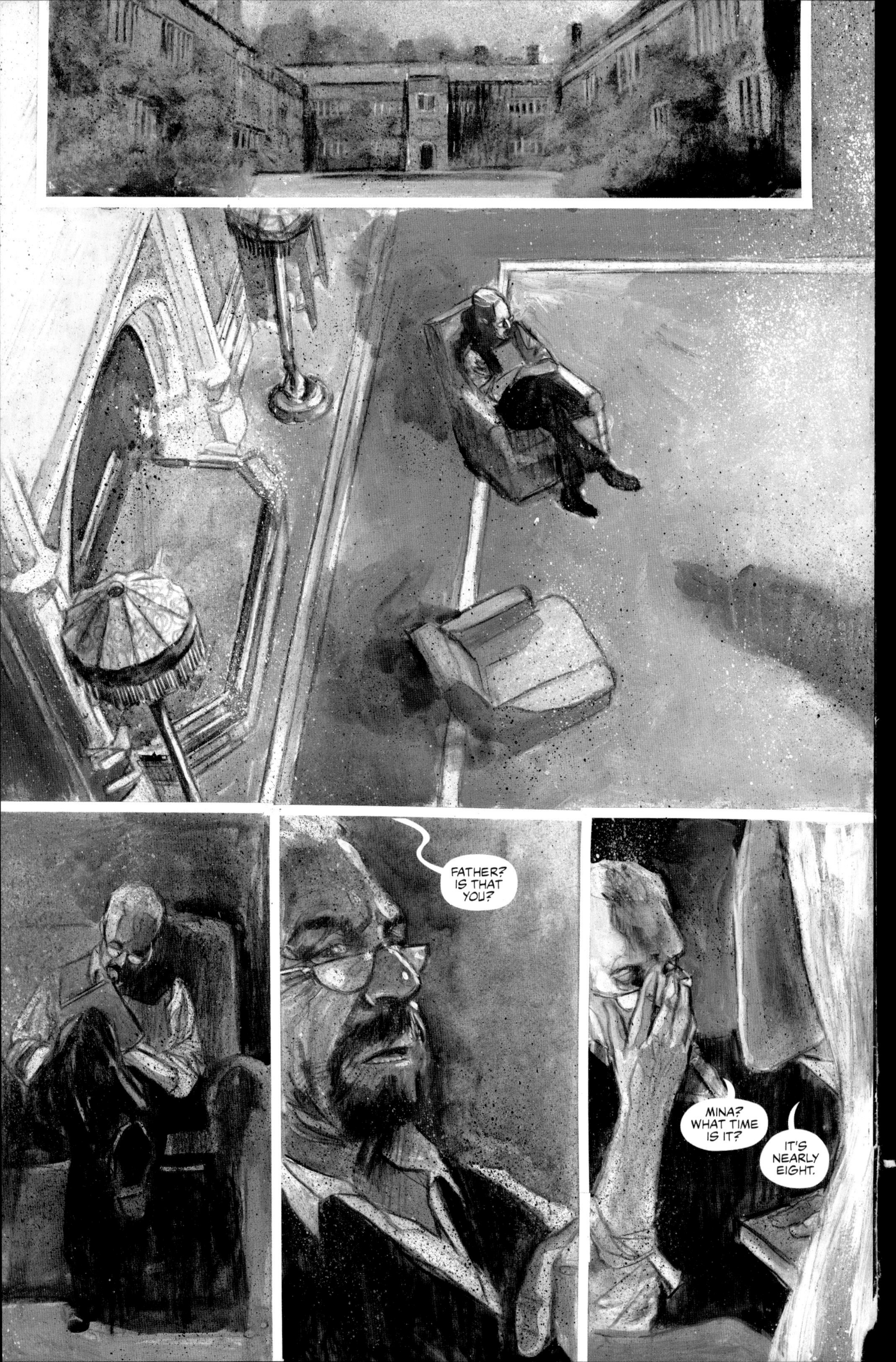
FATHER? IS THAT YOU?
MINA? WHAT TIME IS IT?
IT'S NEARLY EIGHT.

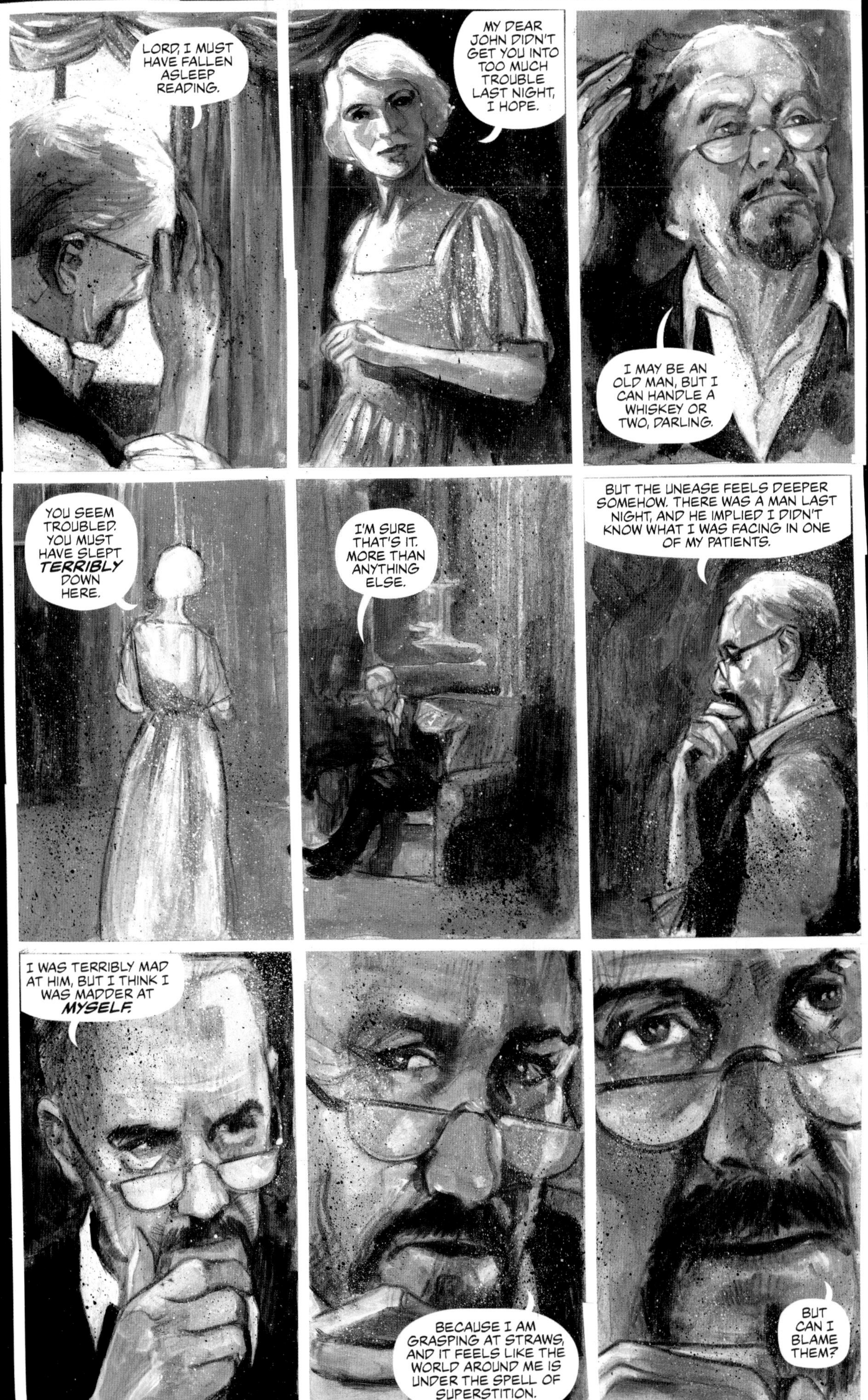
LORD, I MUST HAVE FALLEN ASLEEP READING.
MY DEAR JOHN DIDN'T GET YOU INTO TOO MUCH TROUBLE LAST NIGHT, I HOPE.
I MAY BE AN OLD MAN, BUT I CAN HANDLE A WHISKEY OR TWO, DARLING.
YOU SEEM TROUBLED. YOU MUST HAVE SLEPT TERRIBLY DOWN HERE.
I'M SURE THAT'S IT. MORE THAN ANYTHING ELSE.
BUT THE UNEASE FEELS DEEPER SOMEHOW. THERE WAS A MAN LAST NIGHT, AND HE IMPLIED I DIDN'T KNOW WHAT I WAS FACING IN ONE OF MY PATIENTS.
I WAS TERRIBLY MAD AT HIM, BUT I THINK I WAS MADDER AT MYSELF.
BECAUSE I AM GRASPING AT STRAWS, AND IT FEELS LIKE THE WORLD AROUND ME IS UNDER THE SPELL OF SUPERSTITION.
BUT CAN I BLAME THEM?

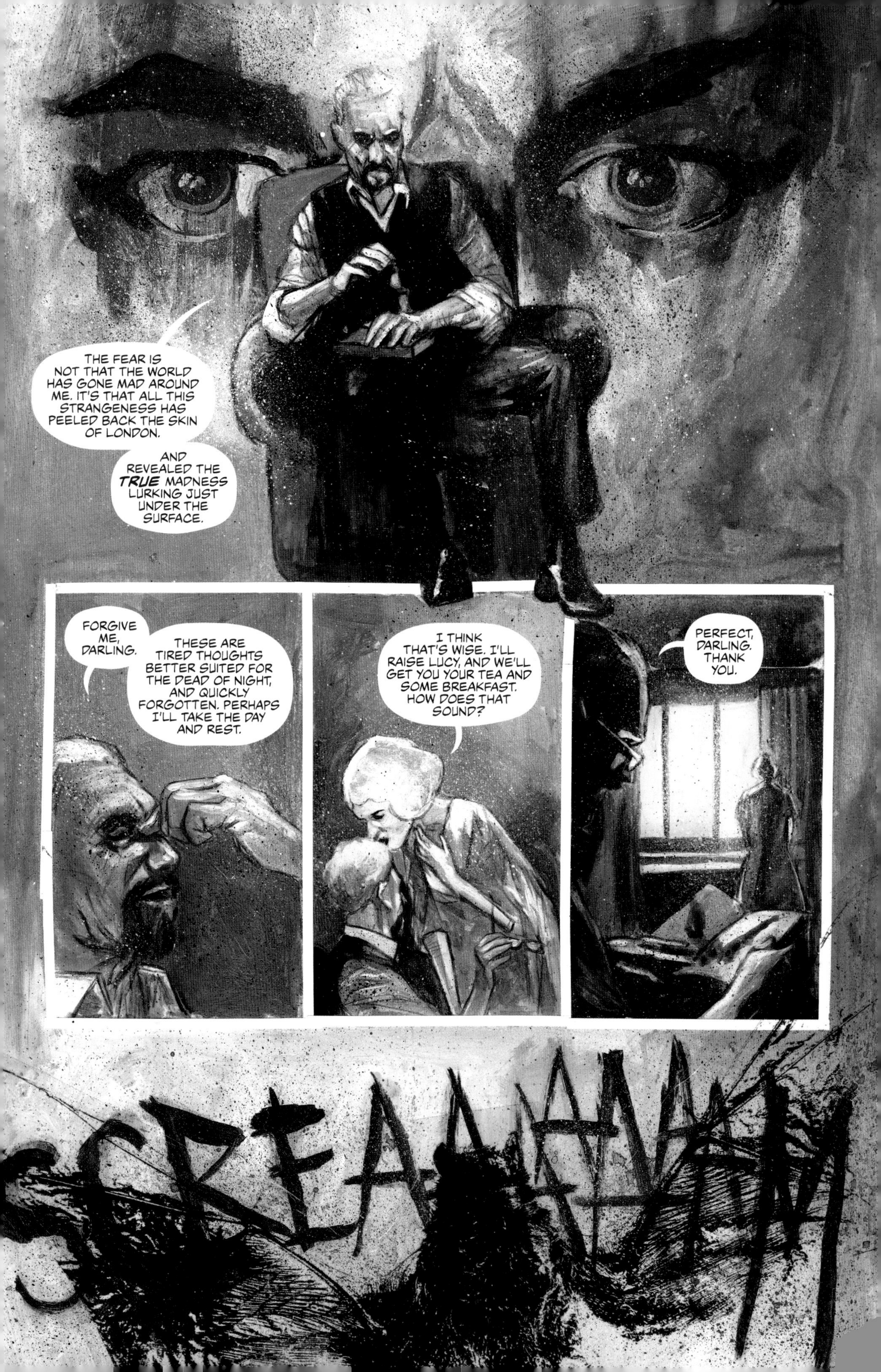
THE FEAR IS NOT THAT THE WORLD HAS GONE MAD AROUND ME. IT'S THAT ALL THIS STRANGENESS HAS PEELED BACK THE SKIN OF LONDON.
AND REVEALED THE *TRUE* MADNESS LURKING JUST UNDER THE SURFACE.
FORGIVE ME, DARLING.
THESE ARE TIRED THOUGHTS BETTER SUITED FOR THE DEAD OF NIGHT, AND QUICKLY FORGOTTEN. PERHAPS I'LL TAKE THE DAY AND REST.
I THINK THAT'S WISE. I'LL RAISE LUCY, AND WE'LL GET YOU YOUR TEA AND SOME BREAKFAST. HOW DOES THAT SOUND?
PERFECT, DARLING. THANK YOU.
SCREAAAAM

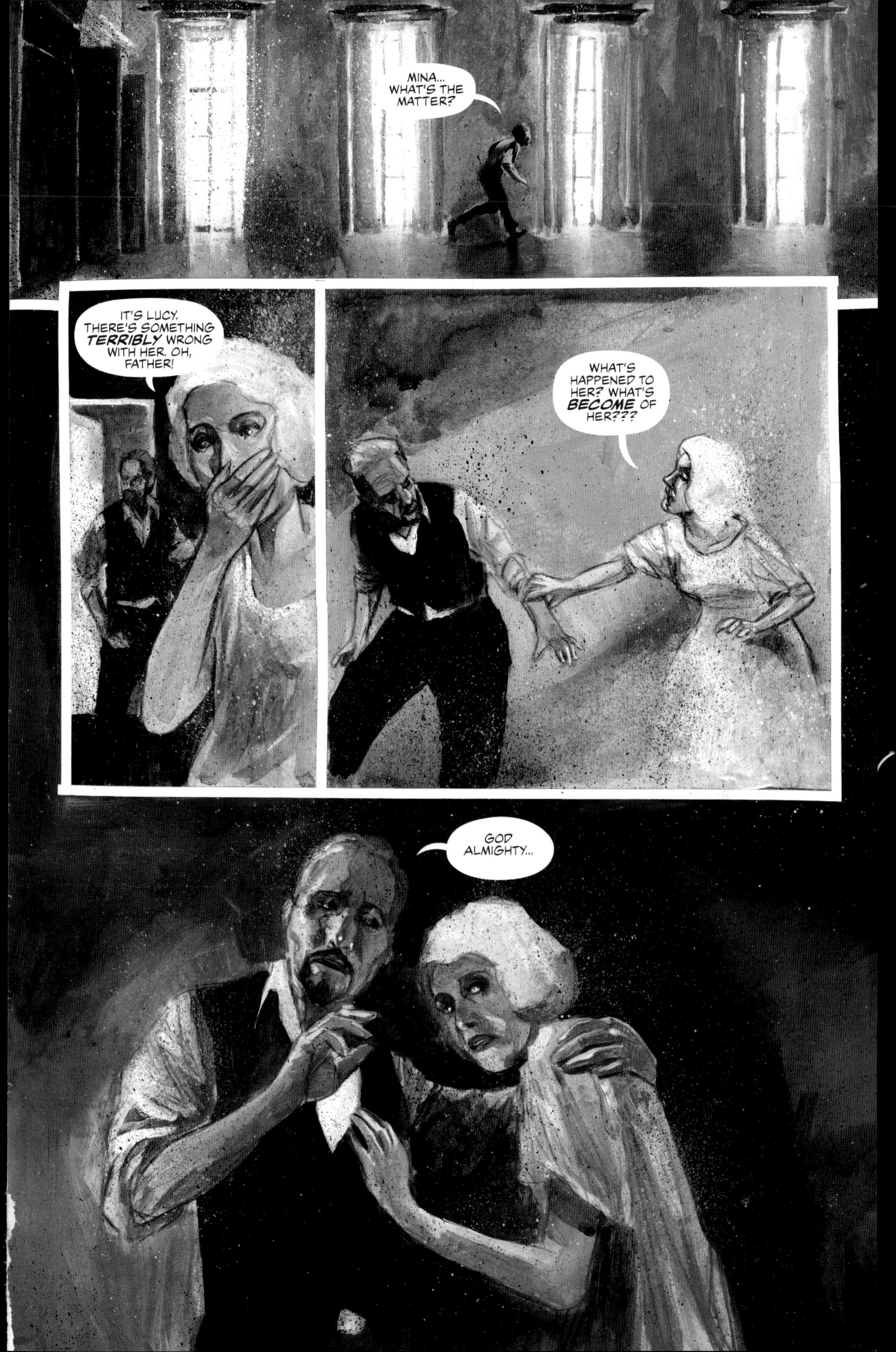
MINA... WHAT'S THE MATTER?
IT'S LUCY. THERE'S SOMETHING TERRIBLY WRONG WITH HER. OH, FATHER!
WHAT'S HAPPENED TO HER? WHAT'S BECOME OF HER???
GOD ALMIGHTY...

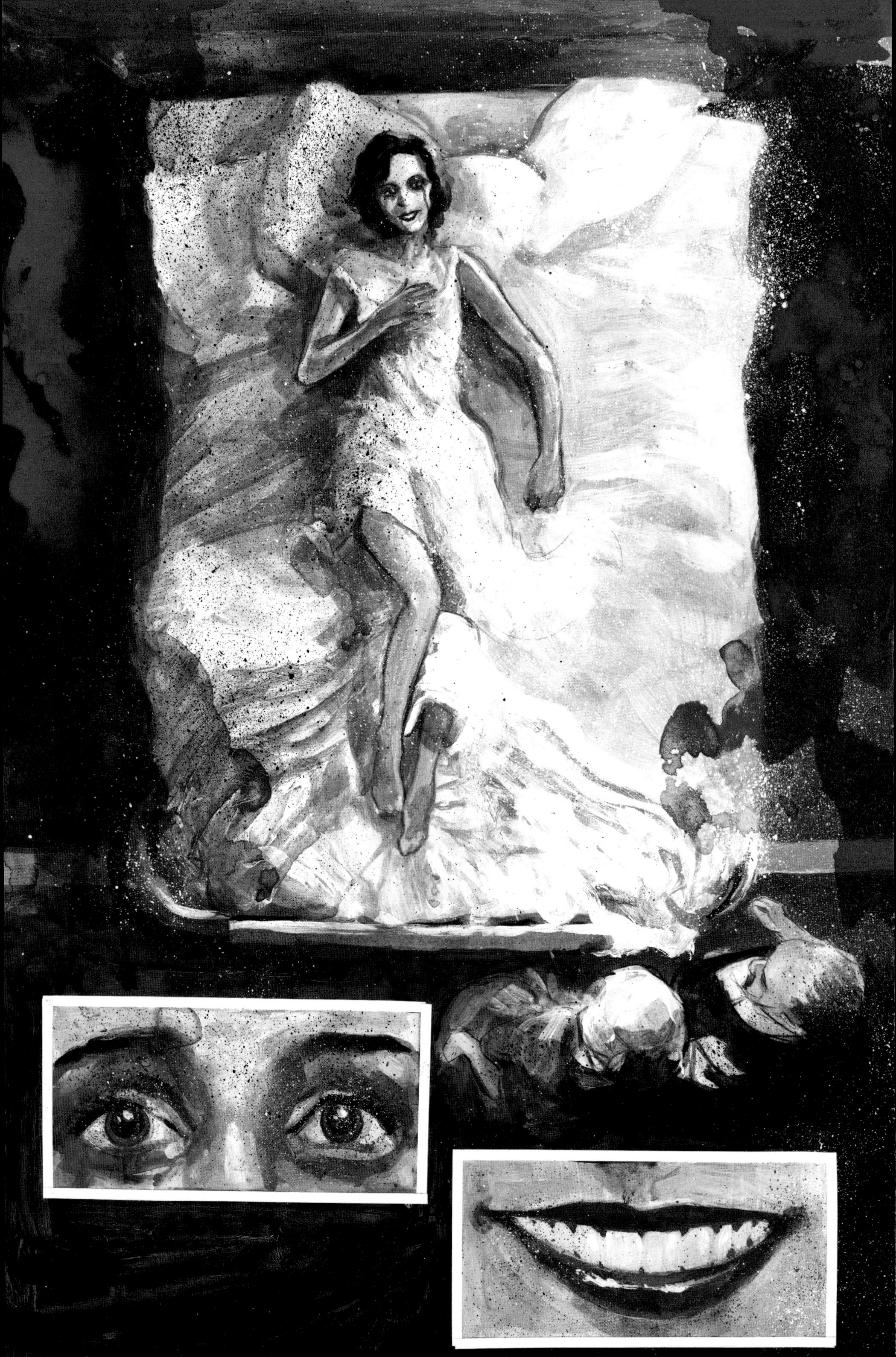

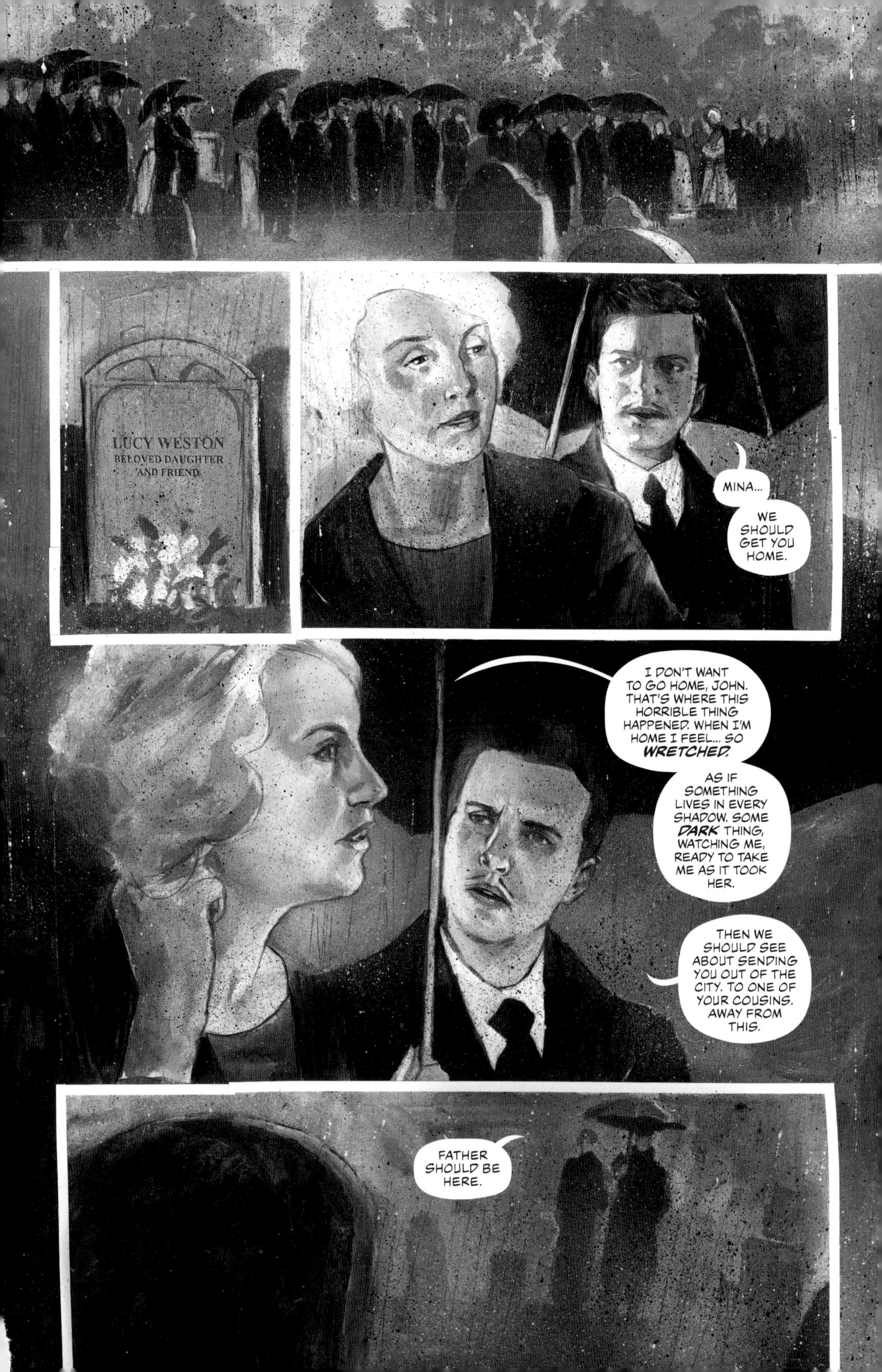
LUCY WESTON
BELOVED DAUGHTER
AND FRIEND
MINA...
WE SHOULD GET YOU HOME.
I DON'T WANT TO GO HOME, JOHN. THAT'S WHERE THIS HORRIBLE THING HAPPENED. WHEN I'M HOME I FEEL... SO WRETCHED.
AS IF SOMETHING LIVES IN EVERY SHADOW. SOME DARK THING, WATCHING ME, READY TO TAKE ME AS IT TOOK HER.
THEN WE SHOULD SEE ABOUT SENDING YOU OUT OF THE CITY. TO ONE OF YOUR COUSINS. AWAY FROM THIS.
FATHER SHOULD BE HERE.

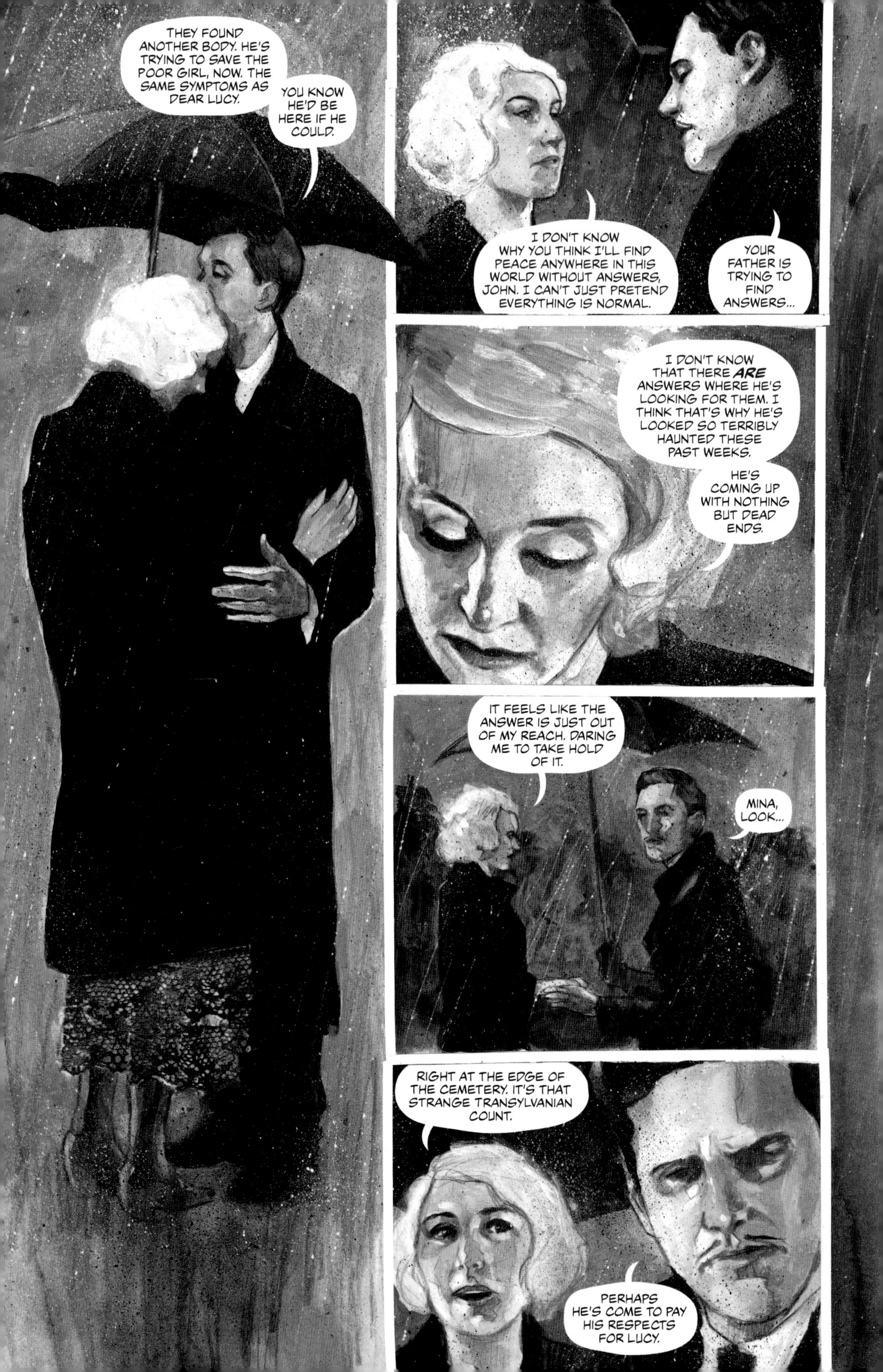
THEY FOUND ANOTHER BODY. HE'S TRYING TO SAVE THE POOR GIRL, NOW. THE SAME SYMPTOMS AS DEAR LUCY.
YOU KNOW HE'D BE HERE IF HE COULD.
I DON'T KNOW WHY YOU THINK I'LL FIND PEACE ANYWHERE IN THIS WORLD WITHOUT ANSWERS, JOHN. I CAN'T JUST PRETEND EVERYTHING IS NORMAL.
YOUR FATHER IS TRYING TO FIND ANSWERS...
I DON'T KNOW THAT THERE **ARE** ANSWERS WHERE HE'S LOOKING FOR THEM. I THINK THAT'S WHY HE'S LOOKED SO TERRIBLY HAUNTED THESE PAST WEEKS.
HE'S COMING UP WITH NOTHING BUT DEAD ENDS.
IT FEELS LIKE THE ANSWER IS JUST OUT OF MY REACH. DARING ME TO TAKE HOLD OF IT.
MINA, LOOK...
RIGHT AT THE EDGE OF THE CEMETERY. IT'S THAT STRANGE TRANSYLVANIAN COUNT.
PERHAPS HE'S COME TO PAY HIS RESPECTS FOR LUCY.

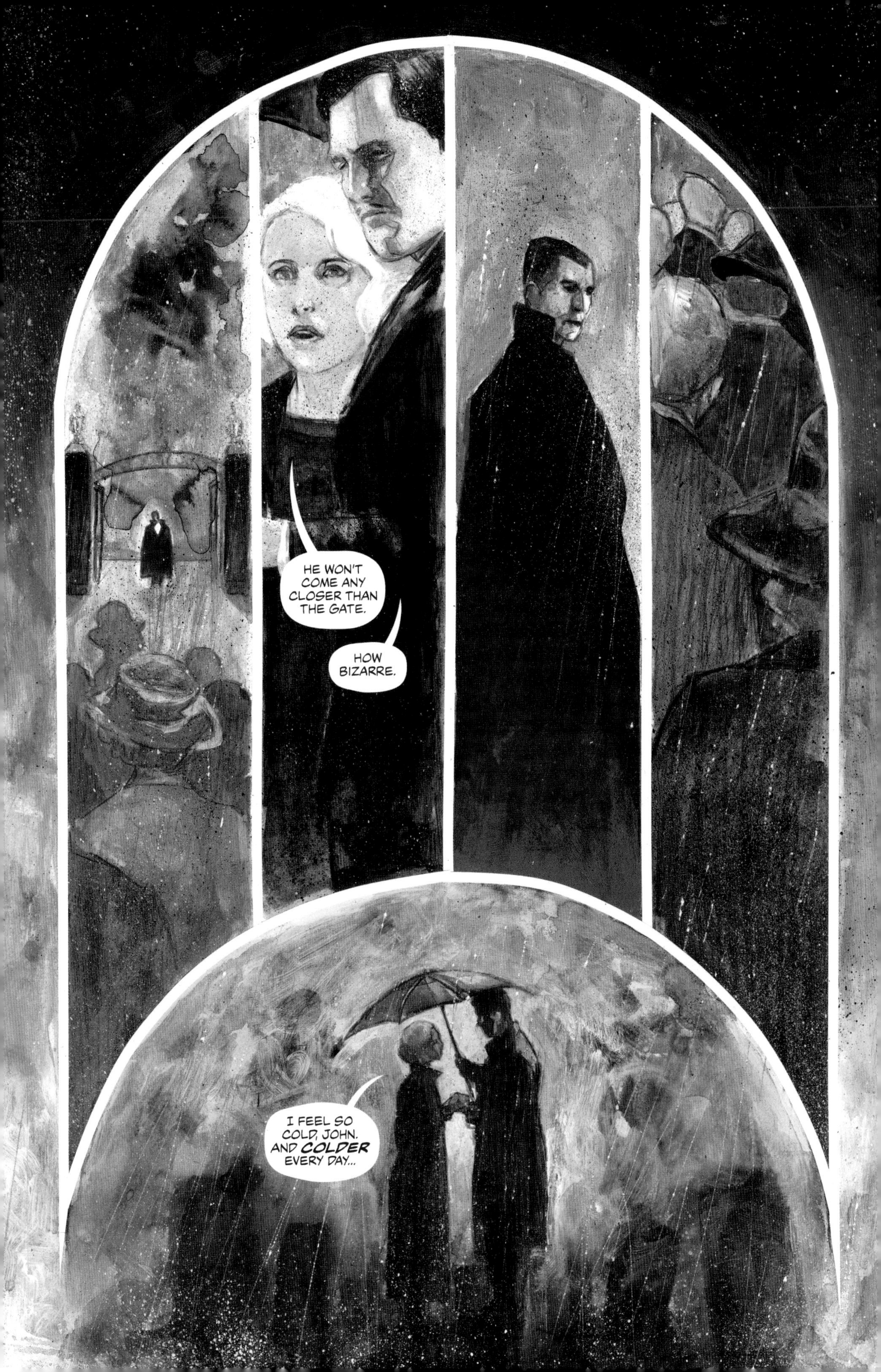
HE WON'T COME ANY CLOSER THAN THE GATE.
HOW BIZARRE.
I FEEL SO COLD, JOHN. AND COLDER EVERY DAY...

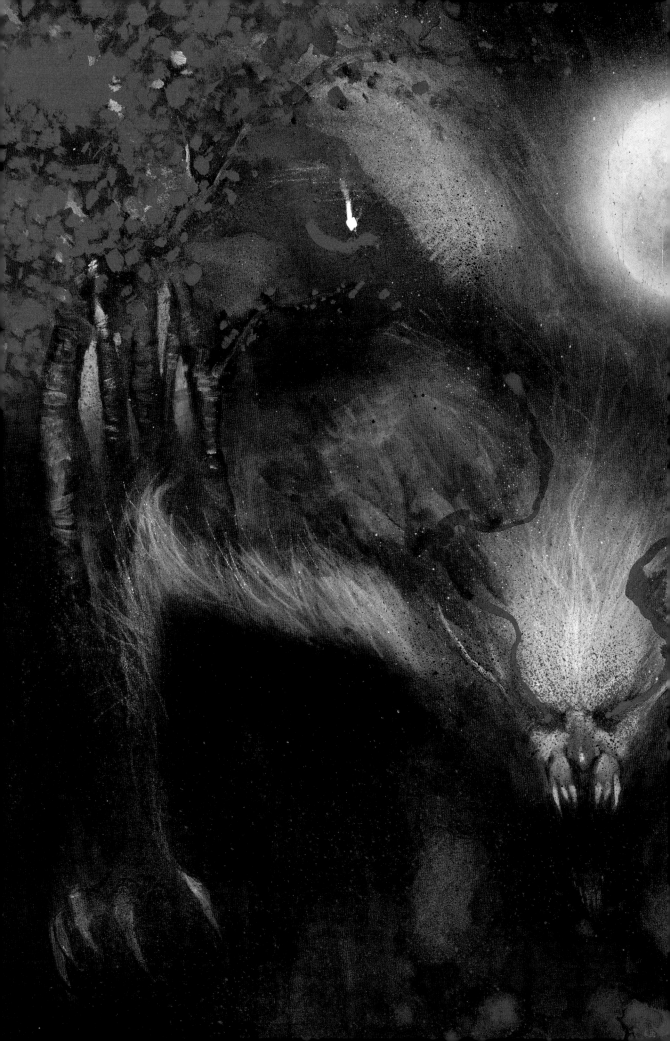

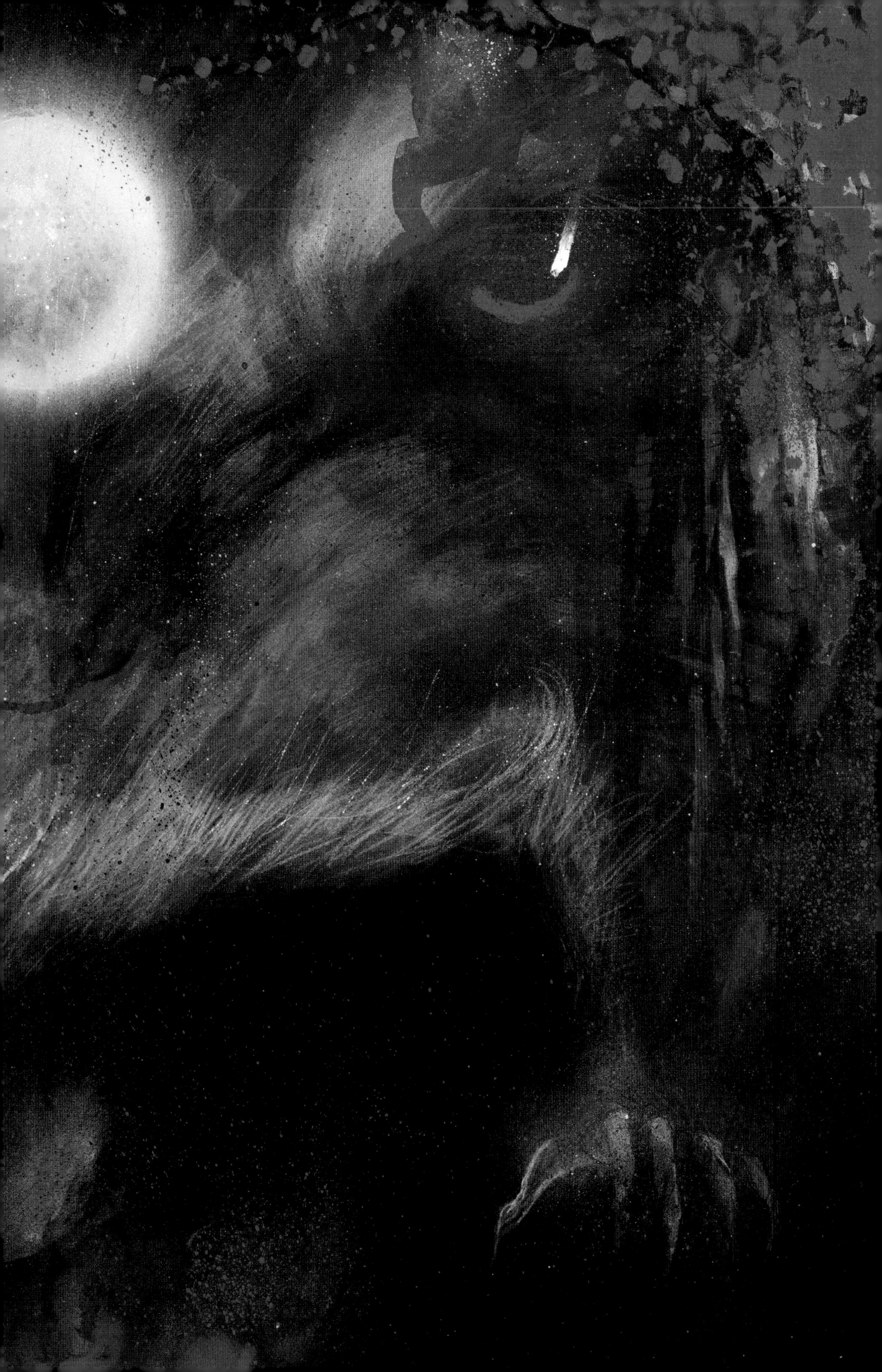

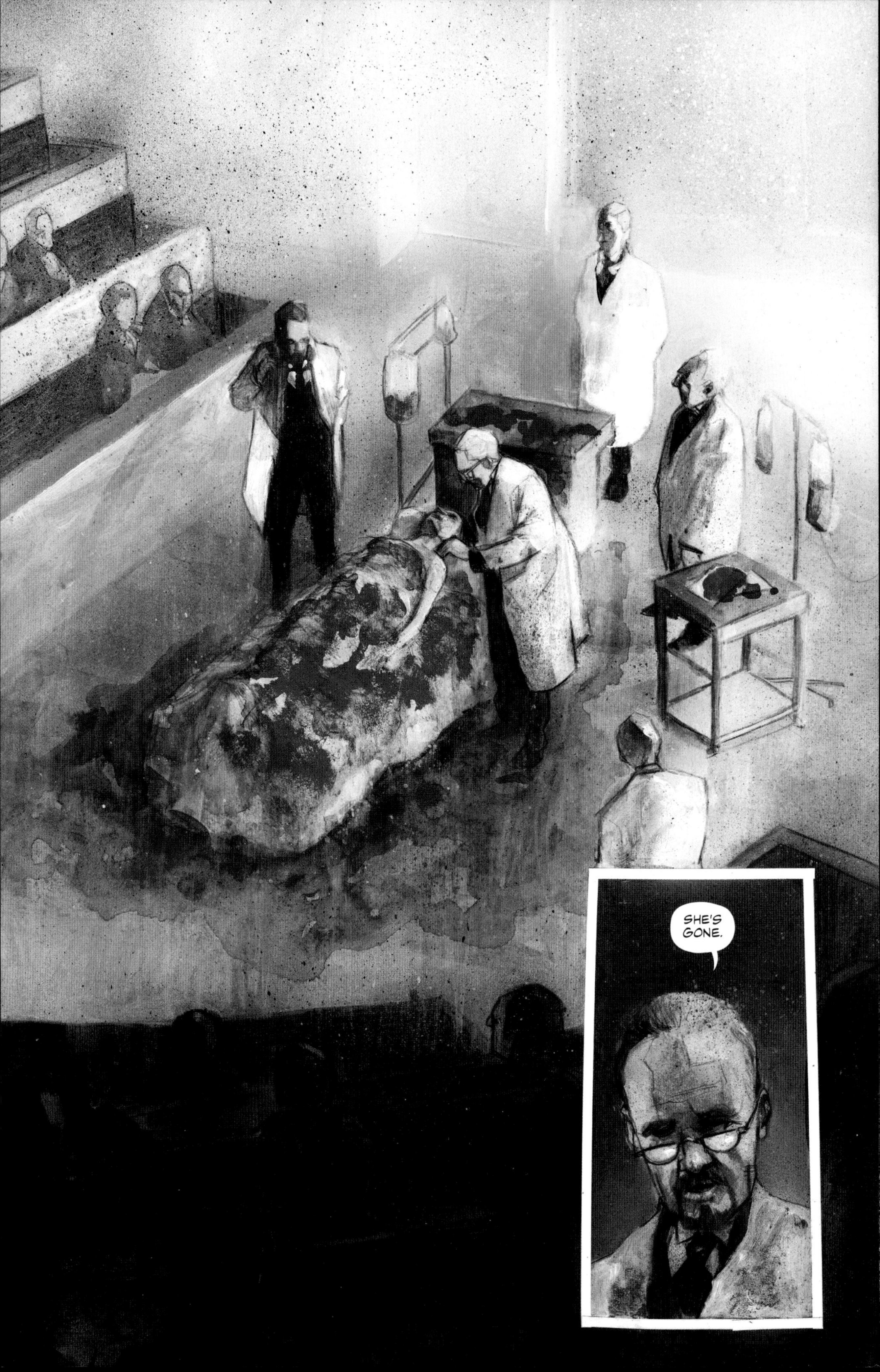
SHE'S GONE.

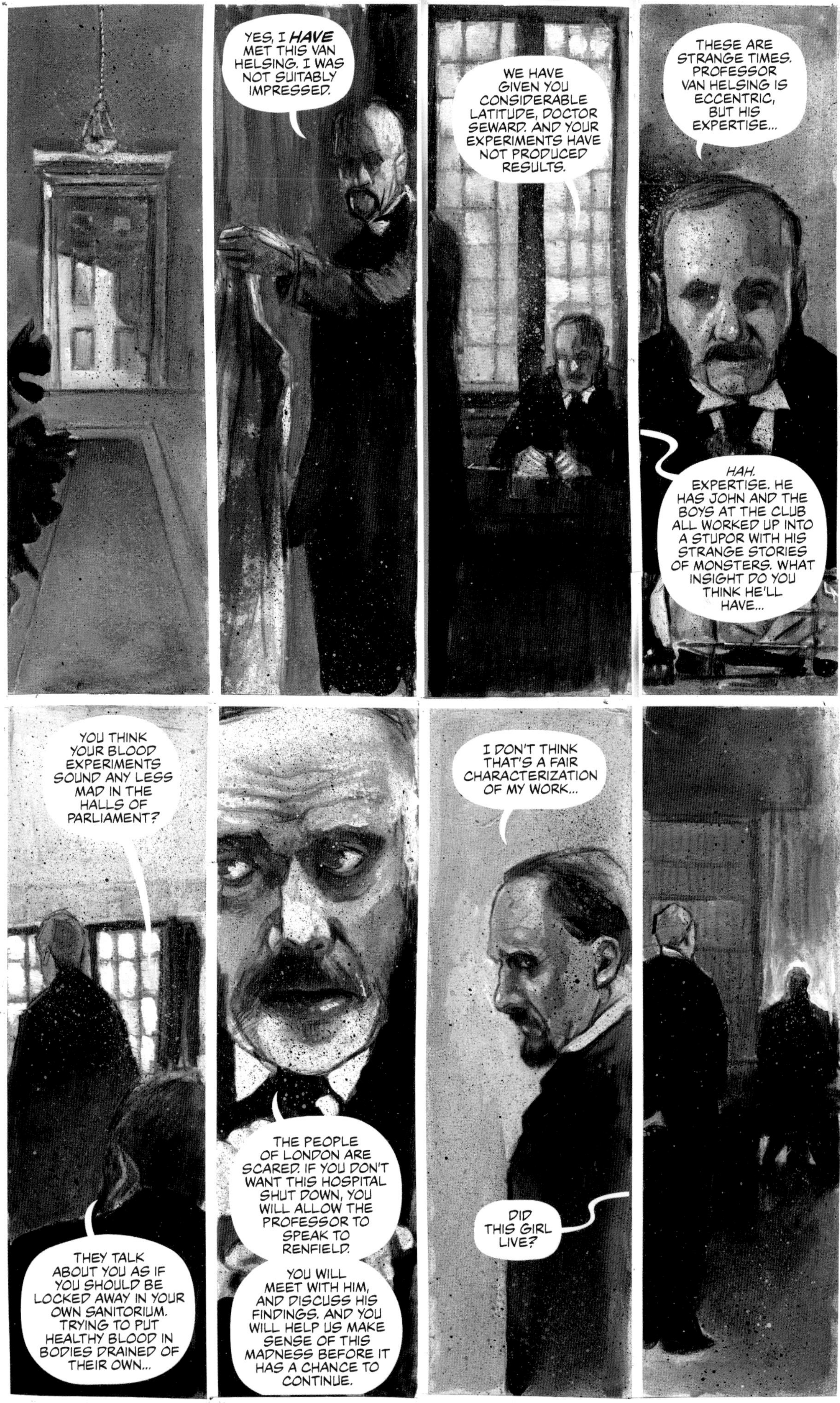
YES, I *HAVE* MET THIS VAN HELSING. I WAS NOT SUITABLY IMPRESSED.
WE HAVE GIVEN YOU CONSIDERABLE LATITUDE, DOCTOR SEWARD. AND YOUR EXPERIMENTS HAVE NOT PRODUCED RESULTS.
THESE ARE STRANGE TIMES. PROFESSOR VAN HELSING IS ECCENTRIC, BUT HIS EXPERTISE...
HAH. EXPERTISE. HE HAS JOHN AND THE BOYS AT THE CLUB ALL WORKED UP INTO A STUPOR WITH HIS STRANGE STORIES OF MONSTERS. WHAT INSIGHT DO YOU THINK HE'LL HAVE...
YOU THINK YOUR BLOOD EXPERIMENTS SOUND ANY LESS MAD IN THE HALLS OF PARLIAMENT?
THEY TALK ABOUT YOU AS IF YOU SHOULD BE LOCKED AWAY IN YOUR OWN SANITORIUM. TRYING TO PUT HEALTHY BLOOD IN BODIES DRAINED OF THEIR OWN...
THE PEOPLE OF LONDON ARE SCARED. IF YOU DON'T WANT THIS HOSPITAL SHUT DOWN, YOU WILL ALLOW THE PROFESSOR TO SPEAK TO RENFIELD.
YOU WILL MEET WITH HIM, AND DISCUSS HIS FINDINGS. AND YOU WILL HELP US MAKE SENSE OF THIS MADNESS BEFORE IT HAS A CHANCE TO CONTINUE.
I DON'T THINK THAT'S A FAIR CHARACTERIZATION OF MY WORK...
DID THIS GIRL LIVE?

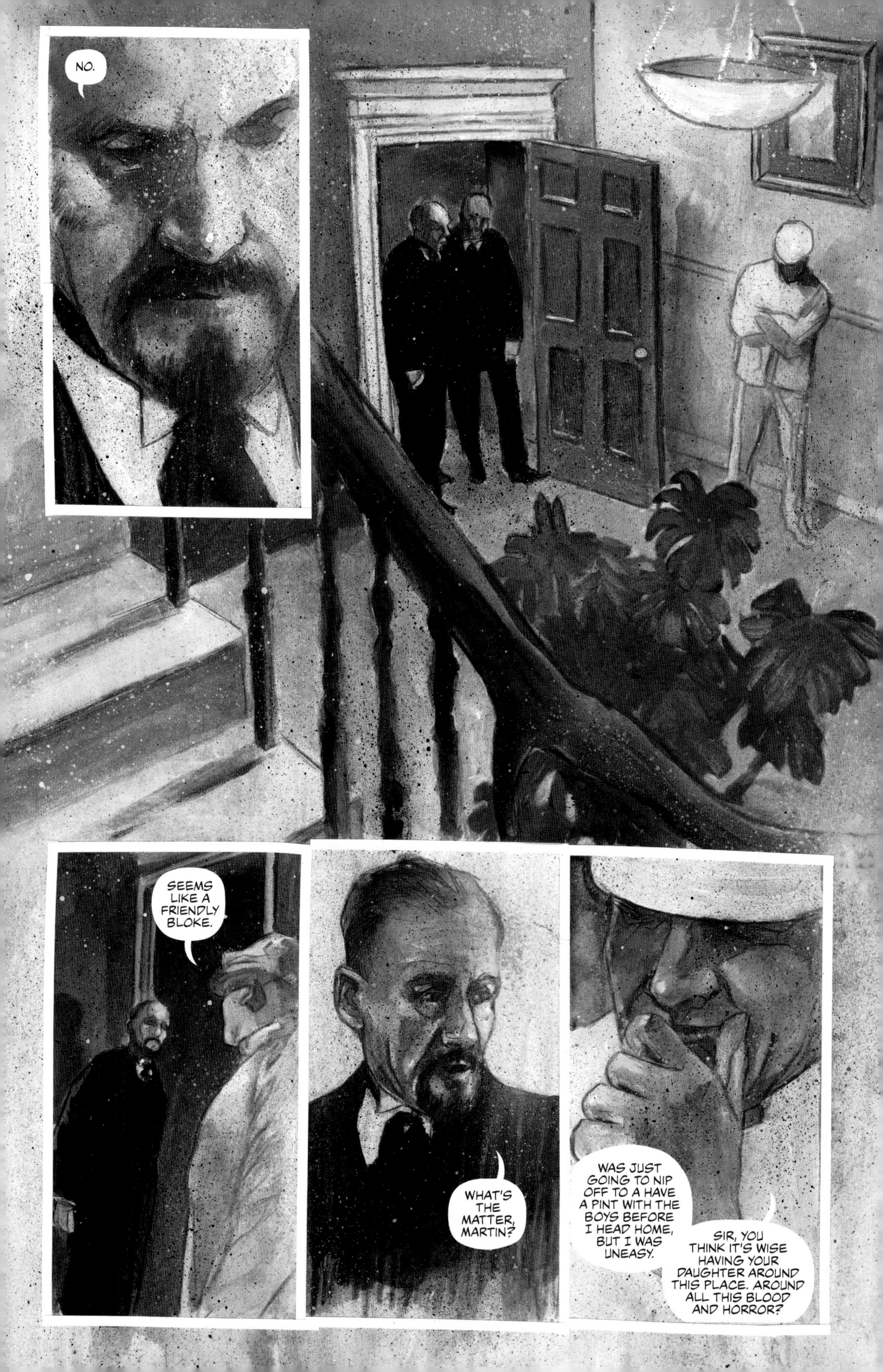
NO.
SEEMS LIKE A FRIENDLY BLOKE.
WHAT'S THE MATTER, MARTIN?
WAS JUST GOING TO NIP OFF TO A HAVE A PINT WITH THE BOYS BEFORE I HEAD HOME, BUT I WAS UNEASY.
SIR, YOU THINK IT'S WISE HAVING YOUR DAUGHTER AROUND THIS PLACE. AROUND ALL THIS BLOOD AND HORROR?

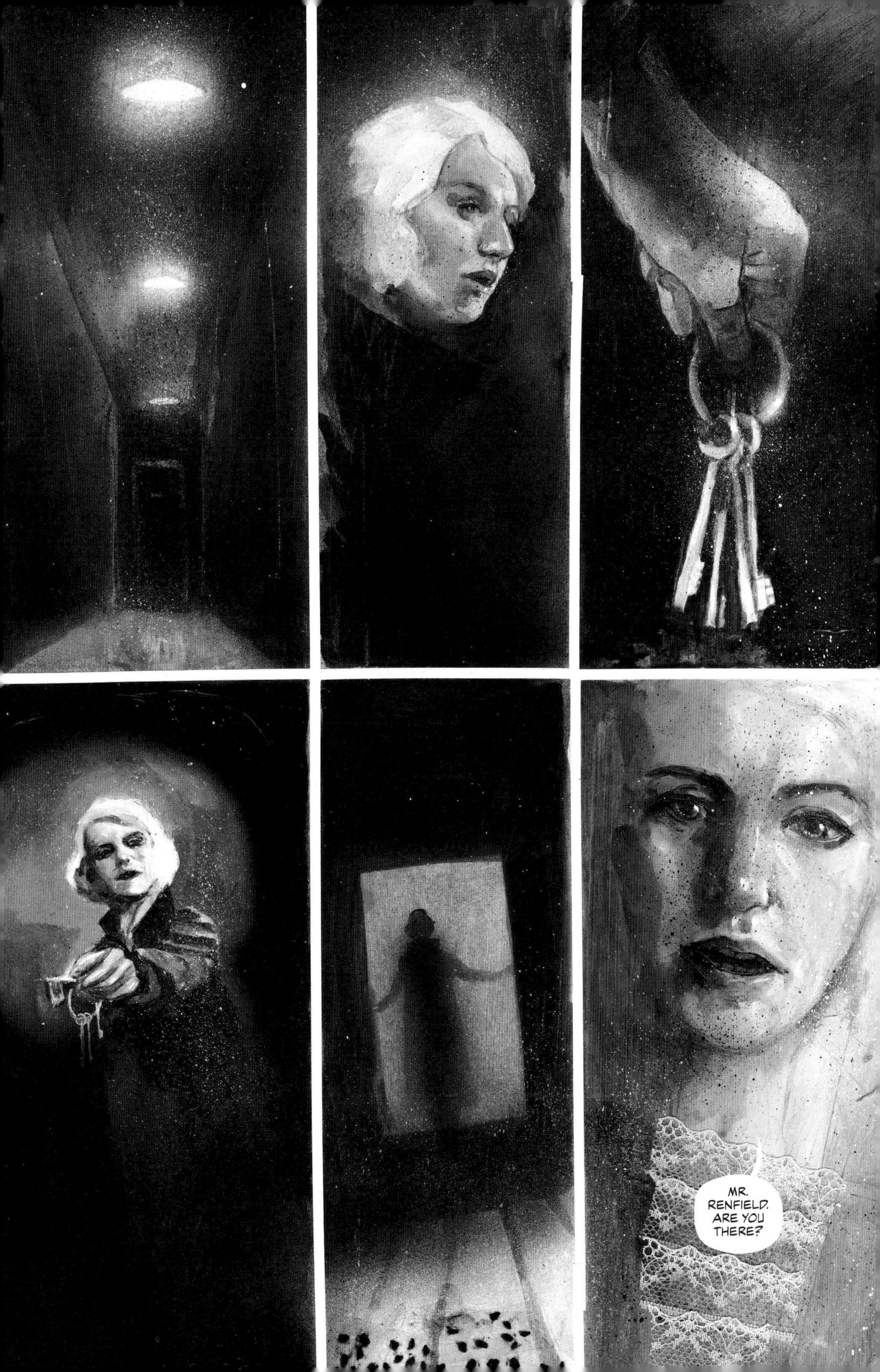
MR. RENFIELD. ARE YOU THERE?

OH, YES. I USUALLY AM. SOMETIMES I LIKE TO GO OUT FOR A LITTLE WALK, BUT IT'S NICE AND SAFE INSIDE THESE WALLS.
YOU... HAVE A KIND VOICE.
DO I KNOW YOU?
I SAW YOU WHEN MY FATHER FIRST BROUGHT YOU INTO HIS SANITORIUM. YOU WERE SHOUTING SOMETHING ABOUT FLIES.
THE DOCTOR'S DAUGHTER, YES.
I'VE SEEN YOU IN MY MIND.
IN HIS MIND.

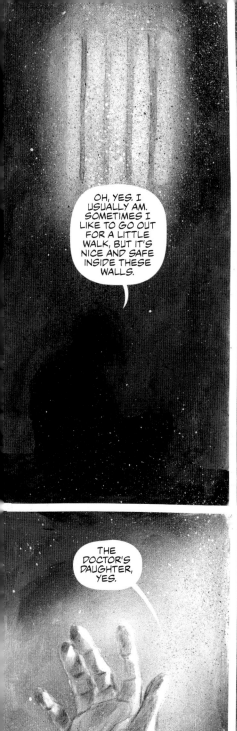

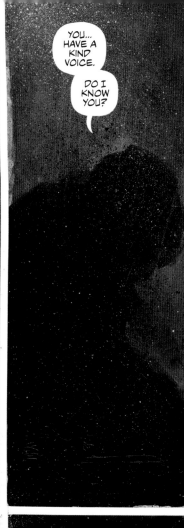

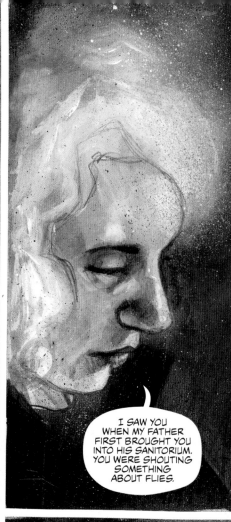

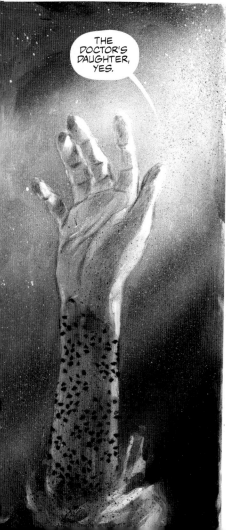

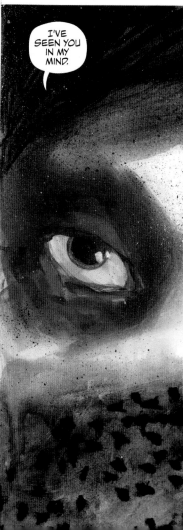

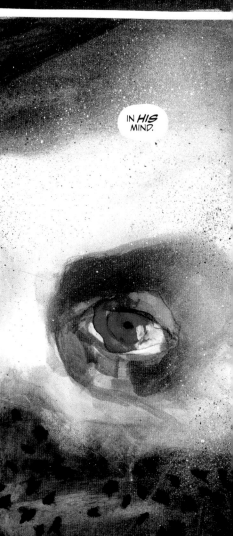

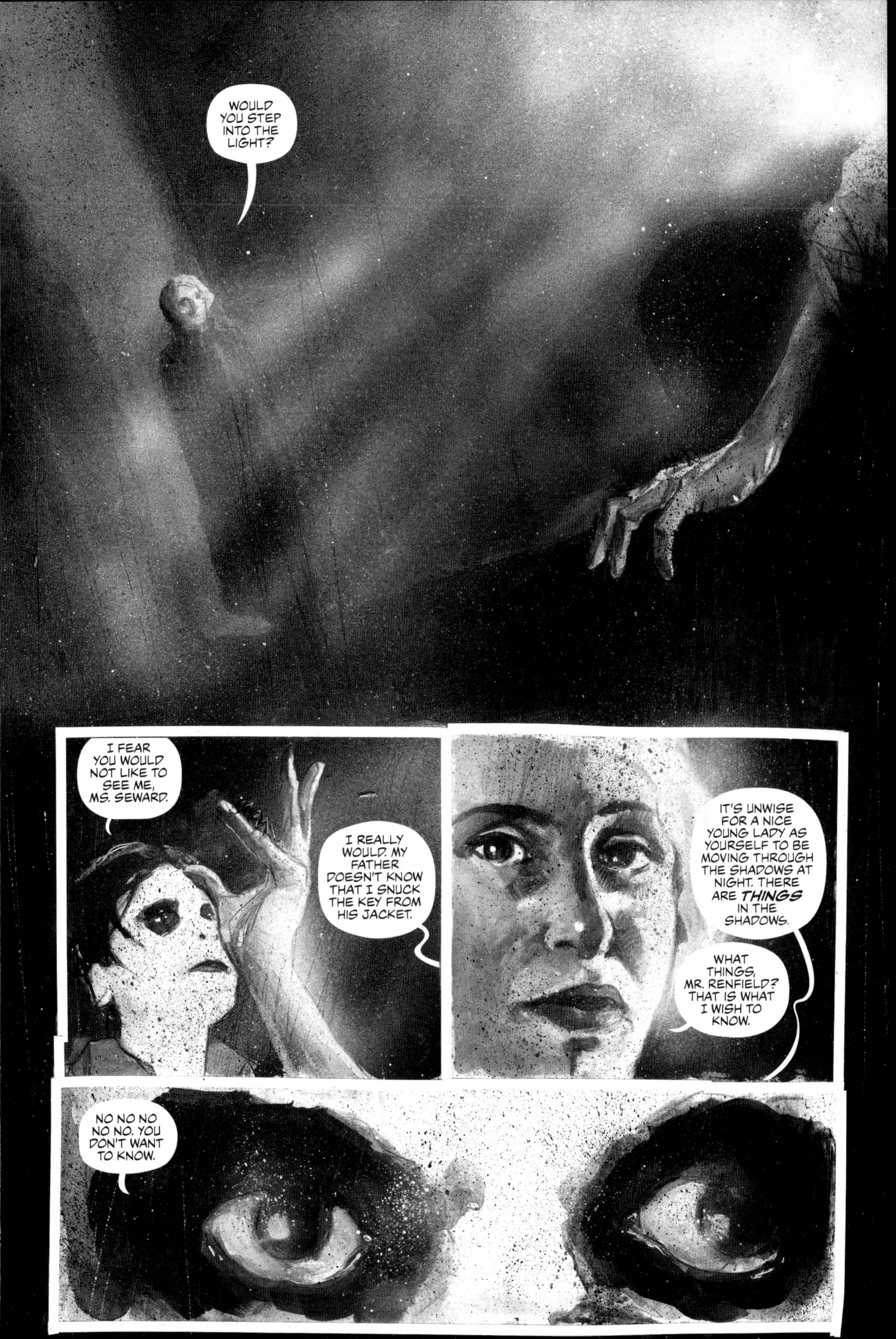
WOULD YOU STEP INTO THE LIGHT?
I FEAR YOU WOULD NOT LIKE TO SEE ME, MS. SEWARD.
I REALLY WOULD. MY FATHER DOESN'T KNOW THAT I SNUCK THE KEY FROM HIS JACKET.
IT'S UNWISE FOR A NICE YOUNG LADY AS YOURSELF TO BE MOVING THROUGH THE SHADOWS AT NIGHT. THERE ARE THINGS IN THE SHADOWS.
WHAT THINGS, MR. RENFIELD? THAT IS WHAT I WISH TO KNOW.
NO NO NO NO NO. YOU DON'T WANT TO KNOW.

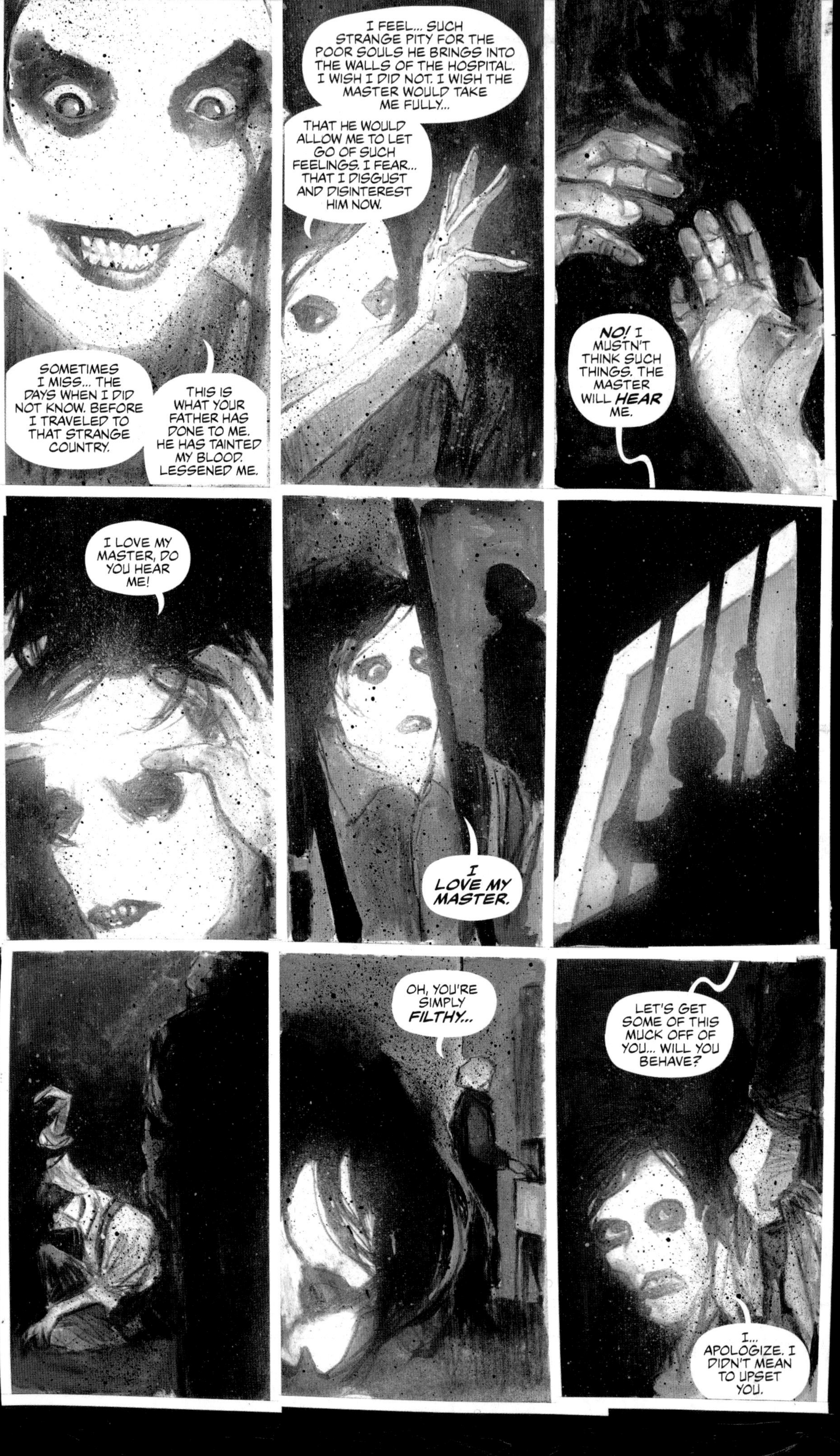
SOMETIMES I MISS... THE DAYS WHEN I DID NOT KNOW. BEFORE I TRAVELED TO THAT STRANGE COUNTRY.
THIS IS WHAT YOUR FATHER HAS DONE TO ME. HE HAS TAINTED MY BLOOD. LESSENED ME.
I FEEL... SUCH STRANGE PITY FOR THE POOR SOULS HE BRINGS INTO THE WALLS OF THE HOSPITAL. I WISH I DID NOT. I WISH THE MASTER WOULD TAKE ME FULLY...
THAT HE WOULD ALLOW ME TO LET GO OF SUCH FEELINGS. I FEAR... THAT I DISGUST AND DISINTEREST HIM NOW.
NO! I MUSTN'T THINK SUCH THINGS. THE MASTER WILL HEAR ME.
I LOVE MY MASTER, DO YOU HEAR ME!
I LOVE MY MASTER.
OH, YOU'RE SIMPLY FILTHY...
LET'S GET SOME OF THIS MUCK OFF OF YOU... WILL YOU BEHAVE?
I... APOLOGIZE. I DIDN'T MEAN TO UPSET YOU.

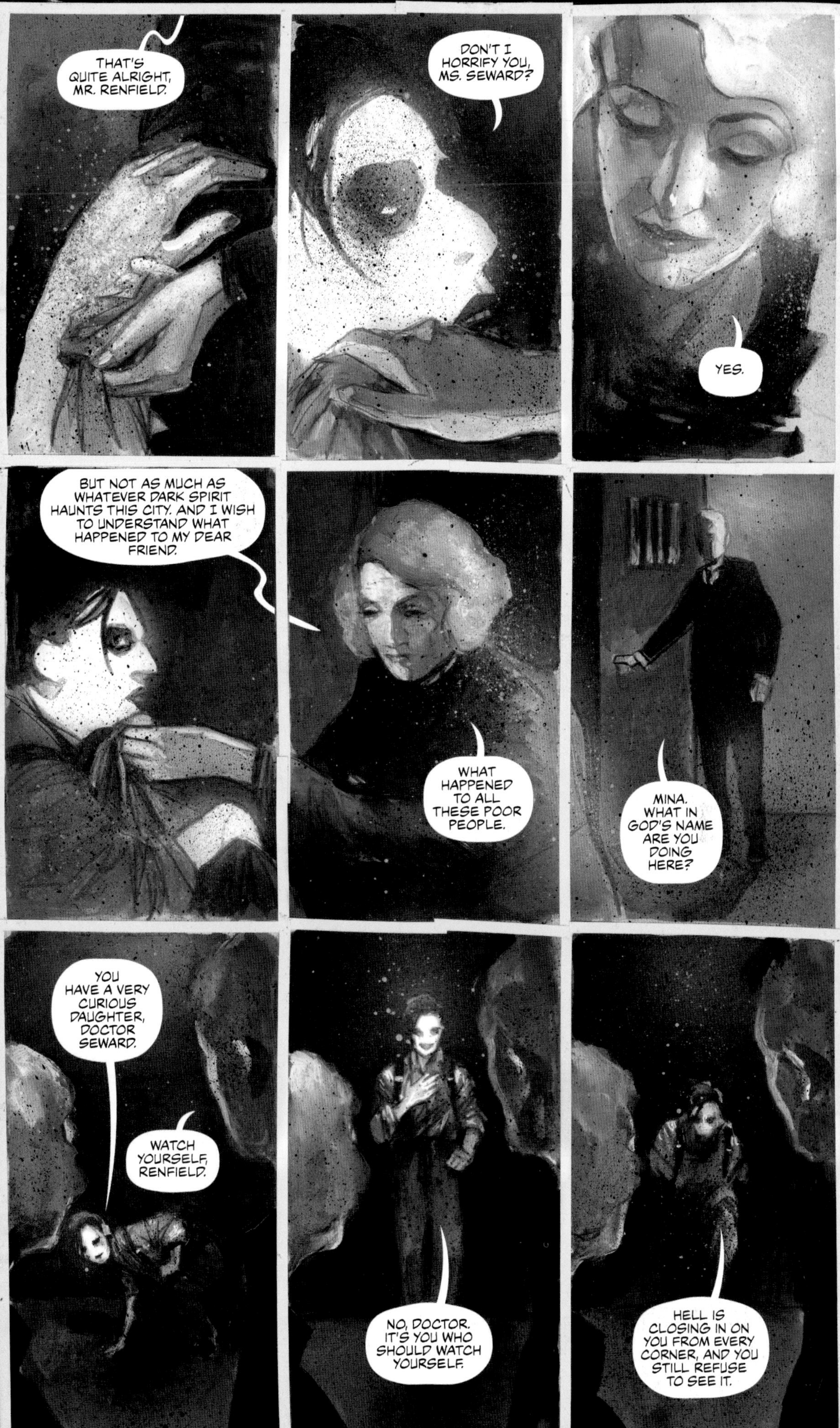
THAT'S QUITE ALRIGHT, MR. RENFIELD.
DON'T I HORRIFY YOU, MS. SEWARD?
YES.
BUT NOT AS MUCH AS WHATEVER DARK SPIRIT HAUNTS THIS CITY. AND I WISH TO UNDERSTAND WHAT HAPPENED TO MY DEAR FRIEND.
WHAT HAPPENED TO ALL THESE POOR PEOPLE.
MINA. WHAT IN GOD'S NAME ARE YOU DOING HERE?
YOU HAVE A VERY CURIOUS DAUGHTER, DOCTOR SEWARD.
WATCH YOURSELF, RENFIELD.
NO, DOCTOR. IT'S YOU WHO SHOULD WATCH YOURSELF.
HELL IS CLOSING IN ON YOU FROM EVERY CORNER, AND YOU STILL REFUSE TO SEE IT.

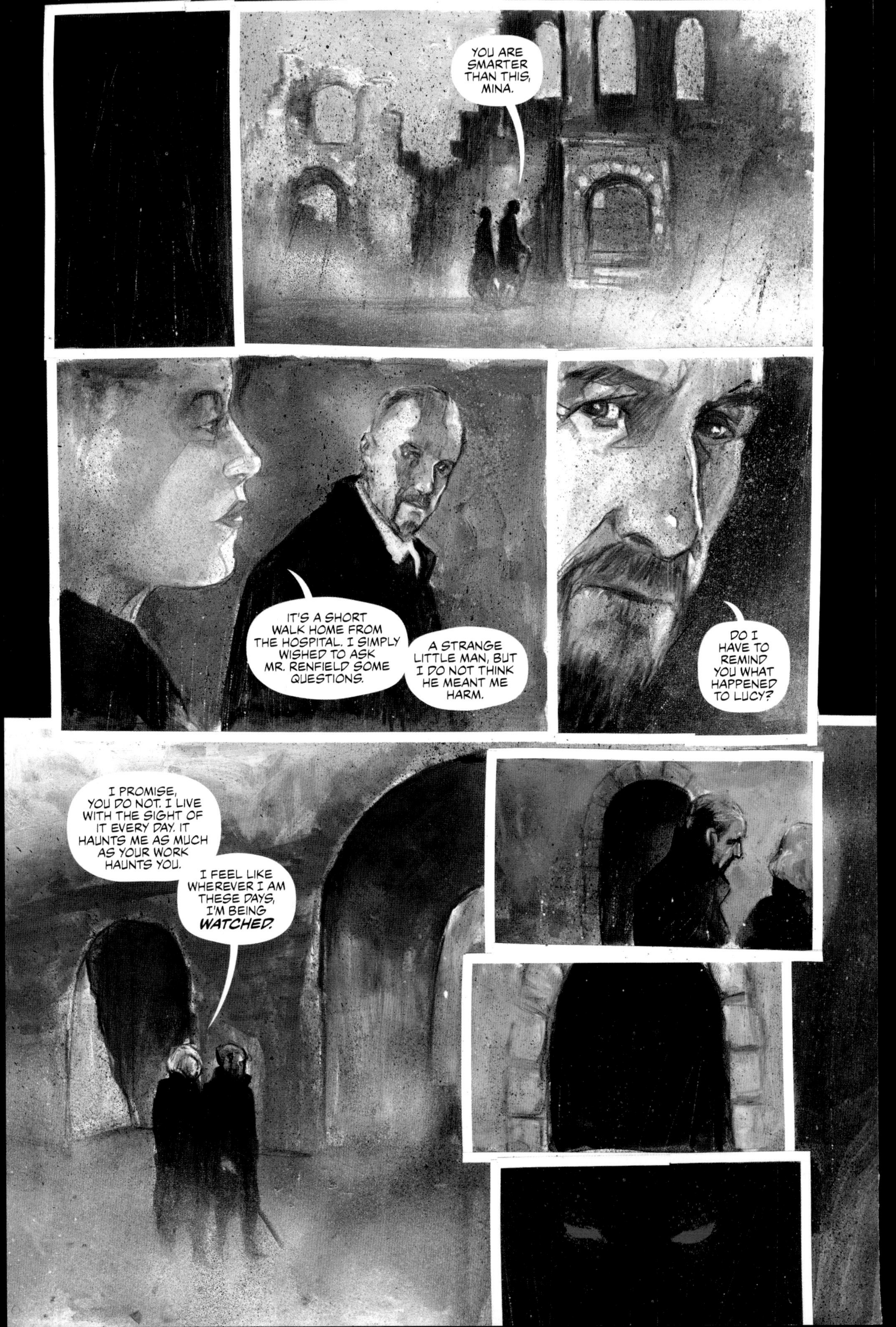
YOU ARE SMARTER THAN THIS, MINA.
IT'S A SHORT WALK HOME FROM THE HOSPITAL. I SIMPLY WISHED TO ASK MR. RENFIELD SOME QUESTIONS.
A STRANGE LITTLE MAN, BUT I DO NOT THINK HE MEANT ME HARM.
DO I HAVE TO REMIND YOU WHAT HAPPENED TO LUCY?
I PROMISE, YOU DO NOT. I LIVE WITH THE SIGHT OF IT EVERY DAY. IT HAUNTS ME AS MUCH AS YOUR WORK HAUNTS YOU.
I FEEL LIKE WHEREVER I AM THESE DAYS, I'M BEING WATCHED.

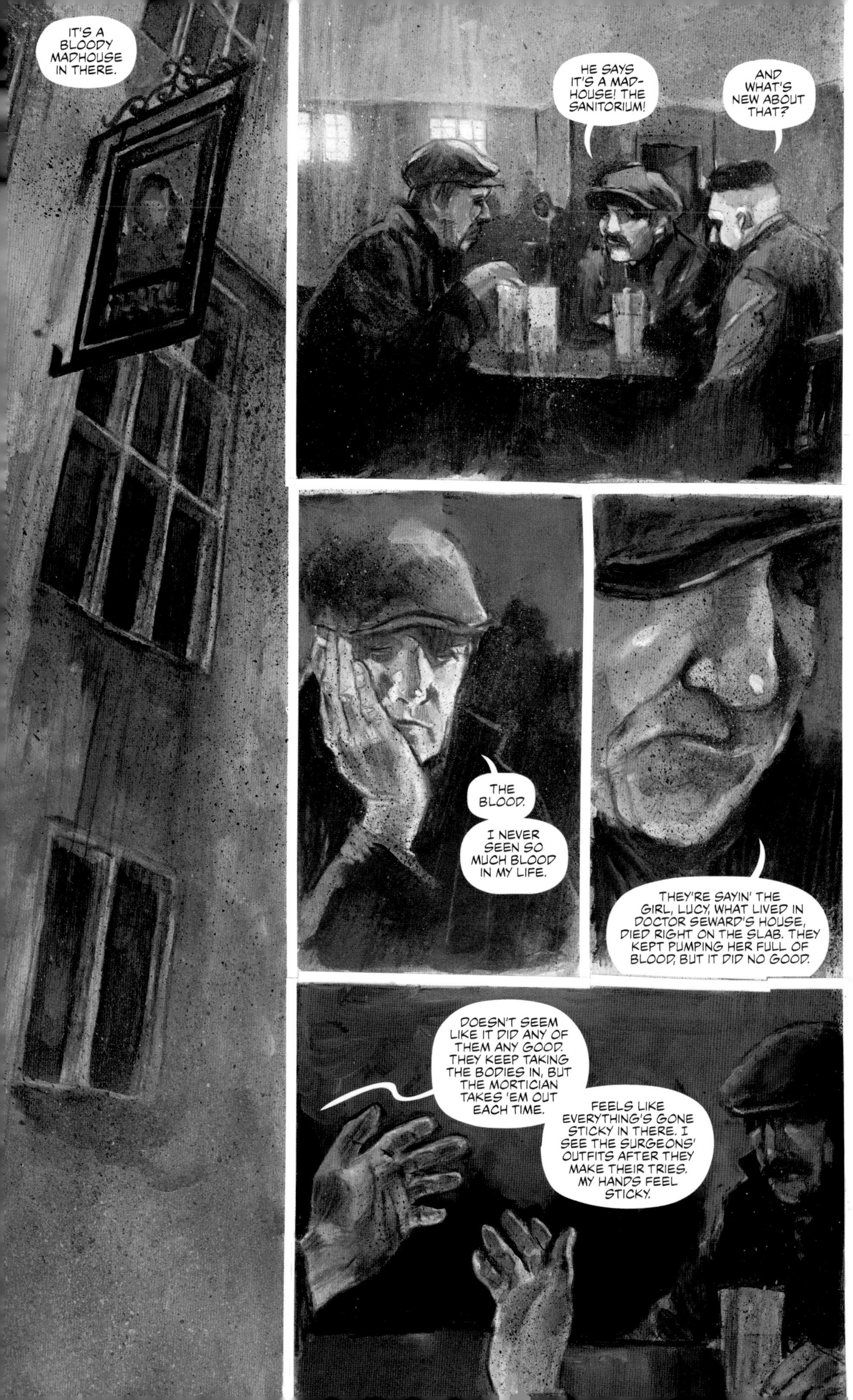
IT'S A BLOODY MADHOUSE IN THERE.
HE SAYS IT'S A MAD-HOUSE! THE SANITORIUM!
AND WHAT'S NEW ABOUT THAT?
THE BLOOD.
I NEVER SEEN SO MUCH BLOOD IN MY LIFE.
THEY'RE SAYIN' THE GIRL, LUCY, WHAT LIVED IN DOCTOR SEWARD'S HOUSE, DIED RIGHT ON THE SLAB. THEY KEPT PUMPING HER FULL OF BLOOD, BUT IT DID NO GOOD.
DOESN'T SEEM LIKE IT DID ANY OF THEM ANY GOOD. THEY KEEP TAKING THE BODIES IN, BUT THE MORTICIAN TAKES 'EM OUT EACH TIME.
FEELS LIKE EVERYTHING'S GONE STICKY IN THERE. I SEE THE SURGEONS' OUTFITS AFTER THEY MAKE THEIR TRIES. MY HANDS FEEL STICKY.

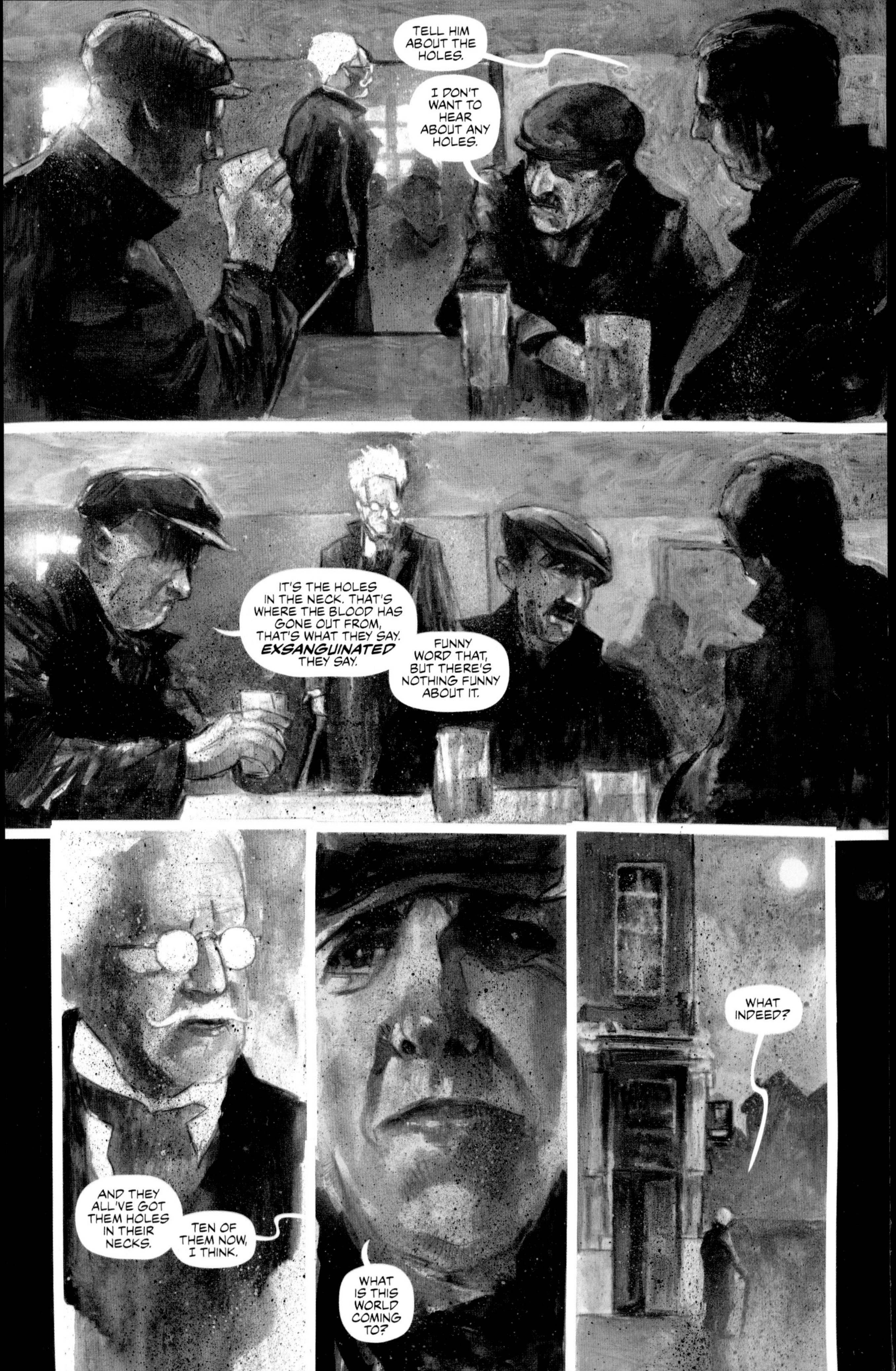
TELL HIM ABOUT THE HOLES.
I DON'T WANT TO HEAR ABOUT ANY HOLES.
IT'S THE HOLES IN THE NECK. THAT'S WHERE THE BLOOD HAS GONE OUT FROM, THAT'S WHAT THEY SAY. **EXSANGUINATED** THEY SAY.
FUNNY WORD THAT, BUT THERE'S NOTHING FUNNY ABOUT IT.
AND THEY ALL'VE GOT THEM HOLES IN THEIR NECKS.
TEN OF THEM NOW, I THINK.
WHAT IS THIS WORLD COMING TO?
WHAT INDEED?

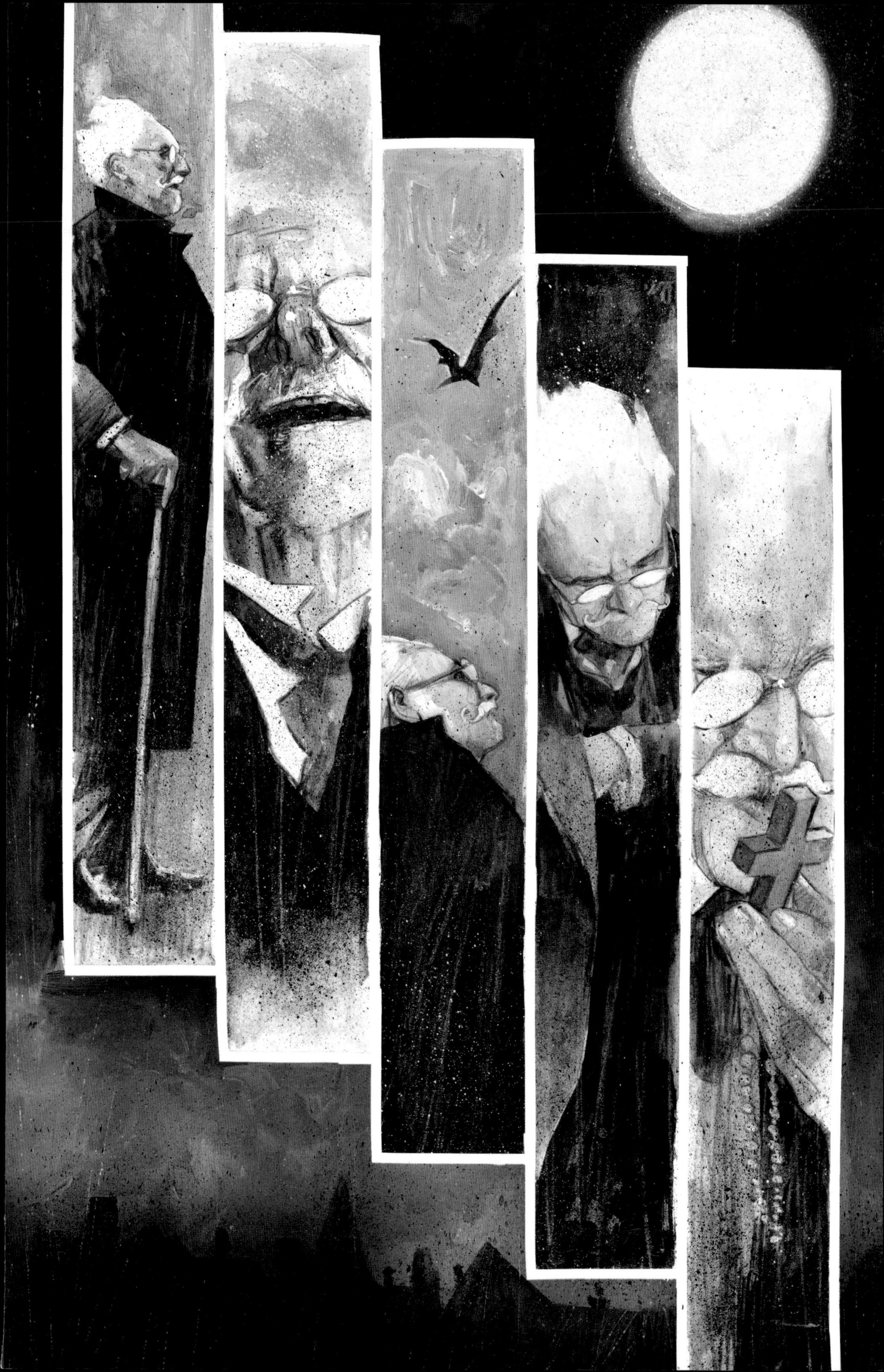

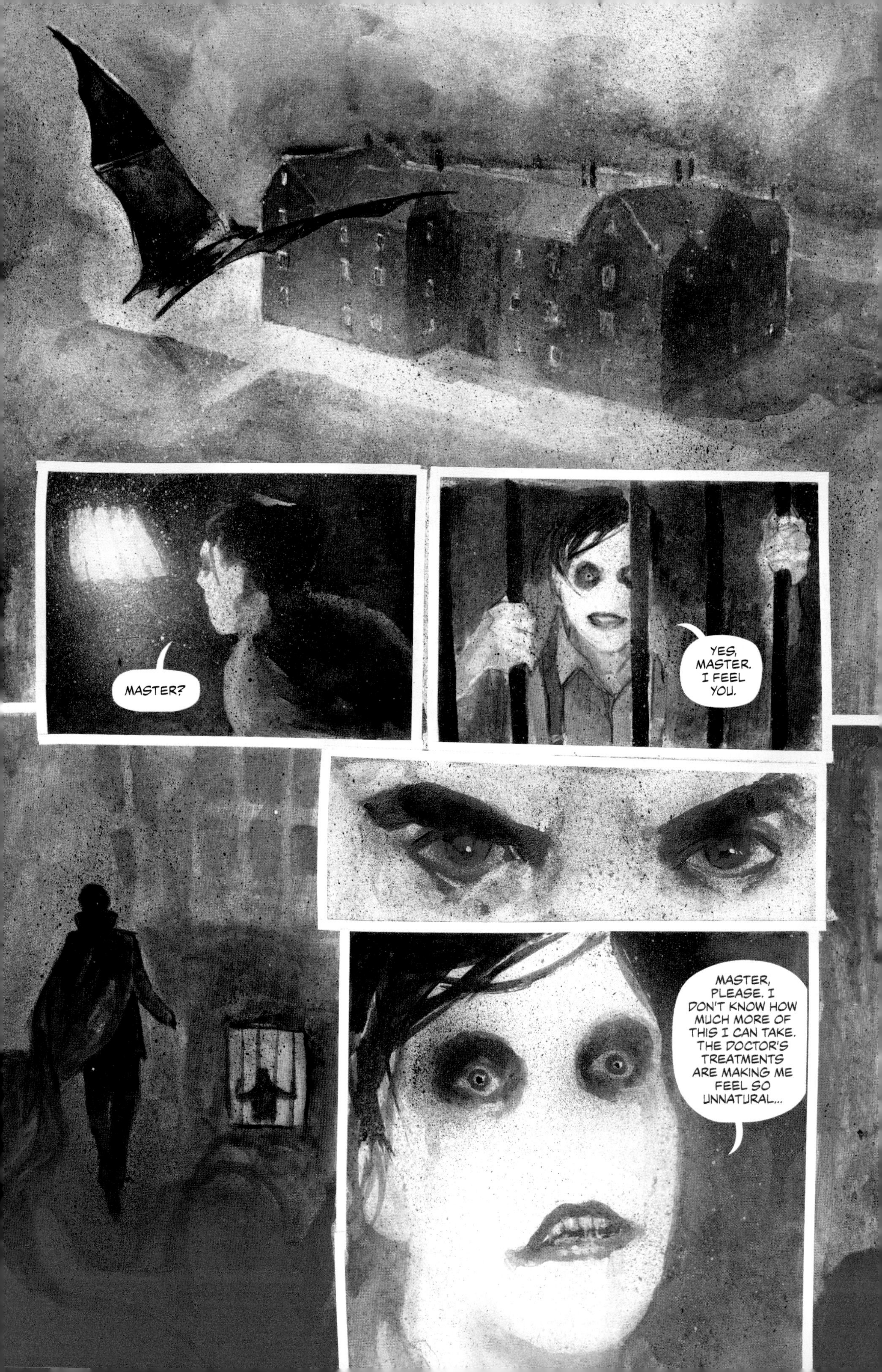
MASTER?
YES, MASTER. I FEEL YOU.
MASTER, PLEASE. I DON'T KNOW HOW MUCH MORE OF THIS I CAN TAKE. THE DOCTOR'S TREATMENTS ARE MAKING ME FEEL SO UNNATURAL...

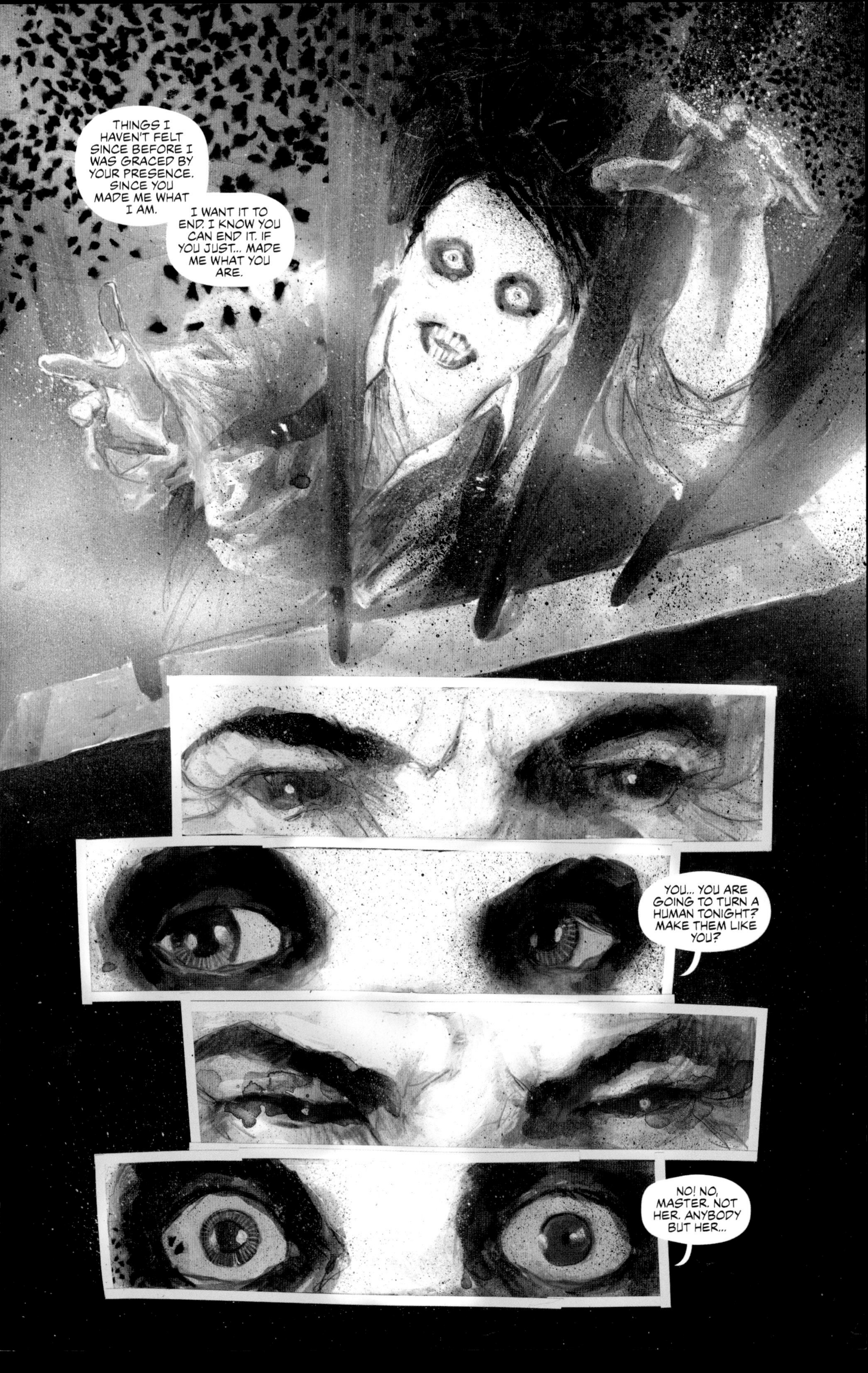
THINGS I HAVEN'T FELT SINCE BEFORE I WAS GRACED BY YOUR PRESENCE. SINCE YOU MADE ME WHAT I AM.
I WANT IT TO END. I KNOW YOU CAN END IT. IF YOU JUST... MADE ME WHAT YOU ARE.
YOU... YOU ARE GOING TO TURN A HUMAN TONIGHT? MAKE THEM LIKE YOU?
NO! NO, MASTER. NOT HER. ANYBODY BUT HER...

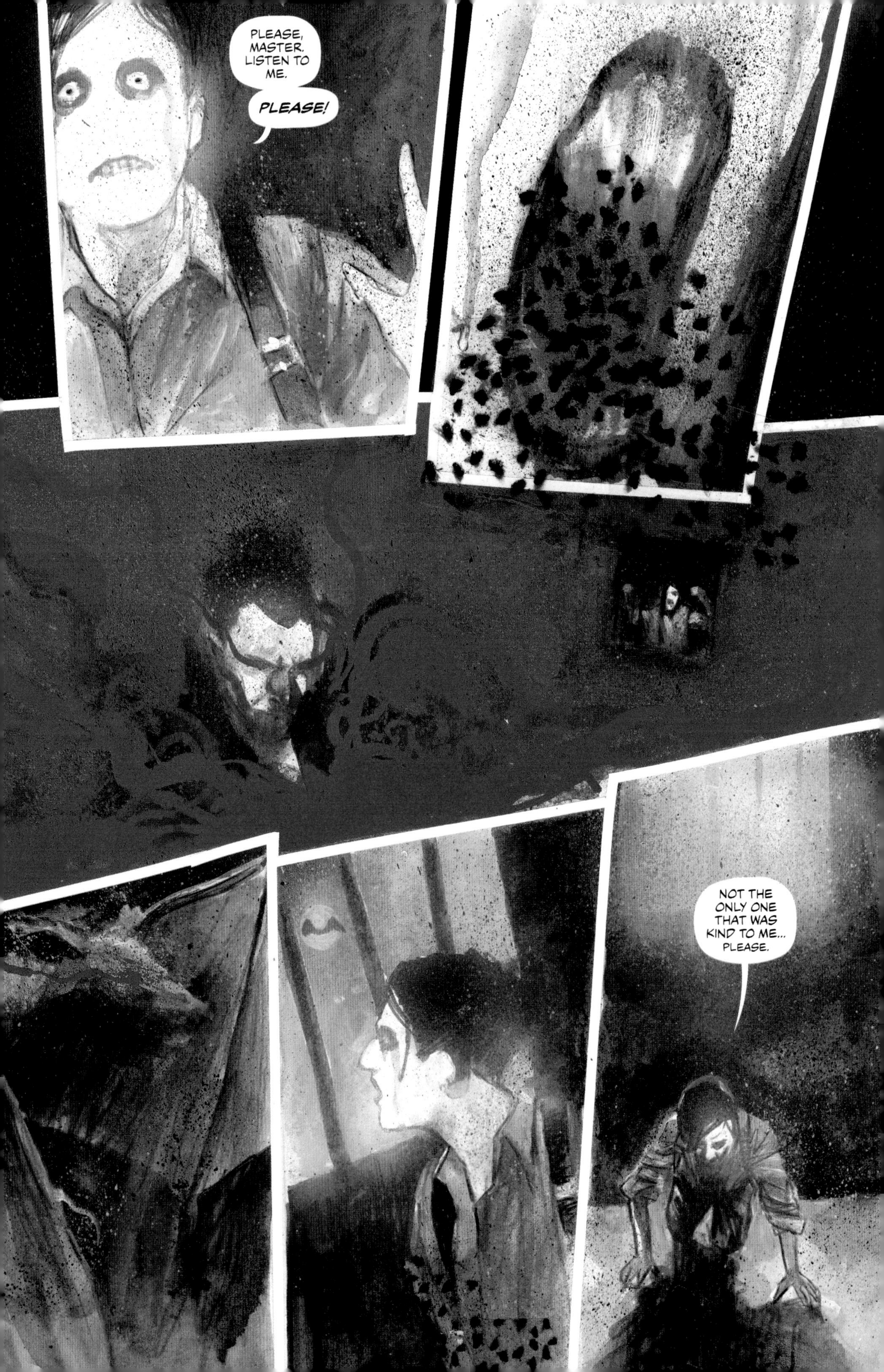
PLEASE, MASTER. LISTEN TO ME.
PLEASE!
NOT THE ONLY ONE THAT WAS KIND TO ME... PLEASE.

DOCTOR SEWARD, I WAS VERY PLEASED TO RECEIVE YOUR MESSAGE.

I'M SURE YOU WERE.

I WOULD HAVE BEEN GLAD TO COME TO YOUR HOME, OR TO YOUR OFFICE. I WAS TAKING A WALK NEAR THERE EARLIER THIS EVENING.

I THOUGHT THE CLUB WOULD BE MORE SUITABLE.

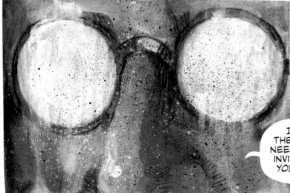

I'M NOT THE ONE YOU NEED TO FEAR INVITING INTO YOUR HOME.

EXCUSE ME?

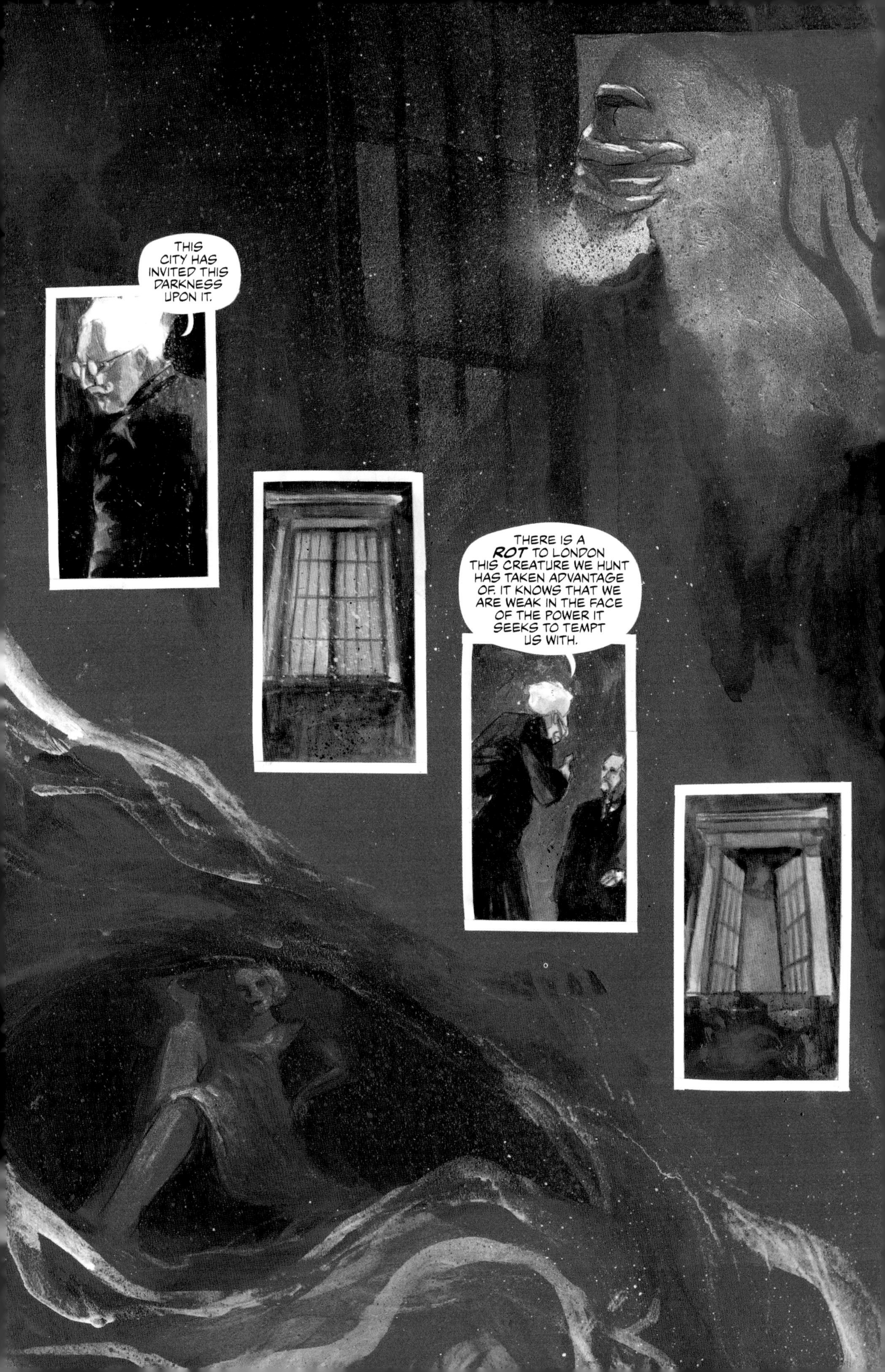
THIS CITY HAS INVITED THIS DARKNESS UPON IT.
THERE IS A ROT TO LONDON THIS CREATURE WE HUNT HAS TAKEN ADVANTAGE OF. IT KNOWS THAT WE ARE WEAK IN THE FACE OF THE POWER IT SEEKS TO TEMPT US WITH.

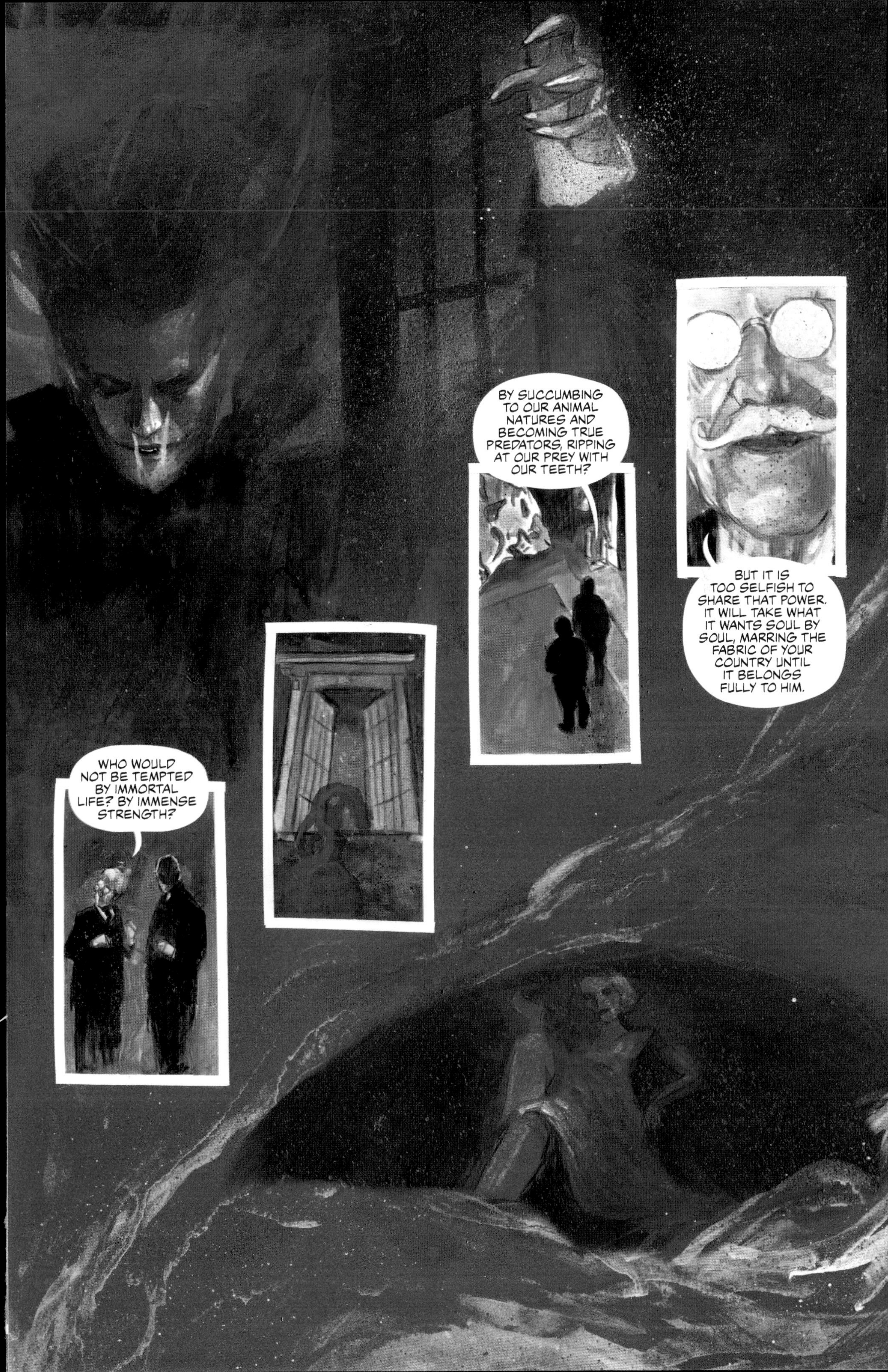
BY SUCCUMBING TO OUR ANIMAL NATURES AND BECOMING TRUE PREDATORS, RIPPING AT OUR PREY WITH OUR TEETH?
BUT IT IS TOO SELFISH TO SHARE THAT POWER. IT WILL TAKE WHAT IT WANTS SOUL BY SOUL, MARRING THE FABRIC OF YOUR COUNTRY UNTIL IT BELONGS FULLY TO HIM.
WHO WOULD NOT BE TEMPTED BY IMMORTAL LIFE? BY IMMENSE STRENGTH?

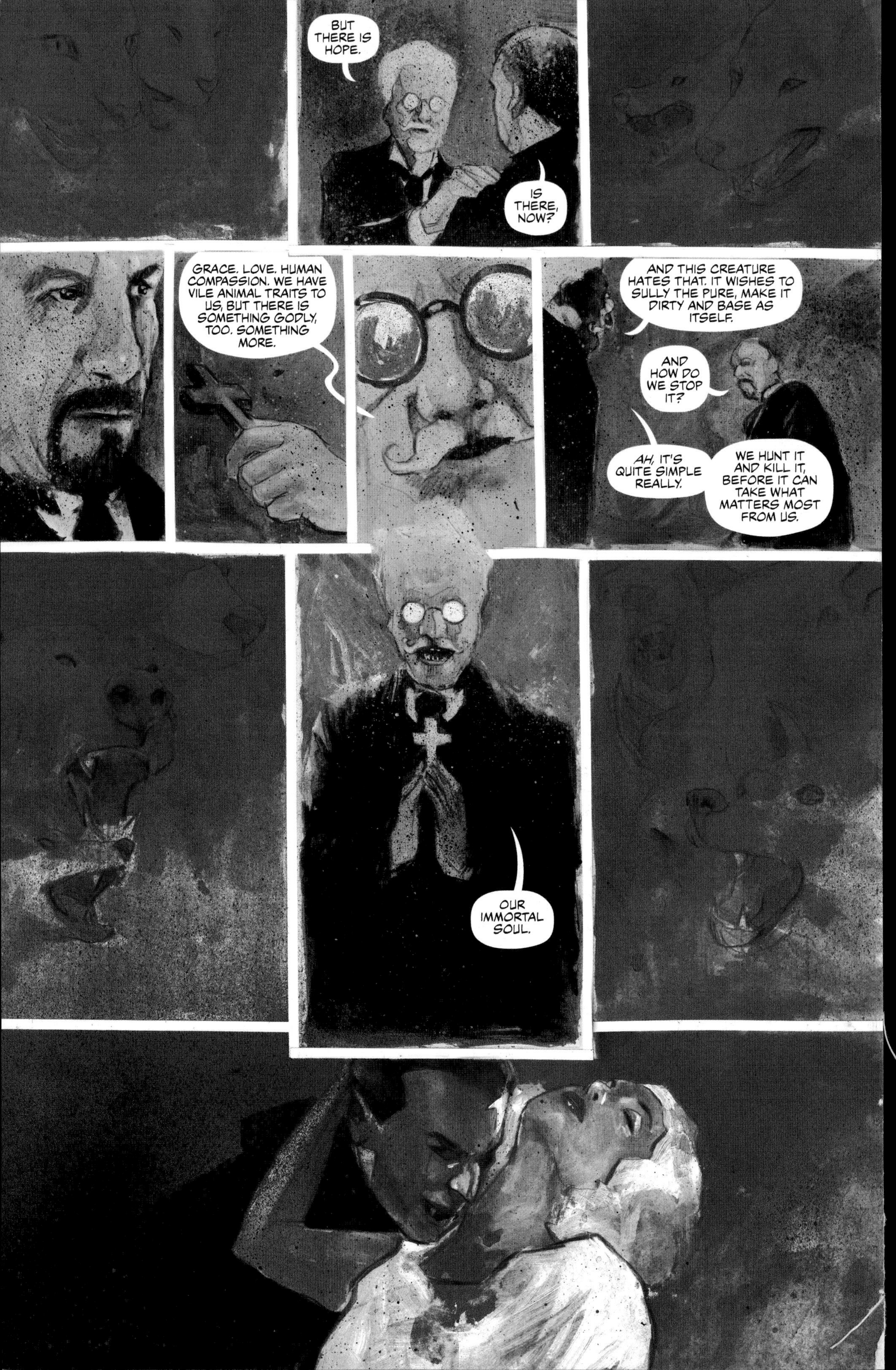
BUT THERE IS HOPE.
IS THERE, NOW?
GRACE. LOVE. HUMAN COMPASSION. WE HAVE VILE ANIMAL TRAITS TO US, BUT THERE IS SOMETHING GODLY, TOO. SOMETHING MORE.
AND THIS CREATURE HATES THAT. IT WISHES TO SULLY THE PURE, MAKE IT DIRTY AND BASE AS ITSELF.
AND HOW DO WE STOP IT?
AH, IT'S QUITE SIMPLE REALLY.
WE HUNT IT AND KILL IT, BEFORE IT CAN TAKE WHAT MATTERS MOST FROM US.
OUR IMMORTAL SOUL.

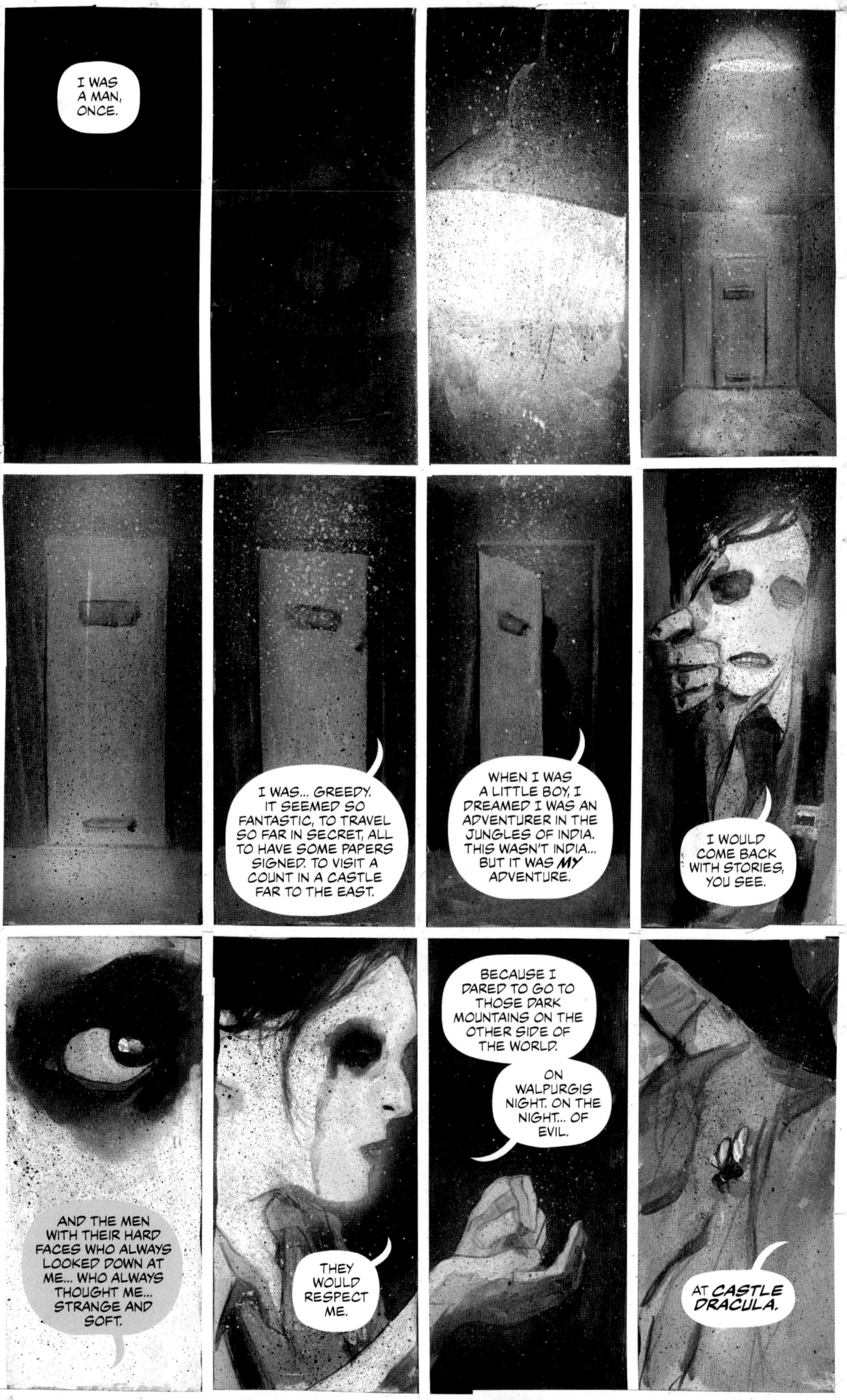
I WAS A MAN, ONCE.
I WAS... GREEDY. IT SEEMED SO FANTASTIC, TO TRAVEL SO FAR IN SECRET, ALL TO HAVE SOME PAPERS SIGNED. TO VISIT A COUNT IN A CASTLE FAR TO THE EAST.
WHEN I WAS A LITTLE BOY, I DREAMED I WAS AN ADVENTURER IN THE JUNGLES OF INDIA. THIS WASN'T INDIA... BUT IT WAS *MY* ADVENTURE.
I WOULD COME BACK WITH STORIES, YOU SEE.
AND THE MEN WITH THEIR HARD FACES WHO ALWAYS LOOKED DOWN AT ME... WHO ALWAYS THOUGHT ME... STRANGE AND SOFT.
THEY WOULD RESPECT ME.
BECAUSE I DARED TO GO TO THOSE DARK MOUNTAINS ON THE OTHER SIDE OF THE WORLD.
ON WALPURGIS NIGHT. ON THE NIGHT... OF EVIL.
AT ***CASTLE DRACULA.***

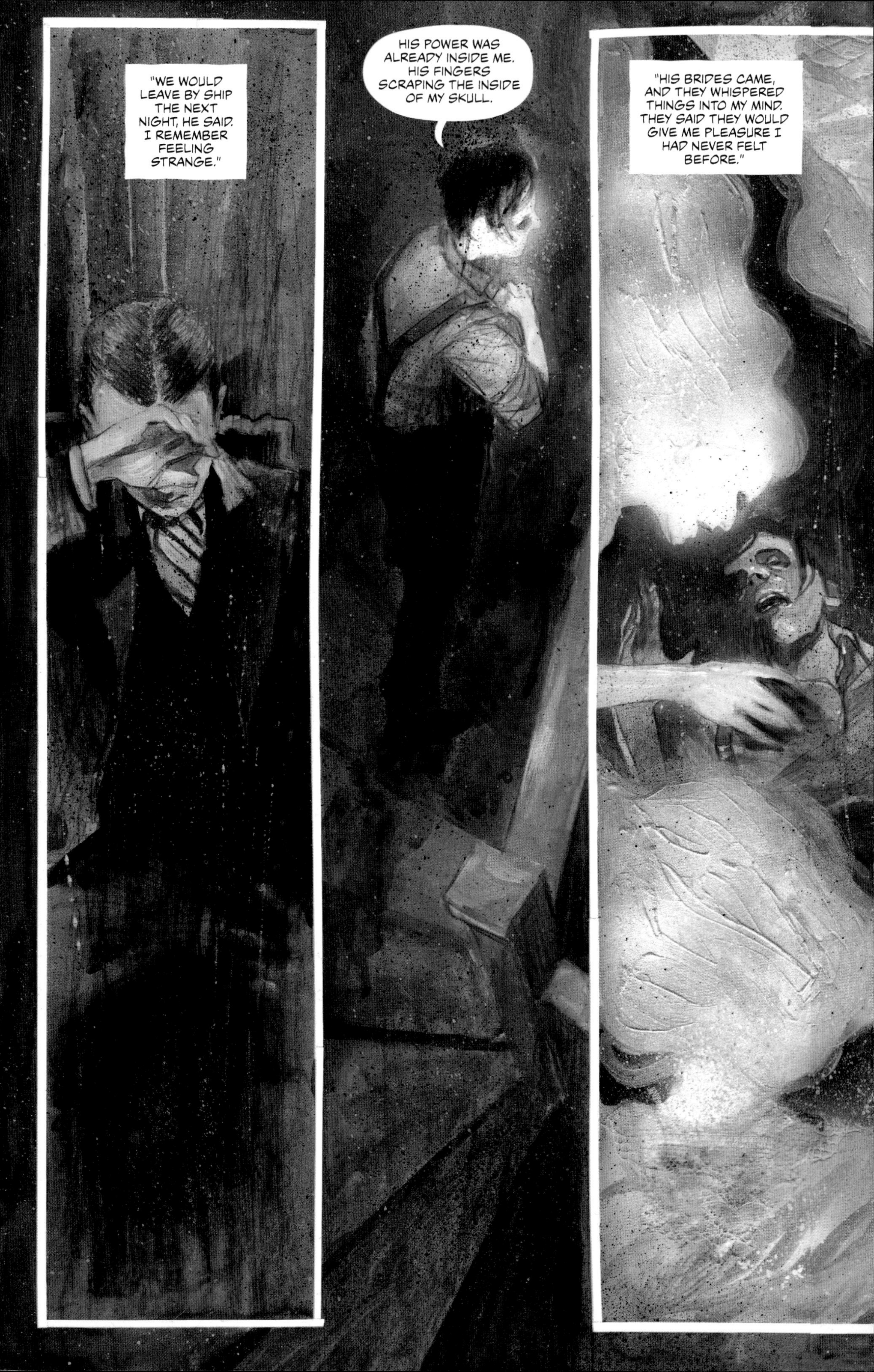
"WE WOULD LEAVE BY SHIP THE NEXT NIGHT, HE SAID. I REMEMBER FEELING STRANGE."
HIS POWER WAS ALREADY INSIDE ME. HIS FINGERS SCRAPING THE INSIDE OF MY SKULL.
"HIS BRIDES CAME, AND THEY WHISPERED THINGS INTO MY MIND. THEY SAID THEY WOULD GIVE ME PLEASURE I HAD NEVER FELT BEFORE."

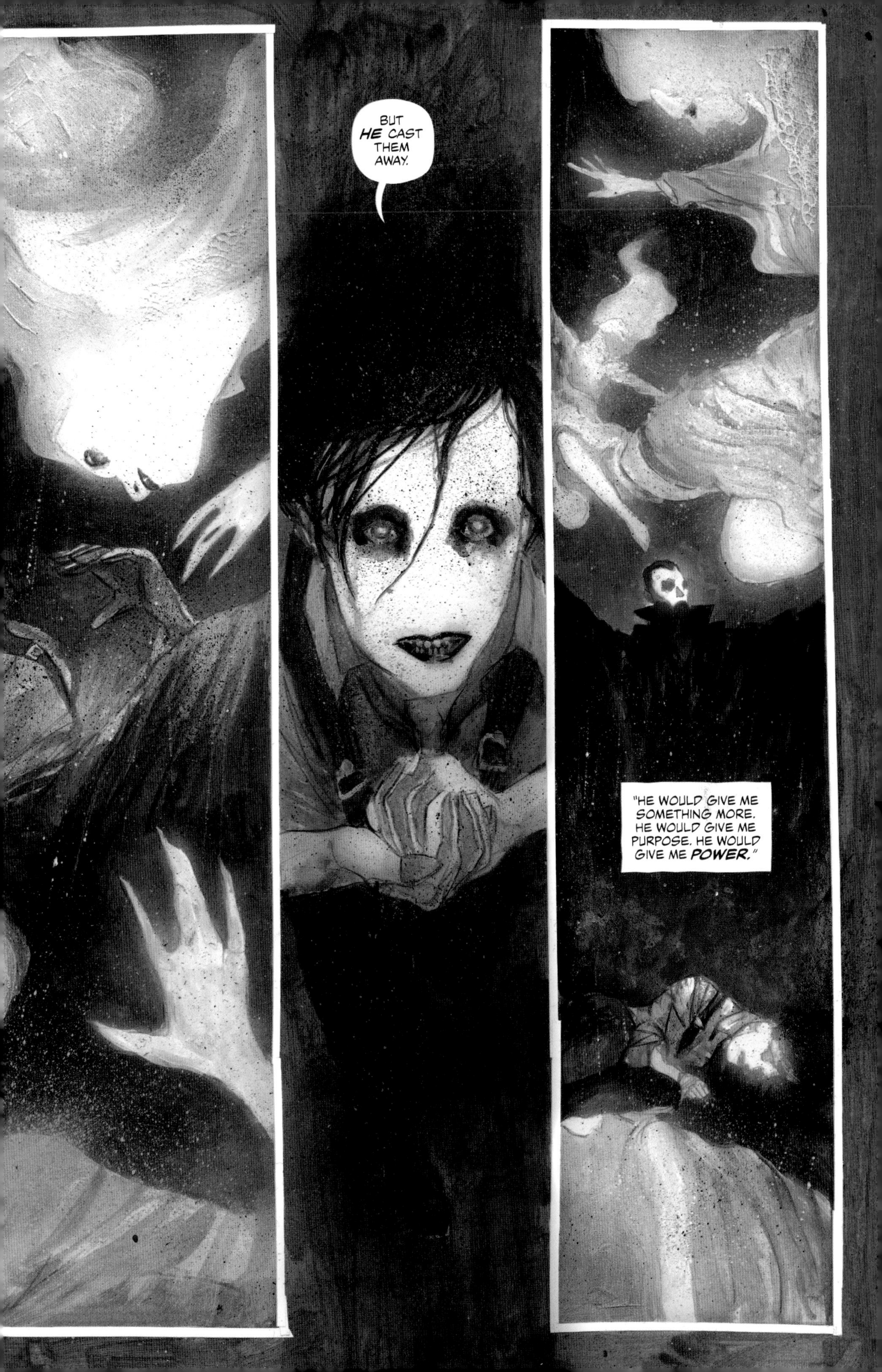
BUT HE CAST THEM AWAY.
"HE WOULD GIVE ME SOMETHING MORE. HE WOULD GIVE ME PURPOSE. HE WOULD GIVE ME POWER."

HE WOULD *CRUSH* THE MEN WHO MADE ME FEEL SMALL. HE WOULD *EAT* LONDON AND REMAKE IT IN HIS DARK IMAGE.

THE WHOLE CITY HIS STRANGE CASTLE.

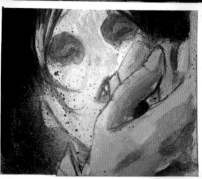

AND I WOULD SIT BY HIS SIDE. I WOULD HAVE DOMINION OF THE VERMIN AND TAKE MY *OWN* POWER FROM THEM.

AND I WANTED IT MORE THAN I HAVE EVER WANTED ANYTHING. BECAUSE MEN ARE *WICKED,* AND THEY DESERVE NO BETTER THAN MY MASTER'S *FANGS.*

BUT THE GIRL MINA...

SHE IS *DIFFERENT.* SHE IS *INNOCENT.* SHE DESERVES *PEACE.*

AND I FEAR... I FEAR ALL I MUST DO TO SAVE HER. I FEAR I DO NOT HAVE THE POWER... TO FACE MY MASTER.

I FEAR I AM BEYOND SAVING IN THE EYES OF GOD, BUT I PRAY... SHE IS NOT.

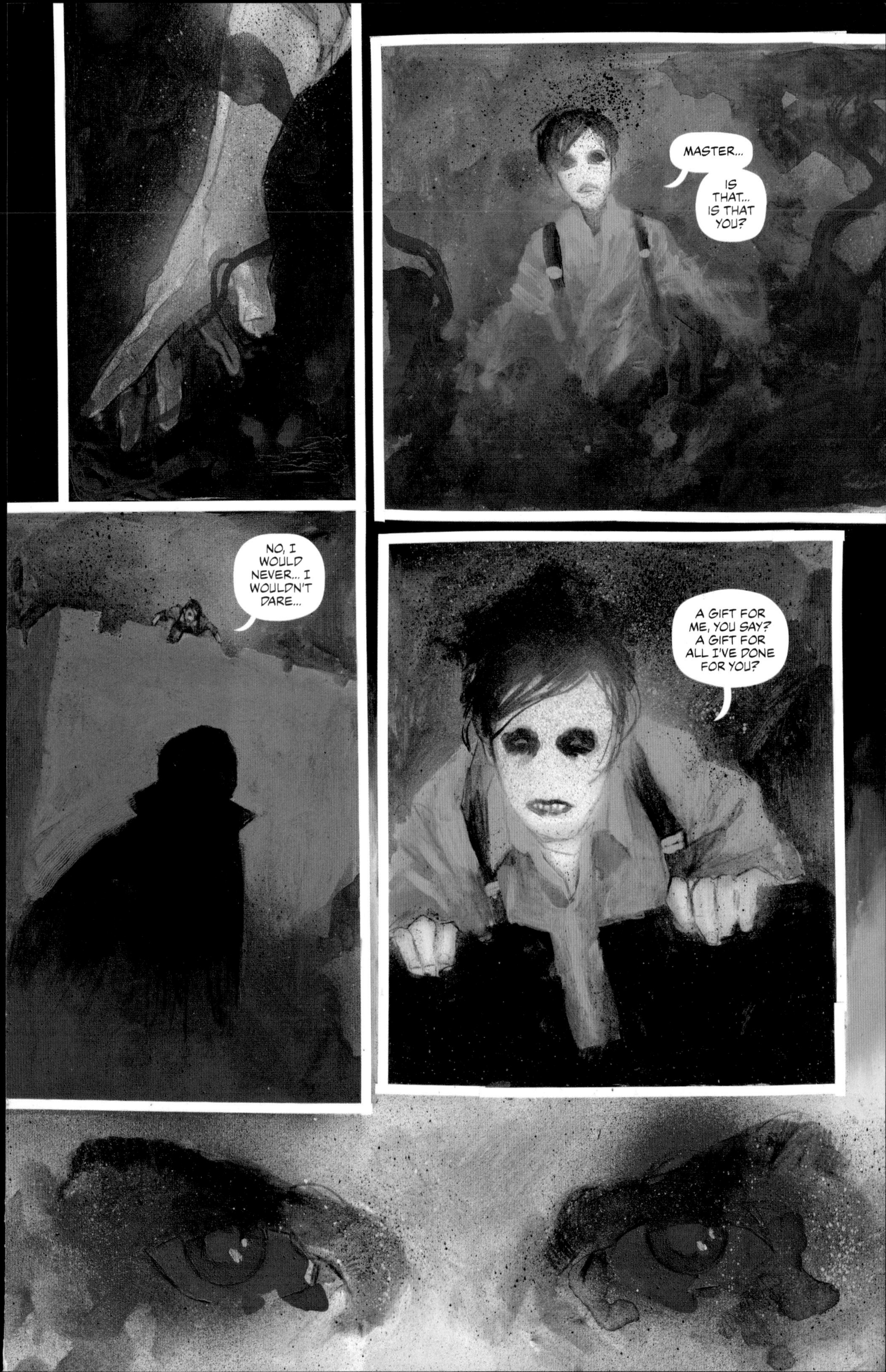
MASTER...
IS THAT... IS THAT YOU?
NO, I WOULD NEVER... I WOULDN'T DARE...
A GIFT FOR ME, YOU SAY? A GIFT FOR ALL I'VE DONE FOR YOU?

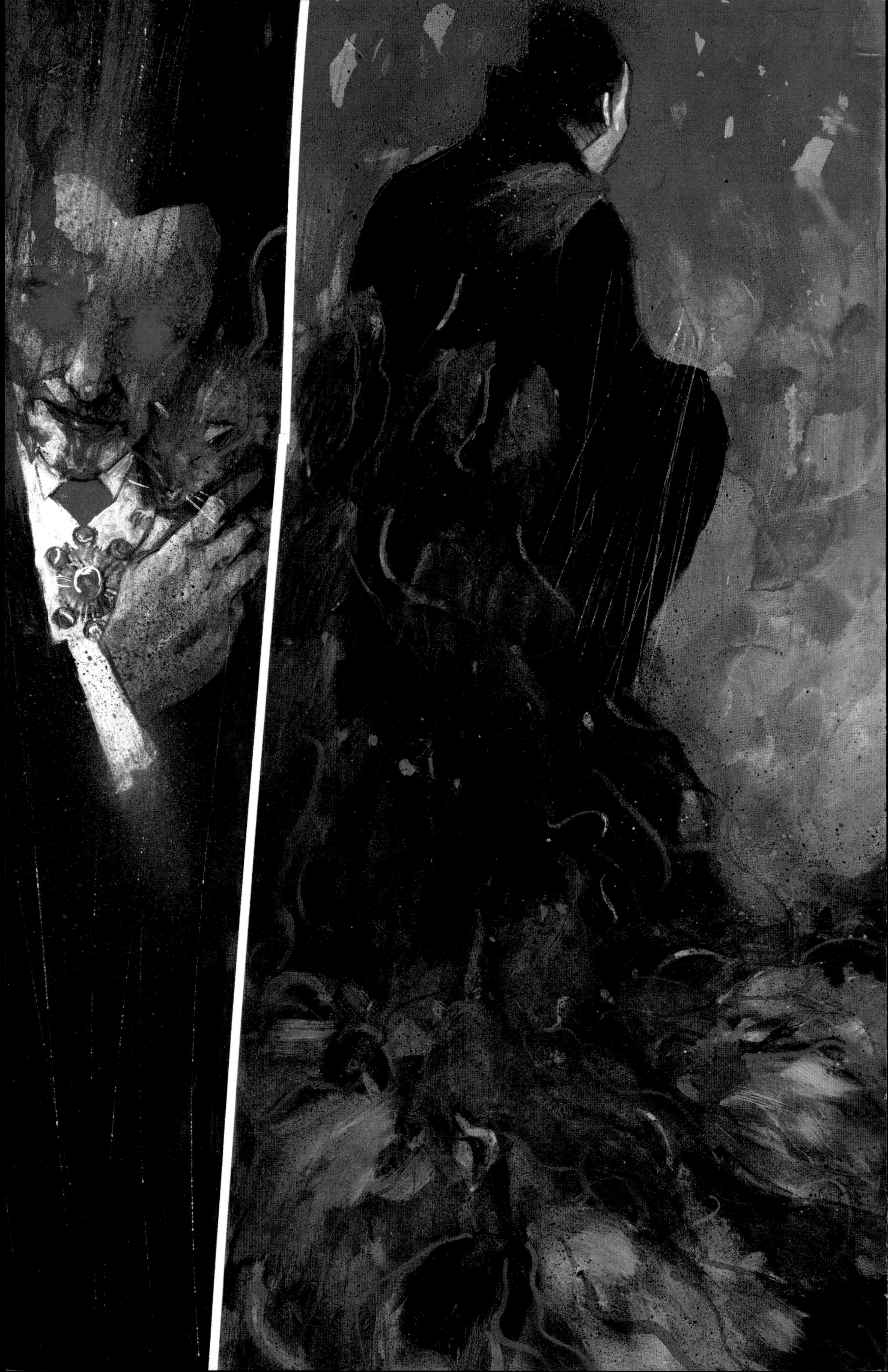

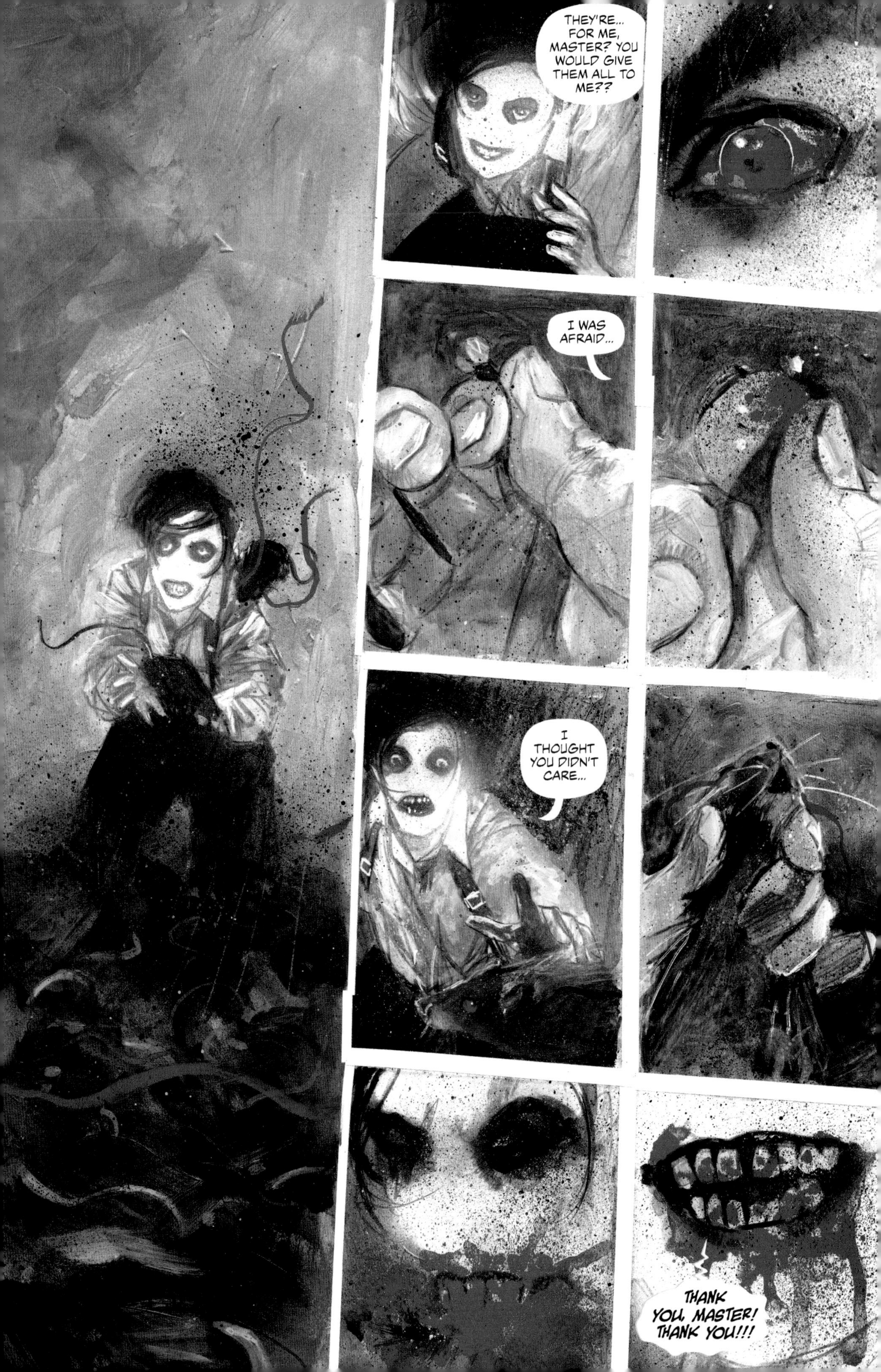
THEY'RE... FOR ME, MASTER? YOU WOULD GIVE THEM ALL TO ME??
I WAS AFRAID...
I THOUGHT YOU DIDN'T CARE...
THANK YOU, MASTER! THANK YOU!!!

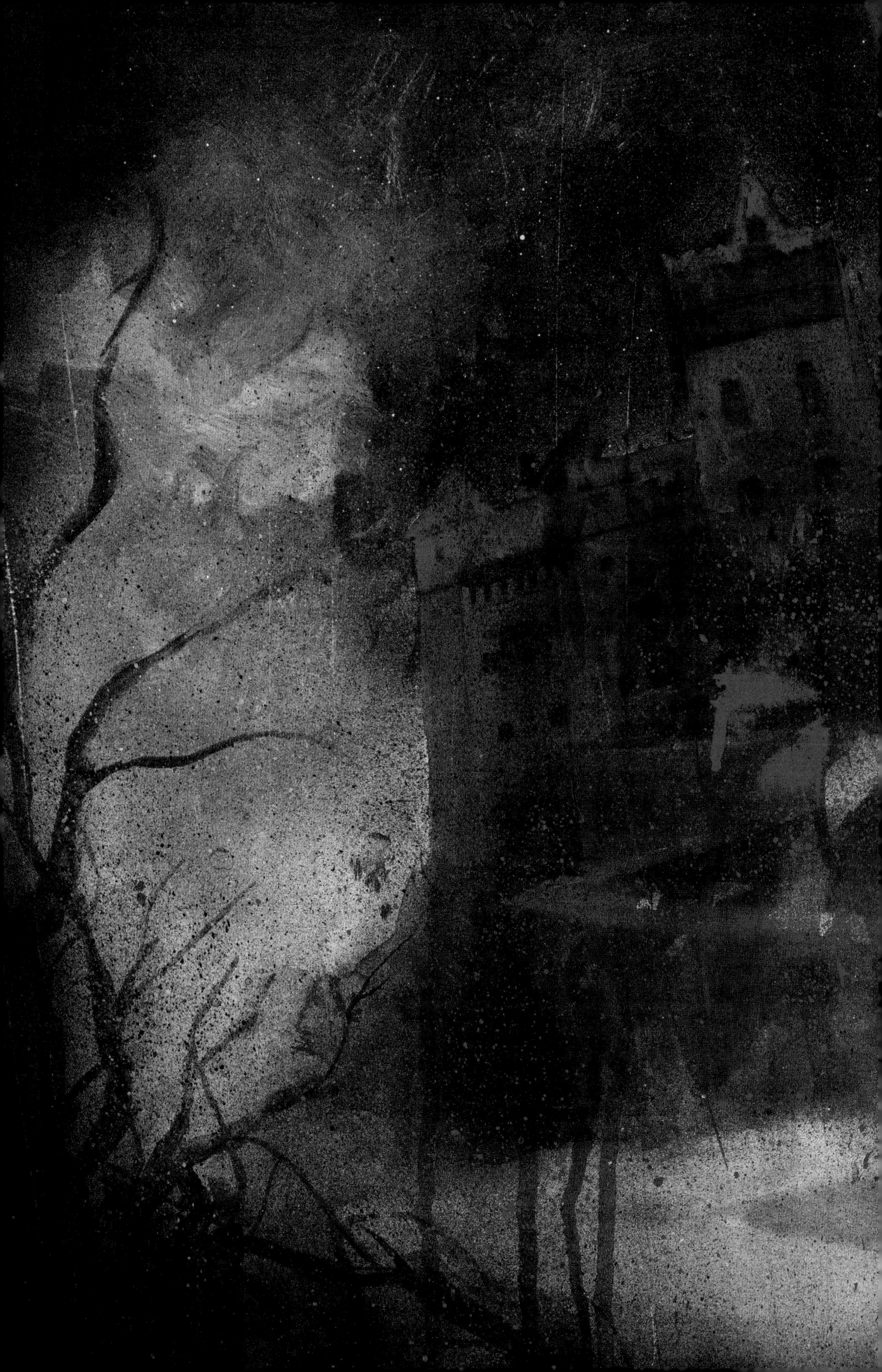

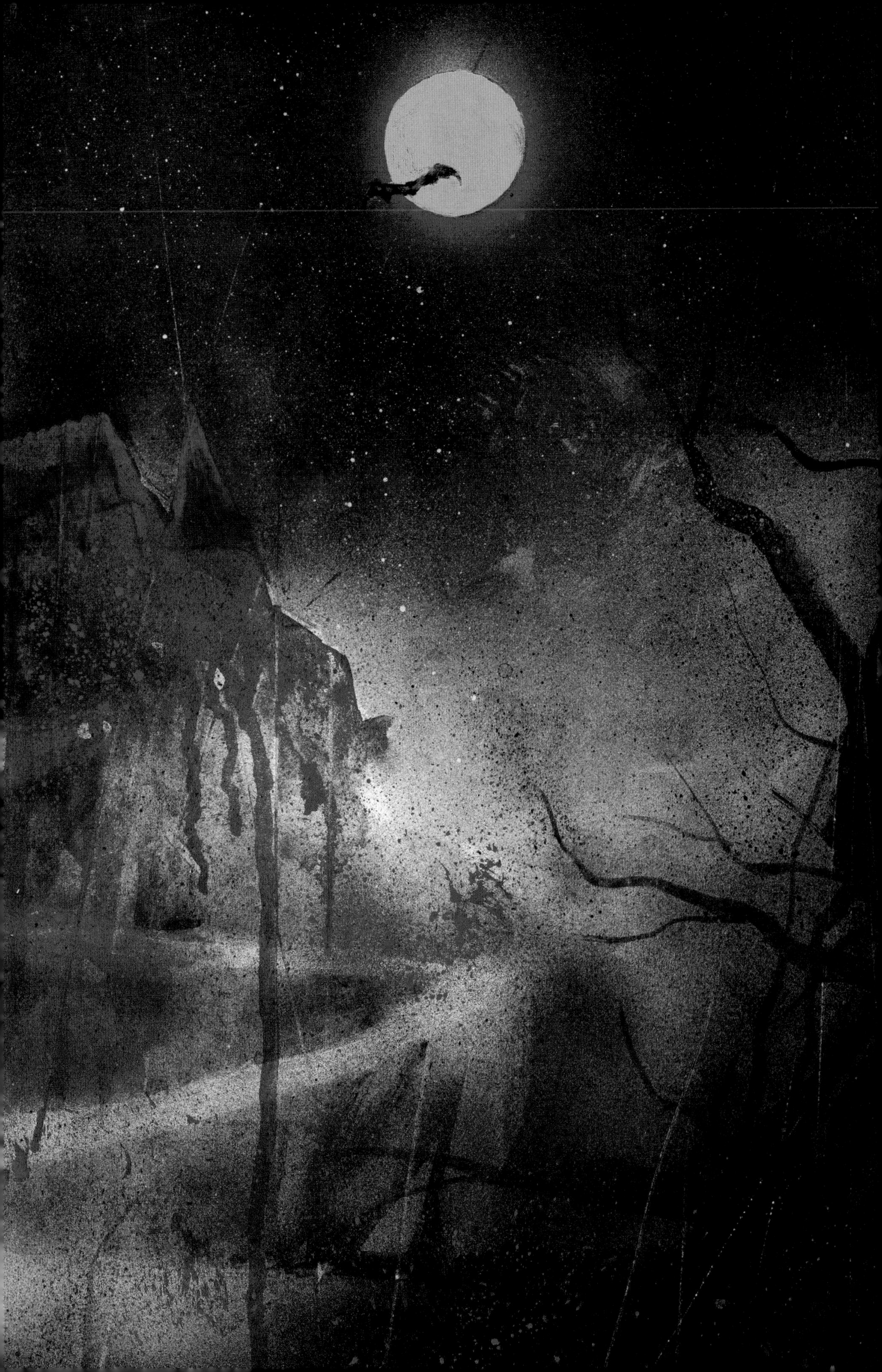

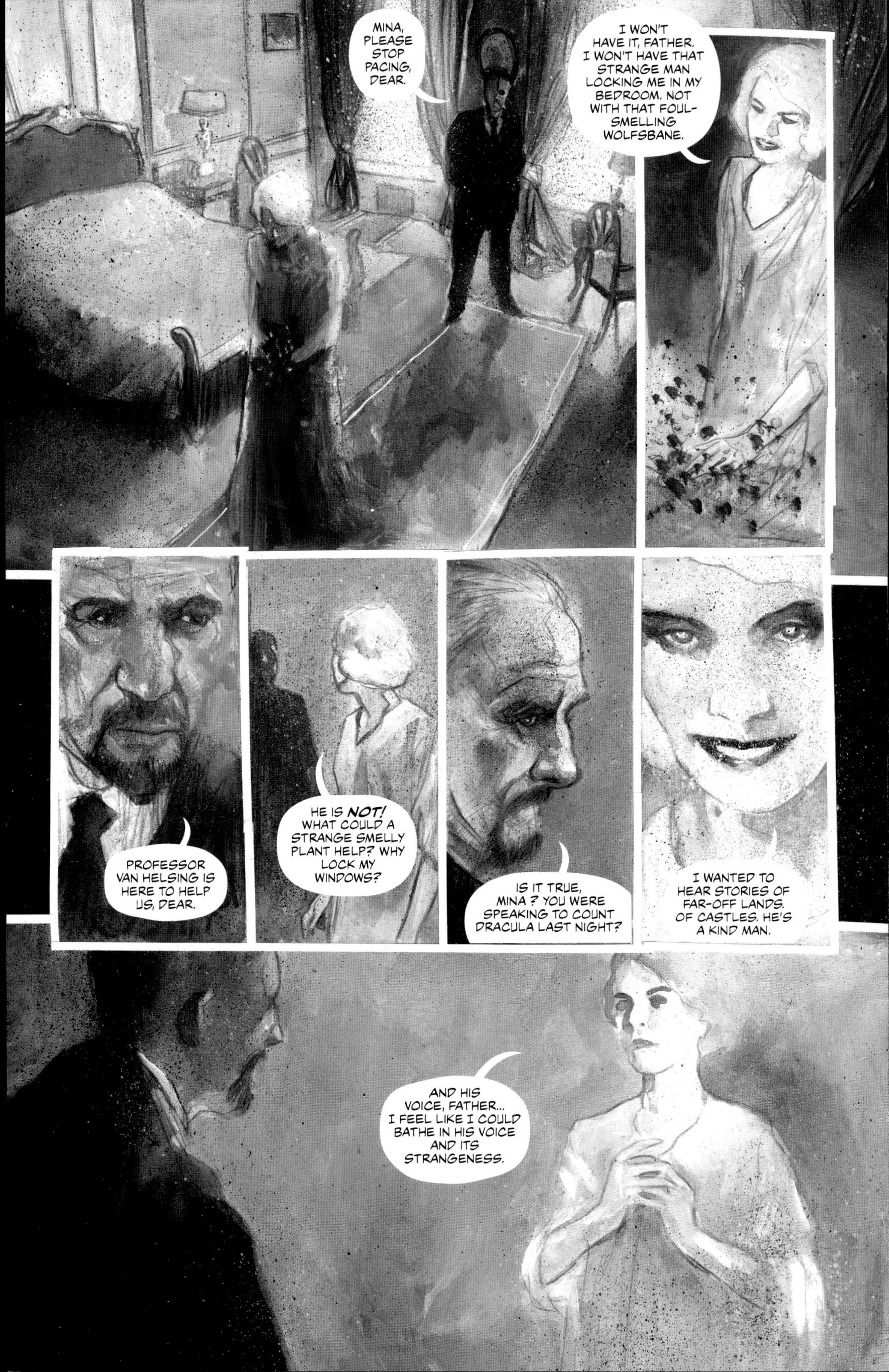
MINA, PLEASE STOP PACING, DEAR.
I WON'T HAVE IT, FATHER. I WON'T HAVE THAT STRANGE MAN LOCKING ME IN MY BEDROOM. NOT WITH THAT FOUL-SMELLING WOLFSBANE.
PROFESSOR VAN HELSING IS HERE TO HELP US, DEAR.
HE IS **NOT!** WHAT COULD A STRANGE SMELLY PLANT HELP? WHY LOCK MY WINDOWS?
IS IT TRUE, MINA ? YOU WERE SPEAKING TO COUNT DRACULA LAST NIGHT?
I WANTED TO HEAR STORIES OF FAR-OFF LANDS. OF CASTLES. HE'S A KIND MAN.
AND HIS VOICE, FATHER... I FEEL LIKE I COULD BATHE IN HIS VOICE AND ITS STRANGENESS.

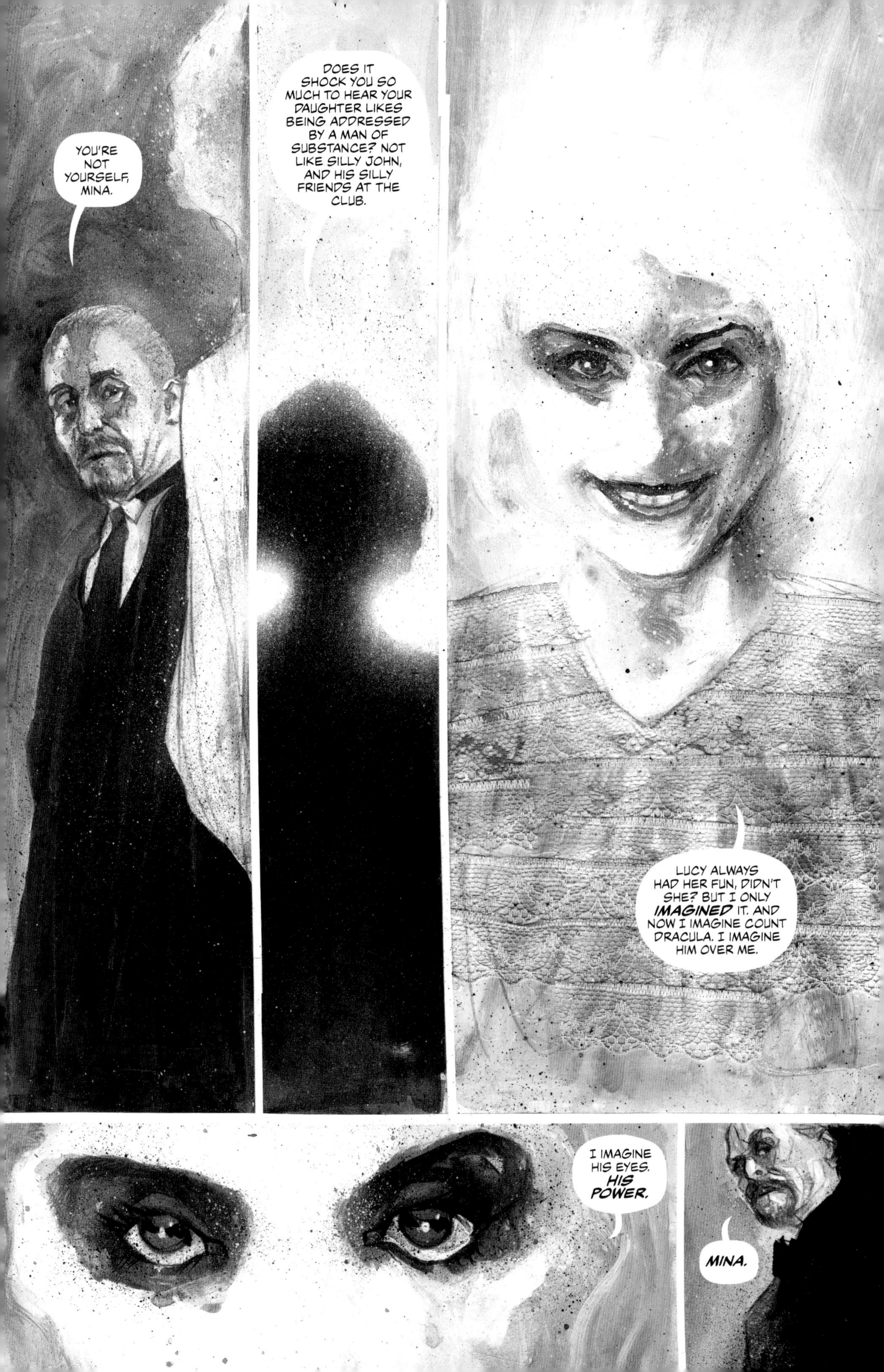
YOU'RE NOT YOURSELF, MINA.
DOES IT SHOCK YOU SO MUCH TO HEAR YOUR DAUGHTER LIKES BEING ADDRESSED BY A MAN OF SUBSTANCE? NOT LIKE SILLY JOHN, AND HIS SILLY FRIENDS AT THE CLUB.
LUCY ALWAYS HAD HER FUN, DIDN'T SHE? BUT I ONLY IMAGINED IT. AND NOW I IMAGINE COUNT DRACULA. I IMAGINE HIM OVER ME.
I IMAGINE HIS EYES. HIS POWER.
MINA.

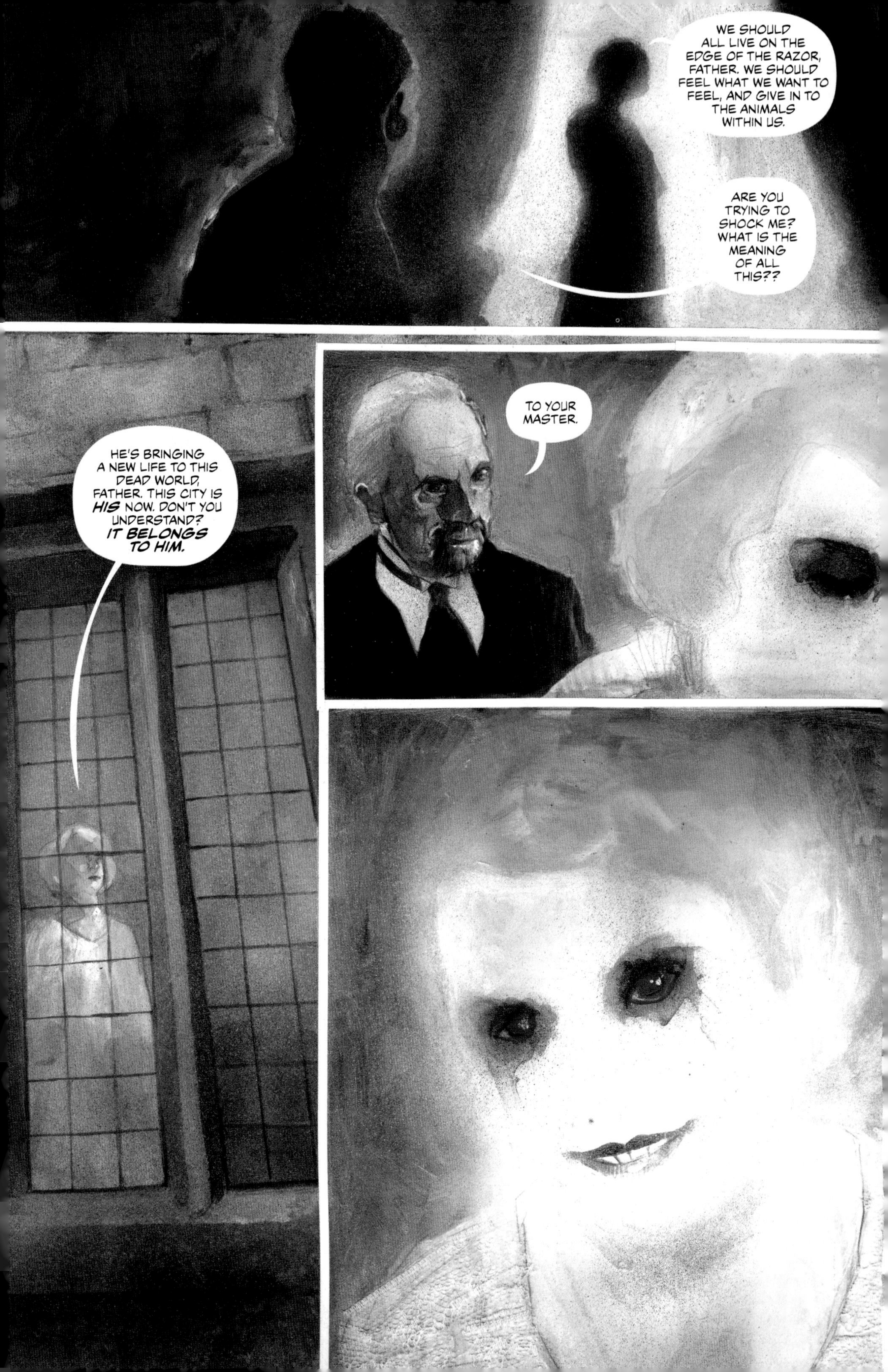
WE SHOULD ALL LIVE ON THE EDGE OF THE RAZOR, FATHER. WE SHOULD FEEL WHAT WE WANT TO FEEL, AND GIVE IN TO THE ANIMALS WITHIN US.
ARE YOU TRYING TO SHOCK ME? WHAT IS THE MEANING OF ALL THIS??
HE'S BRINGING A NEW LIFE TO THIS DEAD WORLD, FATHER. THIS CITY IS *HIS* NOW. DON'T YOU UNDERSTAND? *IT BELONGS TO HIM.*
TO YOUR MASTER.

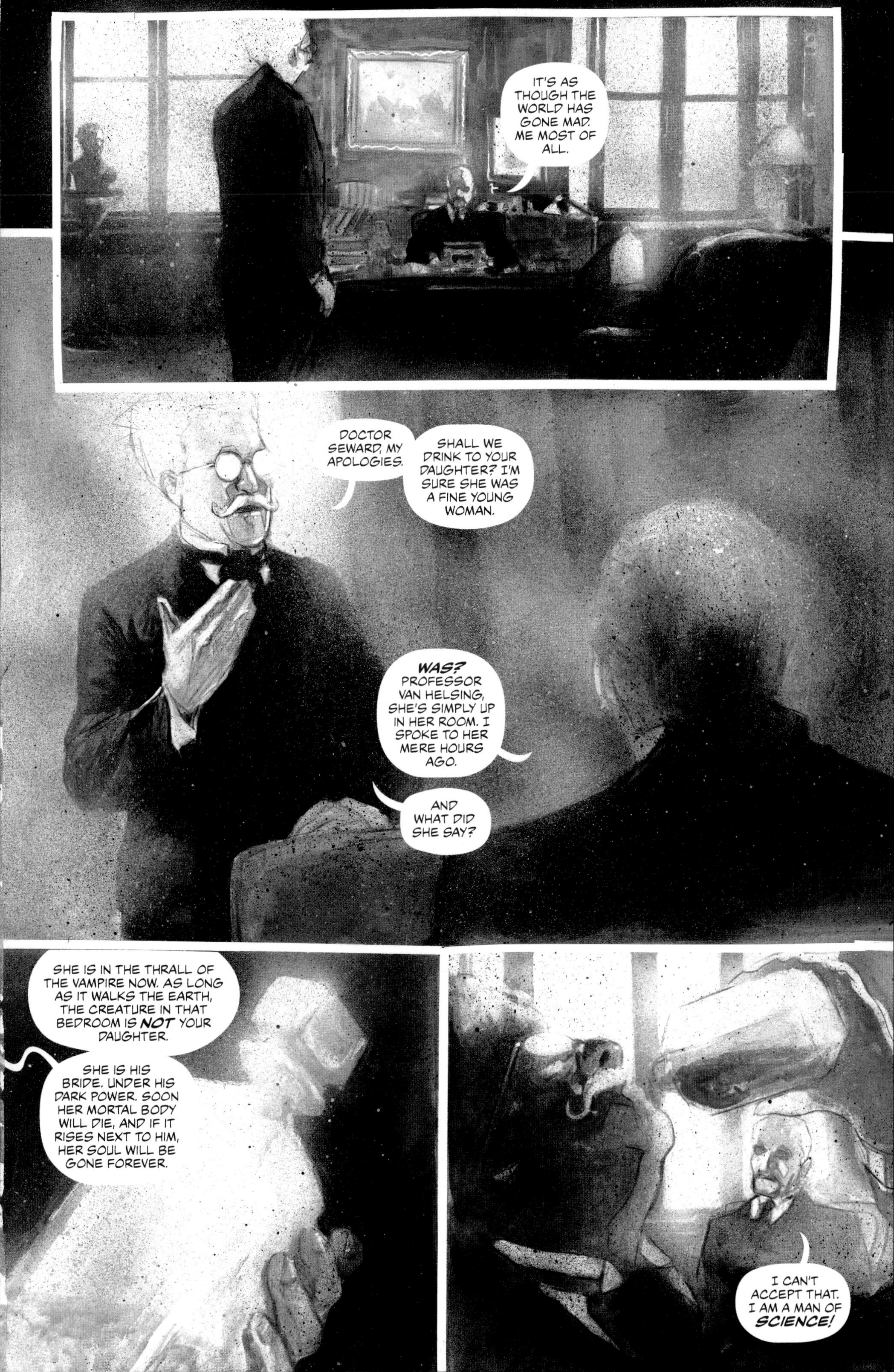
IT'S AS THOUGH THE WORLD HAS GONE MAD. ME MOST OF ALL.
DOCTOR SEWARD, MY APOLOGIES.
SHALL WE DRINK TO YOUR DAUGHTER? I'M SURE SHE WAS A FINE YOUNG WOMAN.
WAS? PROFESSOR VAN HELSING, SHE'S SIMPLY UP IN HER ROOM. I SPOKE TO HER MERE HOURS AGO.
AND WHAT DID SHE SAY?
SHE IS IN THE THRALL OF THE VAMPIRE NOW. AS LONG AS IT WALKS THE EARTH, THE CREATURE IN THAT BEDROOM IS NOT YOUR DAUGHTER.
SHE IS HIS BRIDE. UNDER HIS DARK POWER. SOON HER MORTAL BODY WILL DIE, AND IF IT RISES NEXT TO HIM, HER SOUL WILL BE GONE FOREVER.
I CAN'T ACCEPT THAT. I AM A MAN OF SCIENCE!

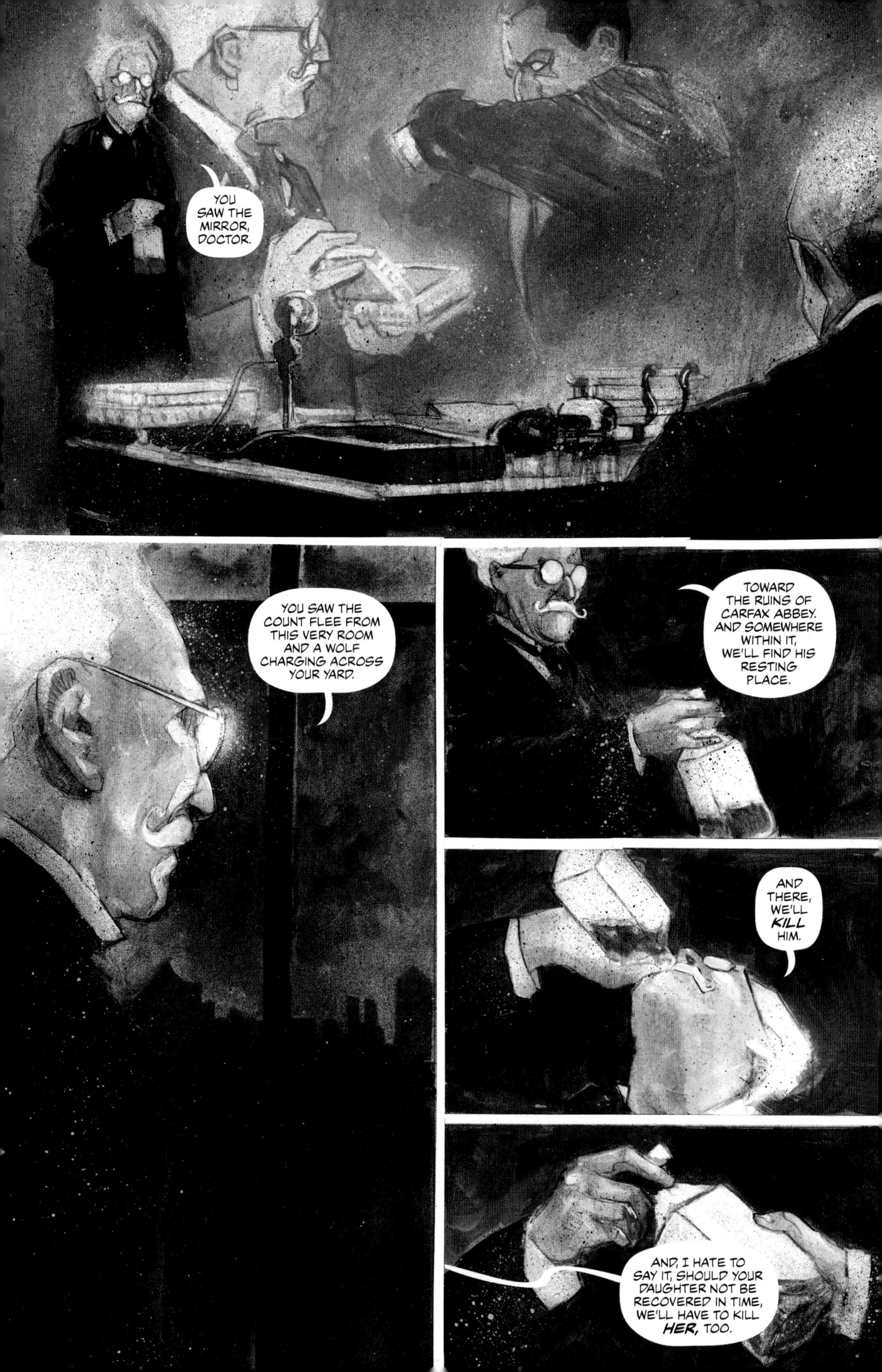

YOU SAW THE MIRROR, DOCTOR.
YOU SAW THE COUNT FLEE FROM THIS VERY ROOM AND A WOLF CHARGING ACROSS YOUR YARD.
TOWARD THE RUINS OF CARFAX ABBEY. AND SOMEWHERE WITHIN IT, WE'LL FIND HIS RESTING PLACE.
AND THERE, WE'LL *KILL* HIM.
AND, I HATE TO SAY IT, SHOULD YOUR DAUGHTER NOT BE RECOVERED IN TIME, WE'LL HAVE TO KILL *HER,* TOO.

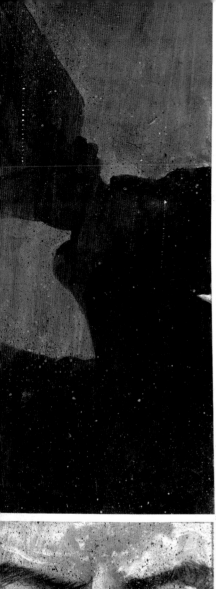

I FEEL AS THOUGH I SHOULD WANT TO STRIKE YOU.

BUT THERE'S NOTHING LEFT IN ME. THE LOOK IN MY DAUGHTER'S EYES...

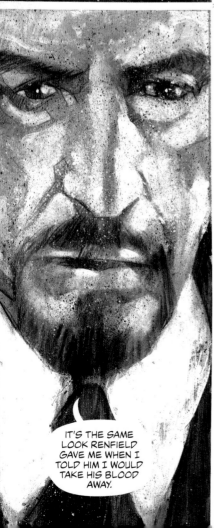

IT'S THE SAME LOOK RENFIELD GAVE ME WHEN I TOLD HIM I WOULD TAKE HIS BLOOD AWAY.

IF ONLY WE COULD WREST HER FROM DAMNATION WITH OUR MINDS, WITH OUR HUMAN CUNNING, WITH OUR WILL.

BUT PRIDE IS A SIN, DOCTOR. AND IT IS ONE THAT DRACULA KNOWS HOW TO FEED UPON.

WE THINK OURSELVES SO MUCH MORE, SO MUCH GREATER, SO MUCH WISER THAN THE BEASTS OF THE FOREST. BUT WE ARE WEAK. FLESH AND BONE.

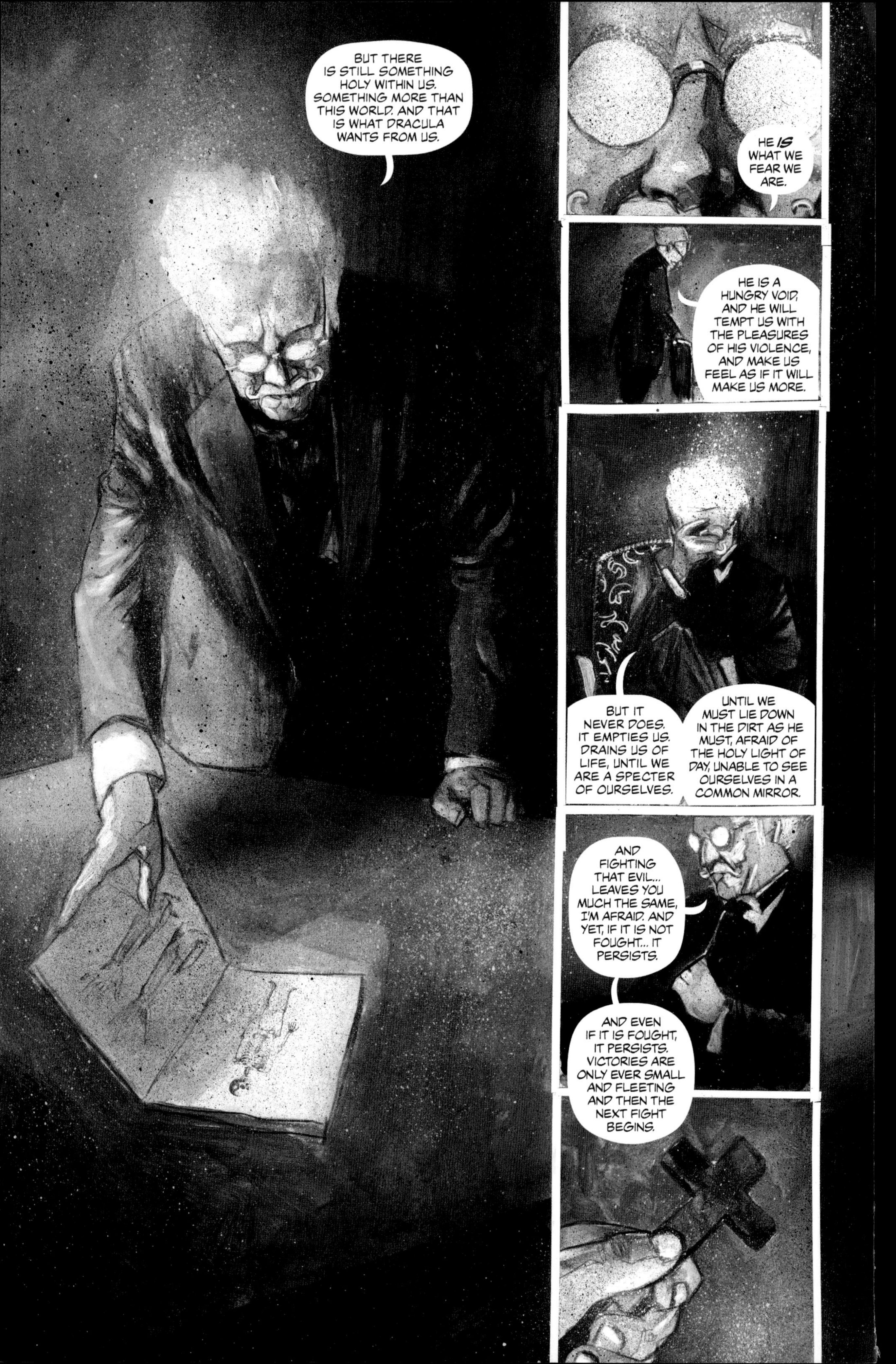
BUT THERE IS STILL SOMETHING HOLY WITHIN US. SOMETHING MORE THAN THIS WORLD. AND THAT IS WHAT DRACULA WANTS FROM US.
HE *IS* WHAT WE FEAR WE ARE.
HE IS A HUNGRY VOID, AND HE WILL TEMPT US WITH THE PLEASURES OF HIS VIOLENCE, AND MAKE US FEEL AS IF IT WILL MAKE US MORE.
BUT IT NEVER DOES. IT EMPTIES US. DRAINS US OF LIFE, UNTIL WE ARE A SPECTER OF OURSELVES.
UNTIL WE MUST LIE DOWN IN THE DIRT AS HE MUST, AFRAID OF THE HOLY LIGHT OF DAY, UNABLE TO SEE OURSELVES IN A COMMON MIRROR.
AND FIGHTING THAT EVIL... LEAVES YOU MUCH THE SAME, I'M AFRAID. AND YET, IF IT IS NOT FOUGHT... IT PERSISTS.
AND EVEN IF IT IS FOUGHT, IT PERSISTS. VICTORIES ARE ONLY EVER SMALL AND FLEETING AND THEN THE NEXT FIGHT BEGINS.

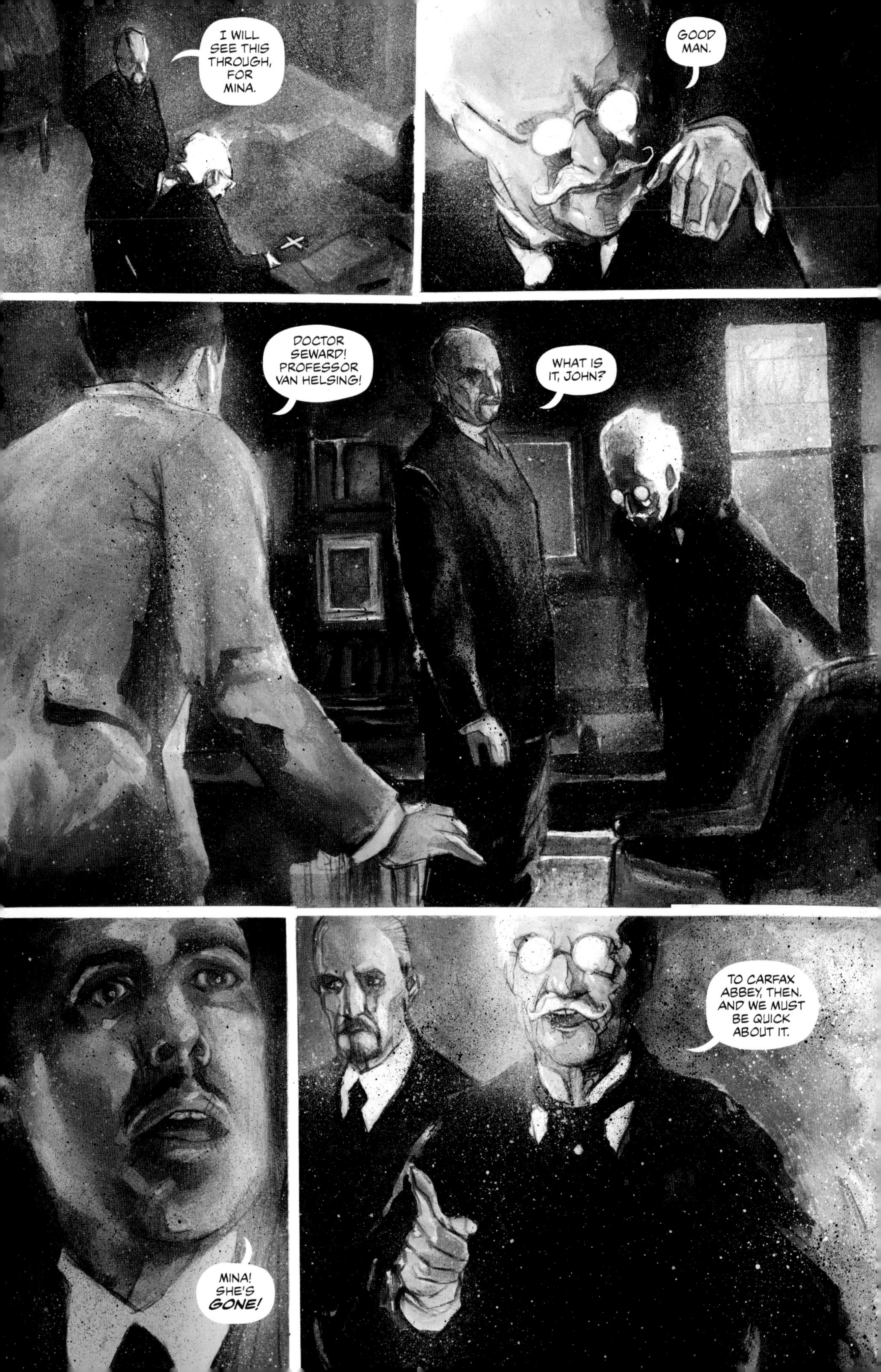
I WILL SEE THIS THROUGH, FOR MINA.
GOOD MAN.
DOCTOR SEWARD! PROFESSOR VAN HELSING!
WHAT IS IT, JOHN?
MINA! SHE'S *GONE!*
TO CARFAX ABBEY, THEN. AND WE MUST BE QUICK ABOUT IT.

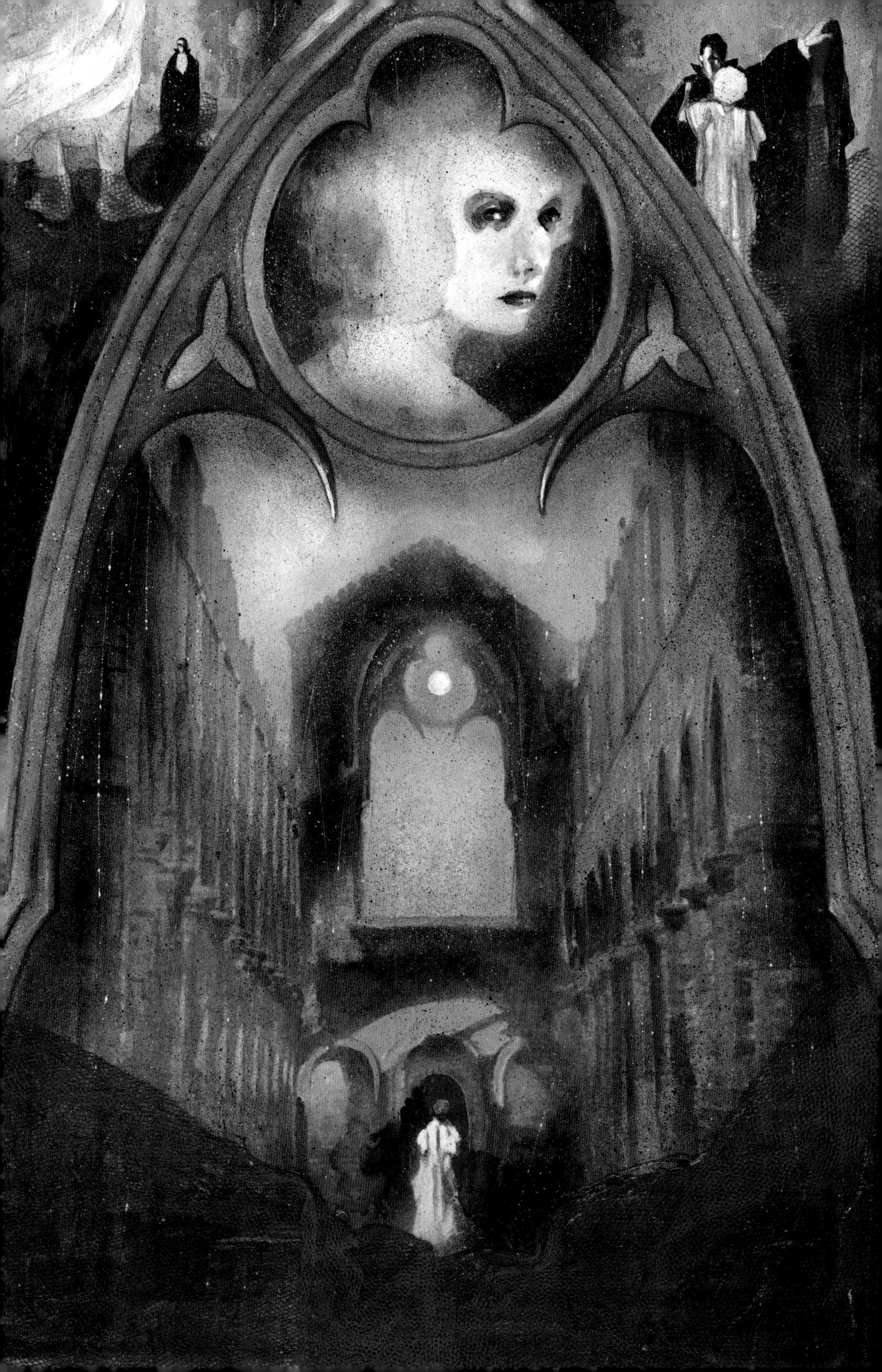

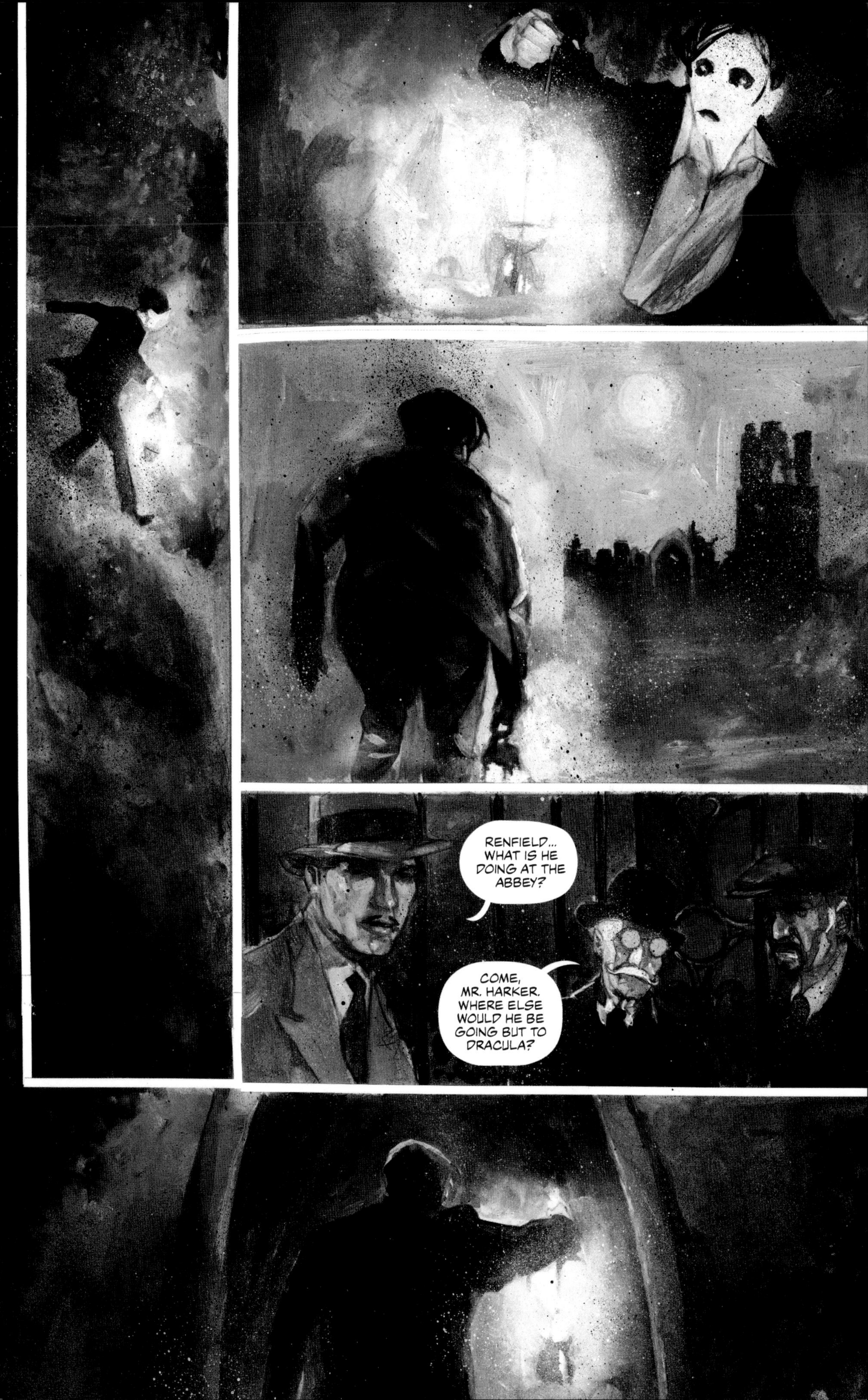
RENFIELD... WHAT IS HE DOING AT THE ABBEY?
COME, MR. HARKER. WHERE ELSE WOULD HE BE GOING BUT TO DRACULA?

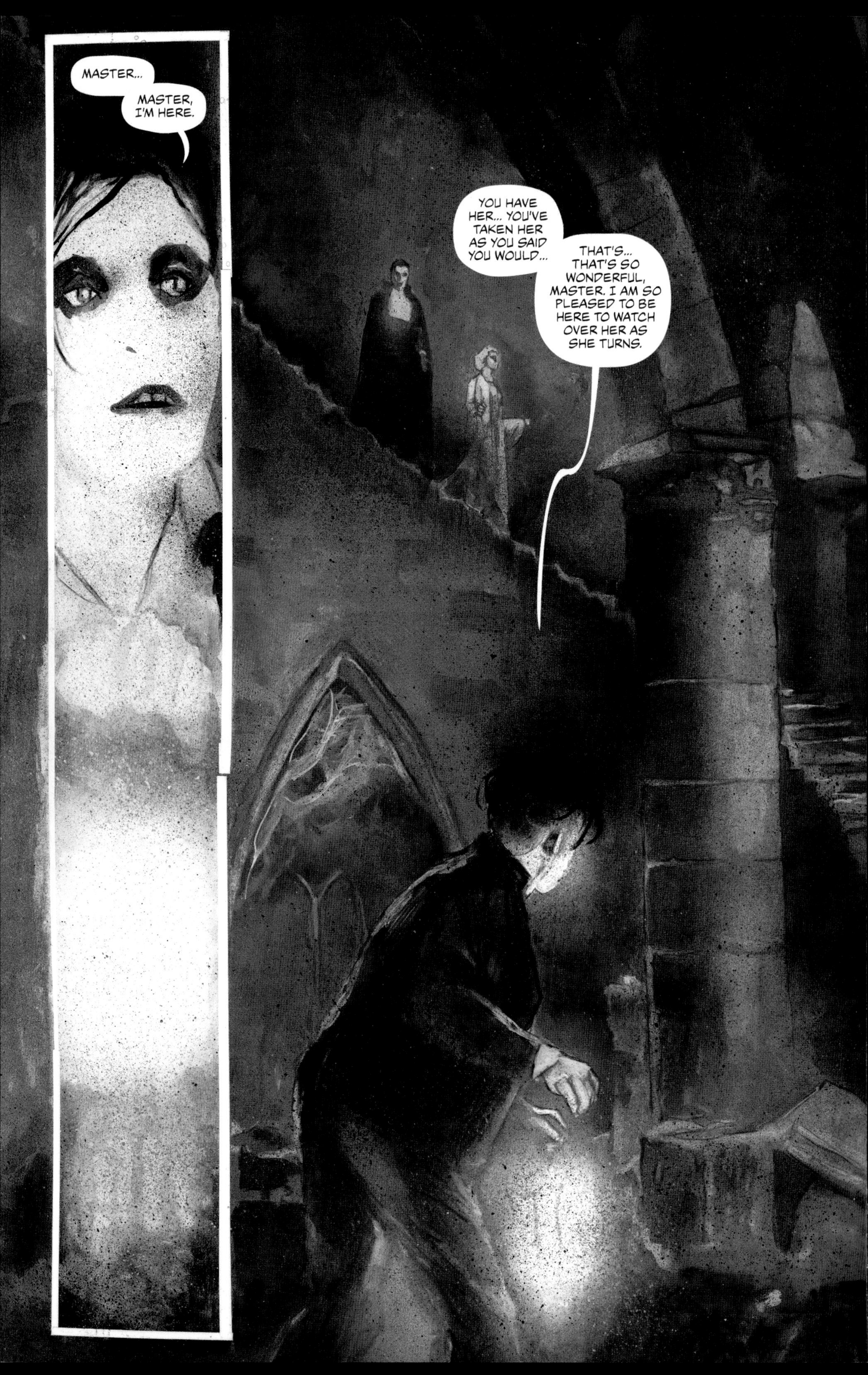
MASTER...
MASTER, I'M HERE.
YOU HAVE HER... YOU'VE TAKEN HER AS YOU SAID YOU WOULD...
THAT'S... THAT'S SO WONDERFUL, MASTER. I AM SO PLEASED TO BE HERE TO WATCH OVER HER AS SHE TURNS.

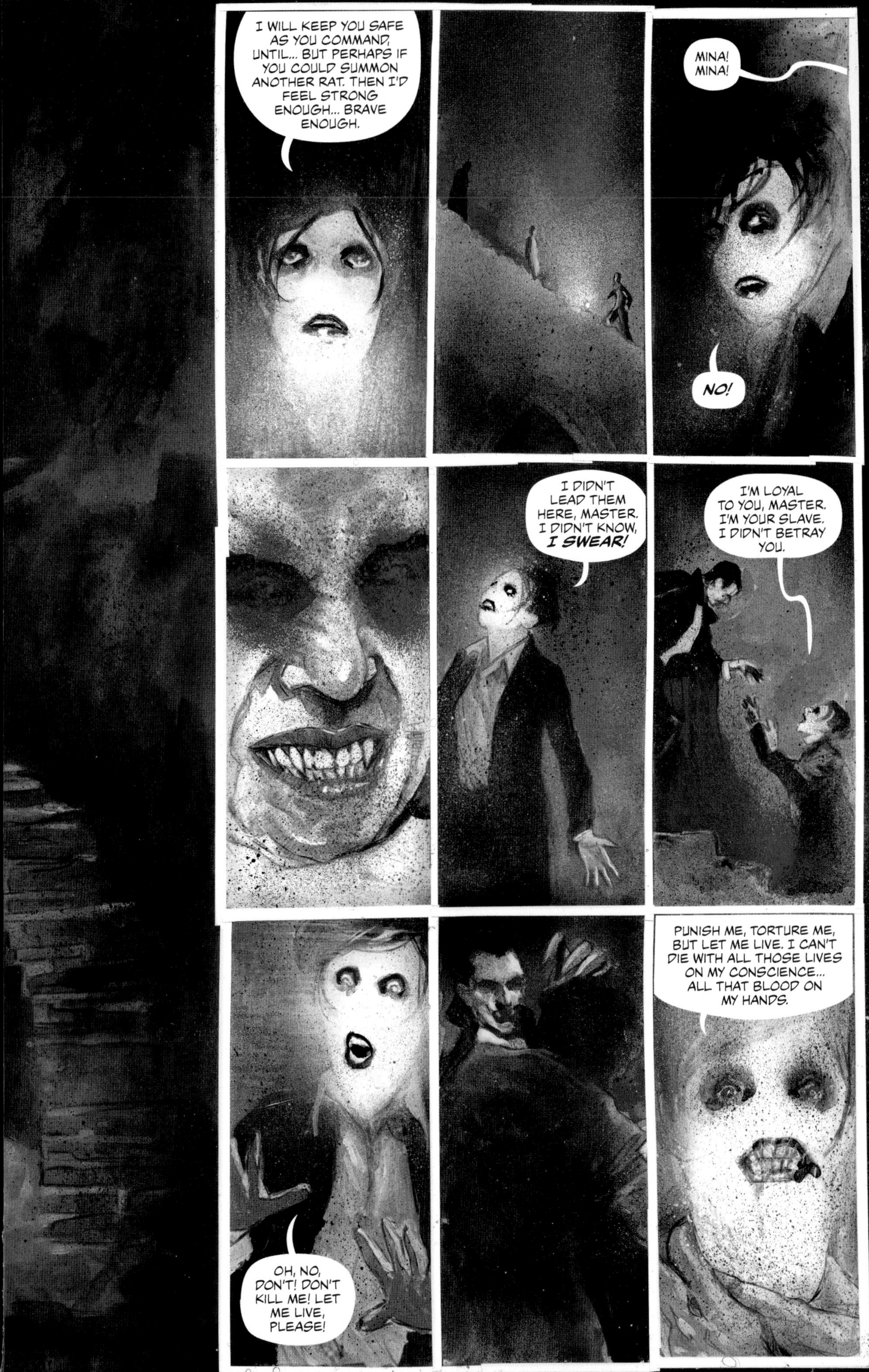
I WILL KEEP YOU SAFE AS YOU COMMAND, UNTIL... BUT PERHAPS IF YOU COULD SUMMON ANOTHER RAT. THEN I'D FEEL STRONG ENOUGH... BRAVE ENOUGH.
MINA! MINA!
NO!
I DIDN'T LEAD THEM HERE, MASTER. I DIDN'T KNOW, *I SWEAR!*
I'M LOYAL TO YOU, MASTER. I'M YOUR SLAVE. I DIDN'T BETRAY YOU.
OH, NO, DON'T! DON'T KILL ME! LET ME LIVE, PLEASE!
PUNISH ME, TORTURE ME, BUT LET ME LIVE. I CAN'T DIE WITH ALL THOSE LIVES ON MY CONSCIENCE... ALL THAT BLOOD ON MY HANDS.

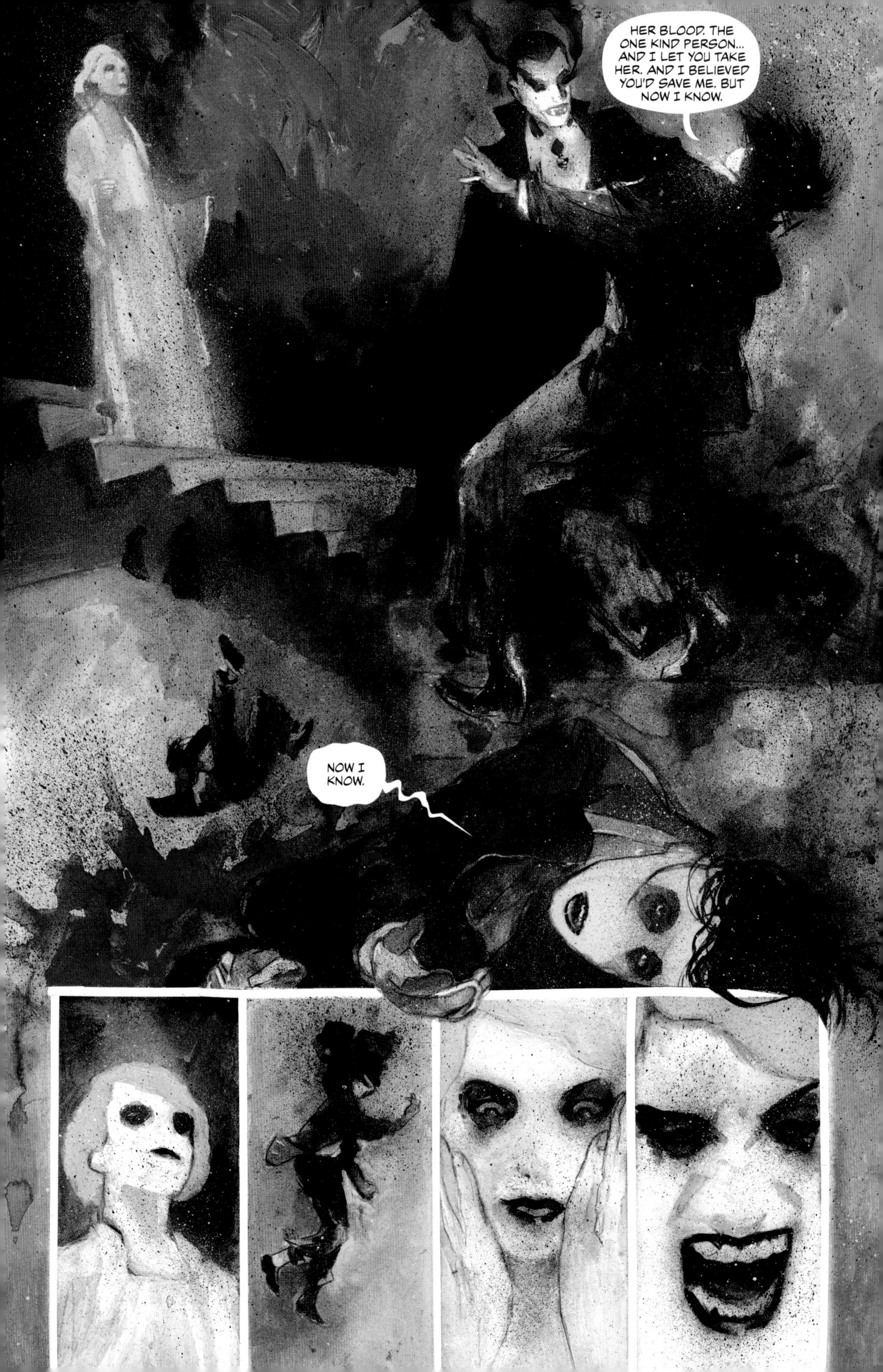
HER BLOOD. THE ONE KIND PERSON... AND I LET YOU TAKE HER. AND I BELIEVED YOU'D SAVE ME. BUT NOW I KNOW.
NOW I KNOW.

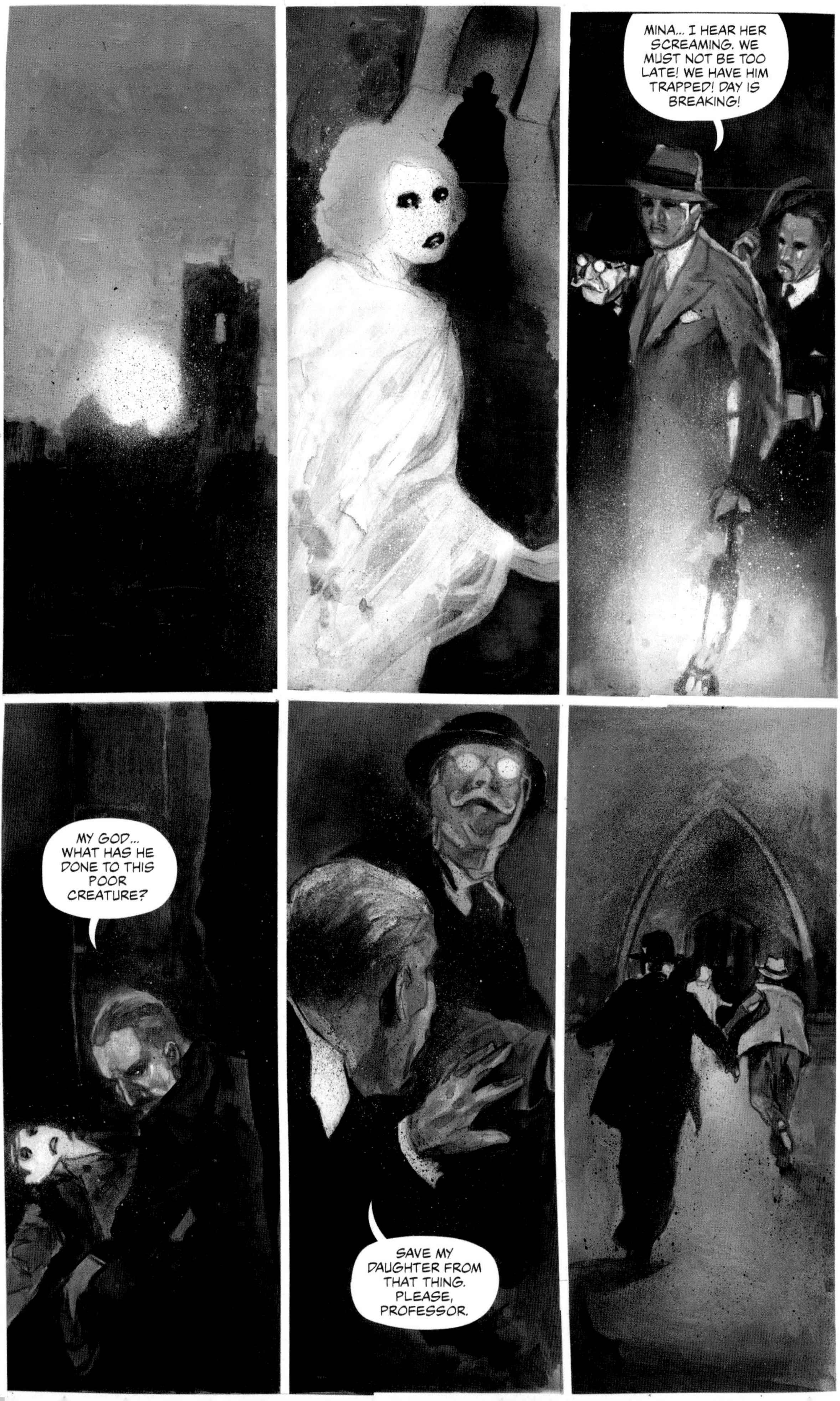
MINA... I HEAR HER SCREAMING. WE MUST NOT BE TOO LATE! WE HAVE HIM TRAPPED! DAY IS BREAKING!
MY GOD... WHAT HAS HE DONE TO THIS POOR CREATURE?
SAVE MY DAUGHTER FROM THAT THING. PLEASE, PROFESSOR.

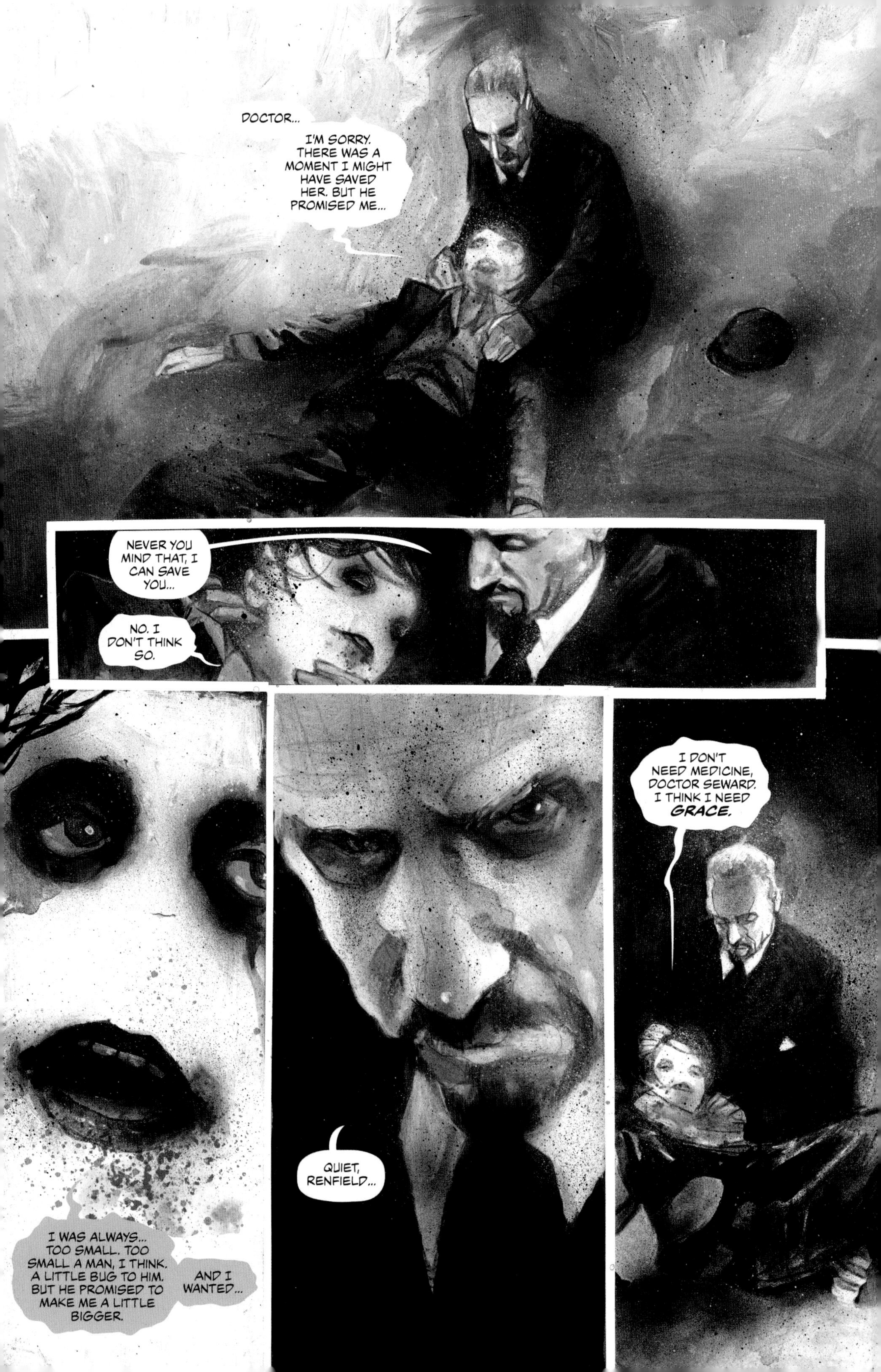
DOCTOR...
I'M SORRY. THERE WAS A MOMENT I MIGHT HAVE SAVED HER. BUT HE PROMISED ME...
NEVER YOU MIND THAT, I CAN SAVE YOU...
NO. I DON'T THINK SO.
I WAS ALWAYS... TOO SMALL. TOO SMALL A MAN, I THINK. A LITTLE BUG TO HIM. BUT HE PROMISED TO MAKE ME A LITTLE BIGGER.
AND I WANTED...
QUIET, RENFIELD...
I DON'T NEED MEDICINE, DOCTOR SEWARD. I THINK I NEED ***GRACE.***

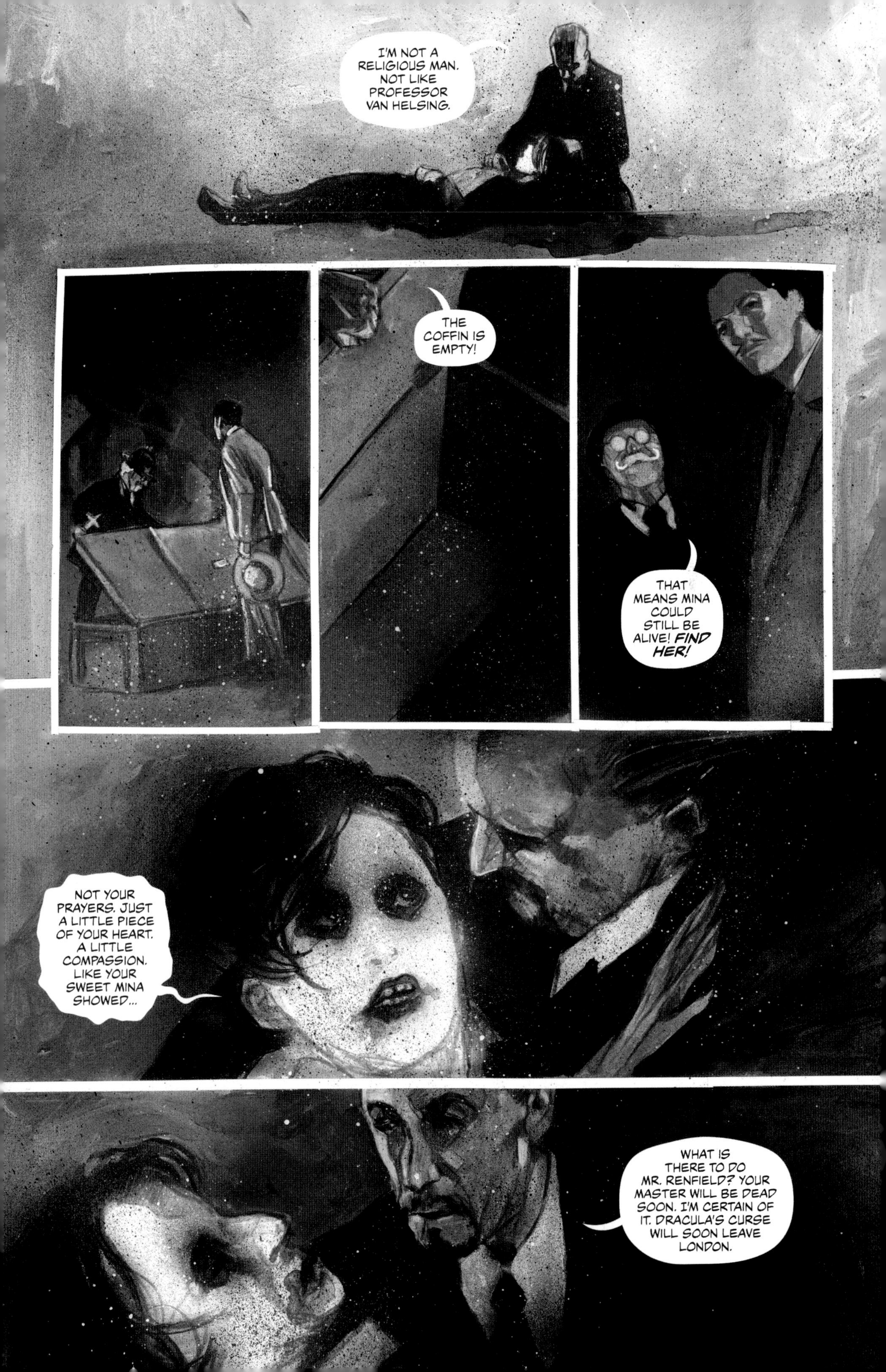
I'M NOT A RELIGIOUS MAN. NOT LIKE PROFESSOR VAN HELSING.
THE COFFIN IS EMPTY!
THAT MEANS MINA COULD STILL BE ALIVE! FIND HER!
NOT YOUR PRAYERS. JUST A LITTLE PIECE OF YOUR HEART. A LITTLE COMPASSION. LIKE YOUR SWEET MINA SHOWED...
WHAT IS THERE TO DO MR. RENFIELD? YOUR MASTER WILL BE DEAD SOON. I'M CERTAIN OF IT. DRACULA'S CURSE WILL SOON LEAVE LONDON.

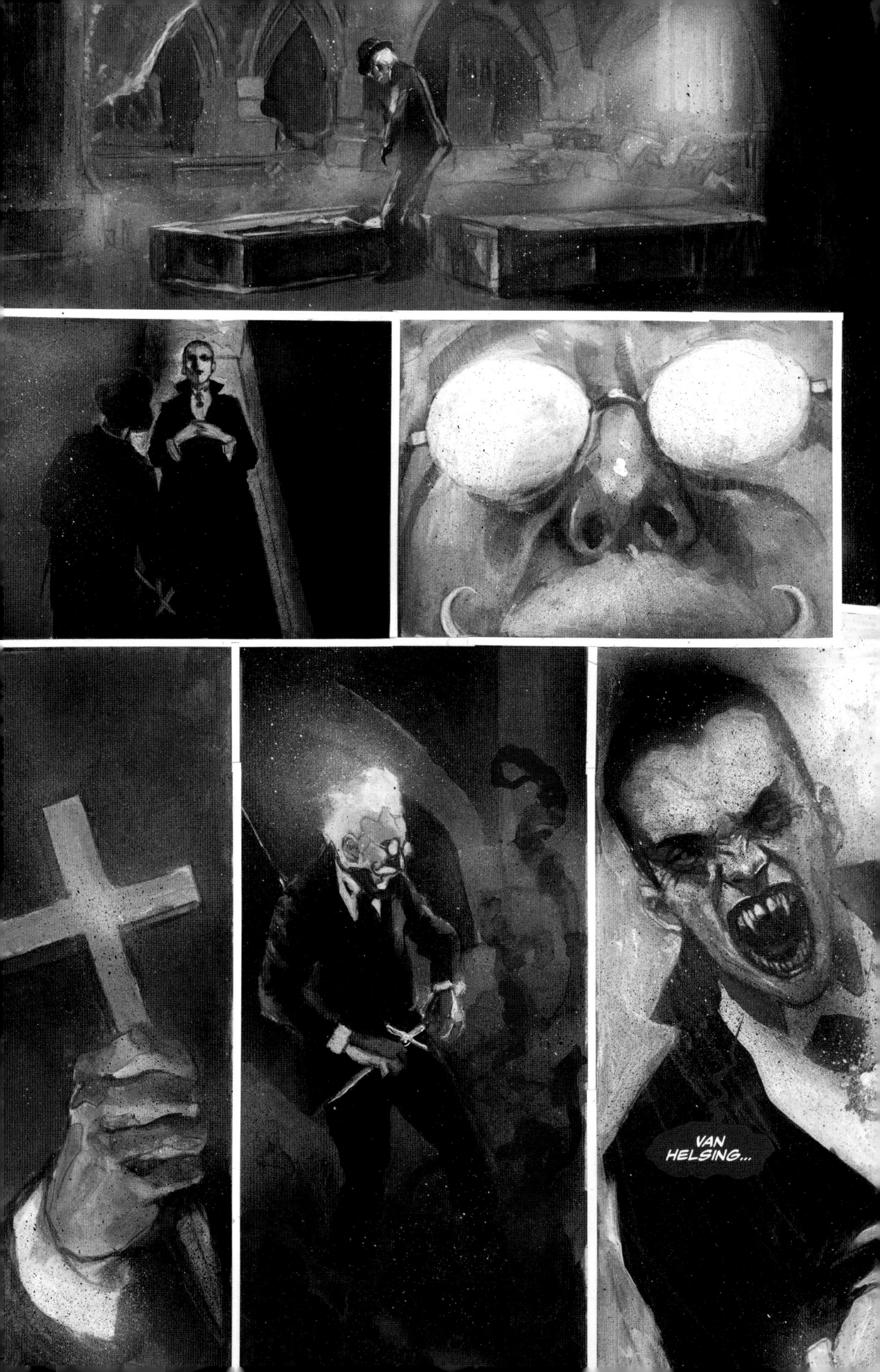
VAN HELSING...

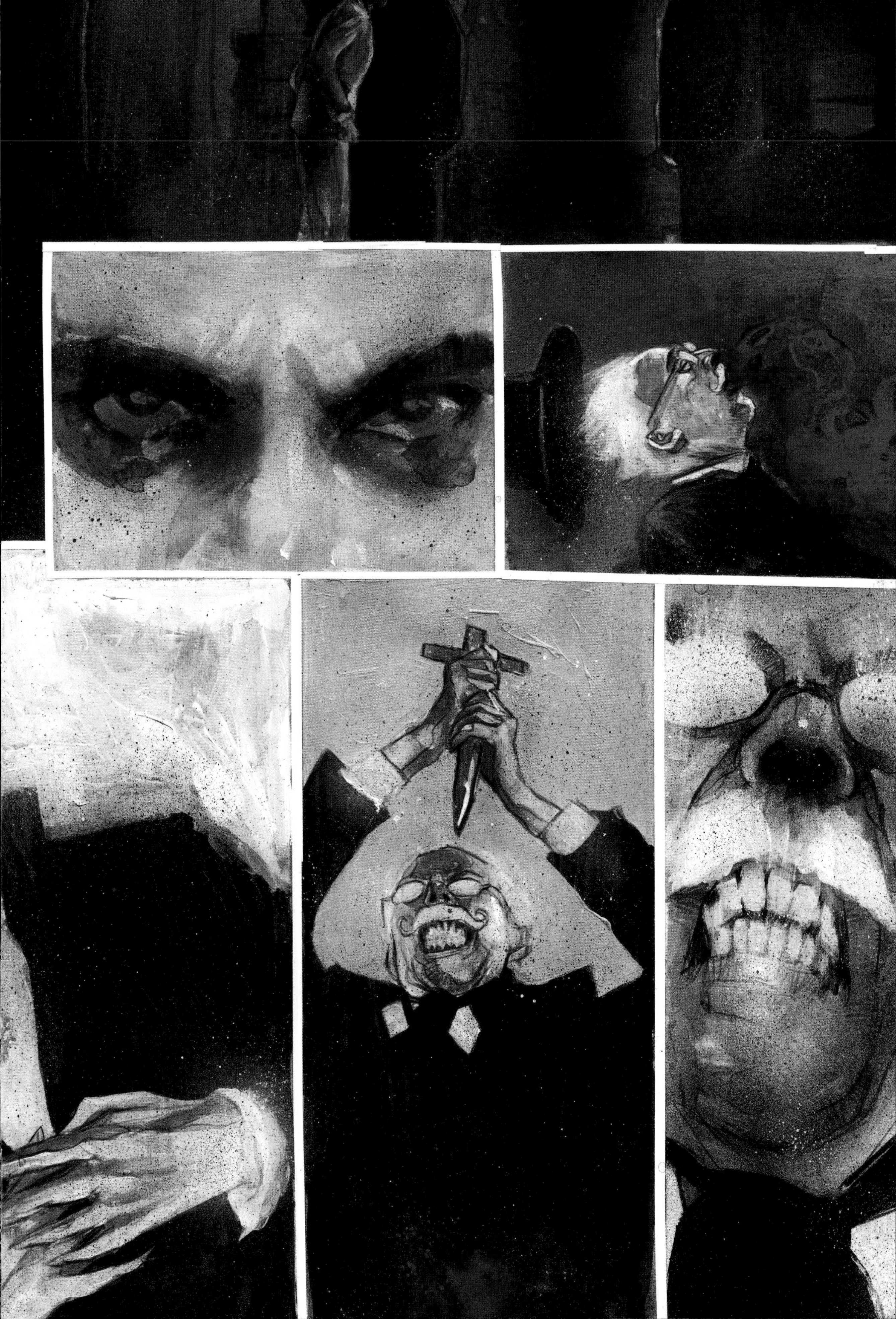

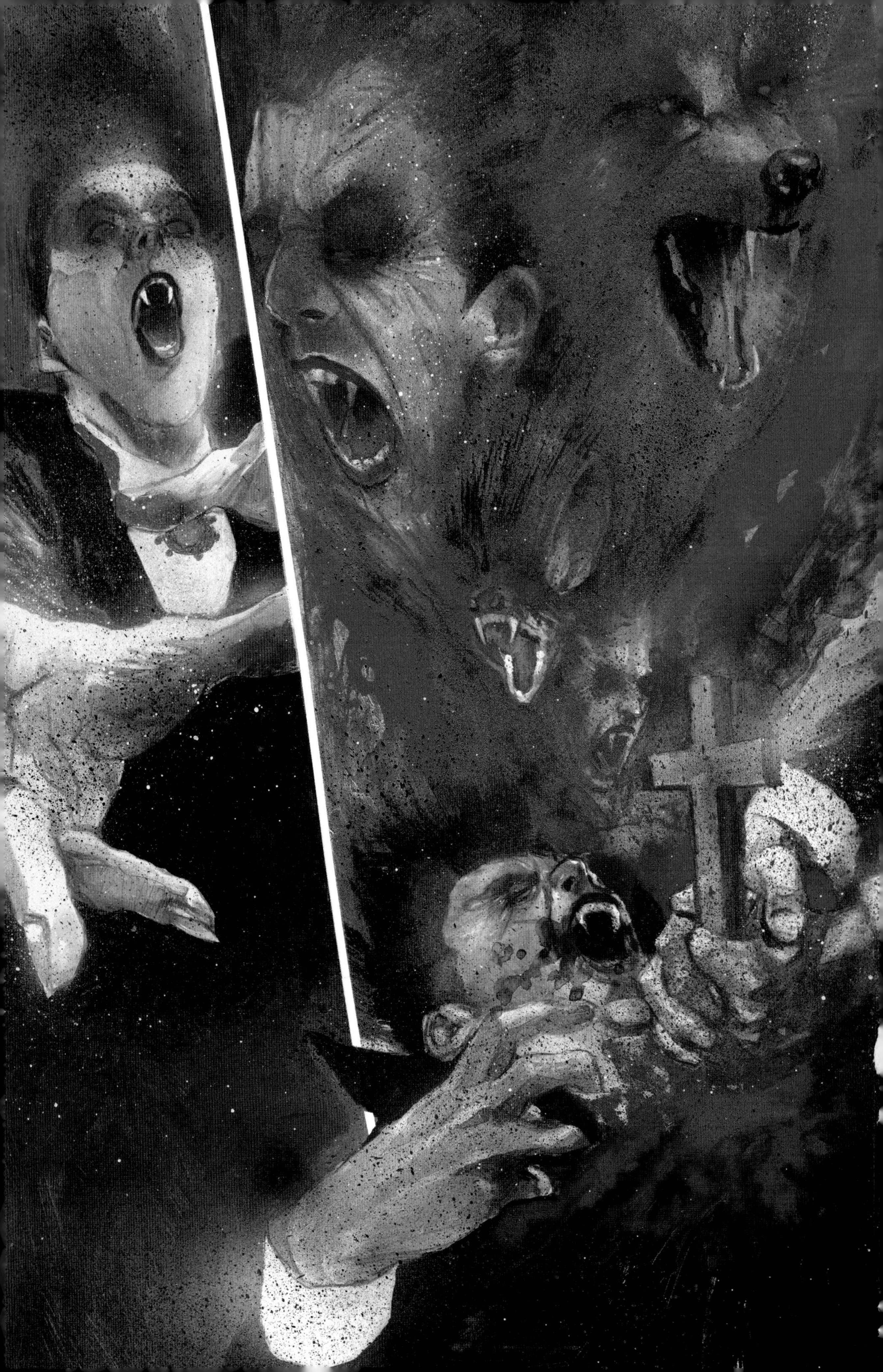

YOU LIVE IN THE WORLD, AND YOU *BELIEVE* THAT? YOU DON'T BELIEVE THAT OTHER LITTLE MEN LIKE ME WON'T LOOK TO BUILD THEMSELVES UP ON GREAT POWER? THAT THEY WON'T GO SEARCHING FOR IT?

DRACULA ISN'T A MAN. DRACULA IS IMMORTAL. *FOREVER.* WHAT HAPPENS IN THE CRYPT BELOW DOESN'T MATTER. HE WILL HAVE THE WORLD.

BUT YOU WILL HAVE YOUR DAUGHTER, I HOPE.

WE THOUGHT HE'D KILLED YOU, DEAR...

AND I WILL HAVE...

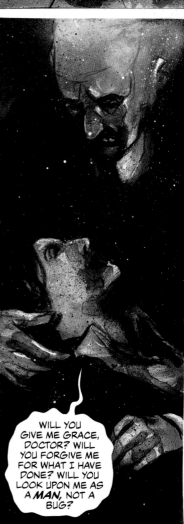

WILL YOU GIVE ME GRACE, DOCTOR? WILL YOU FORGIVE ME FOR WHAT I HAVE DONE? WILL YOU LOOK UPON ME AS A *MAN*, NOT A BUG?

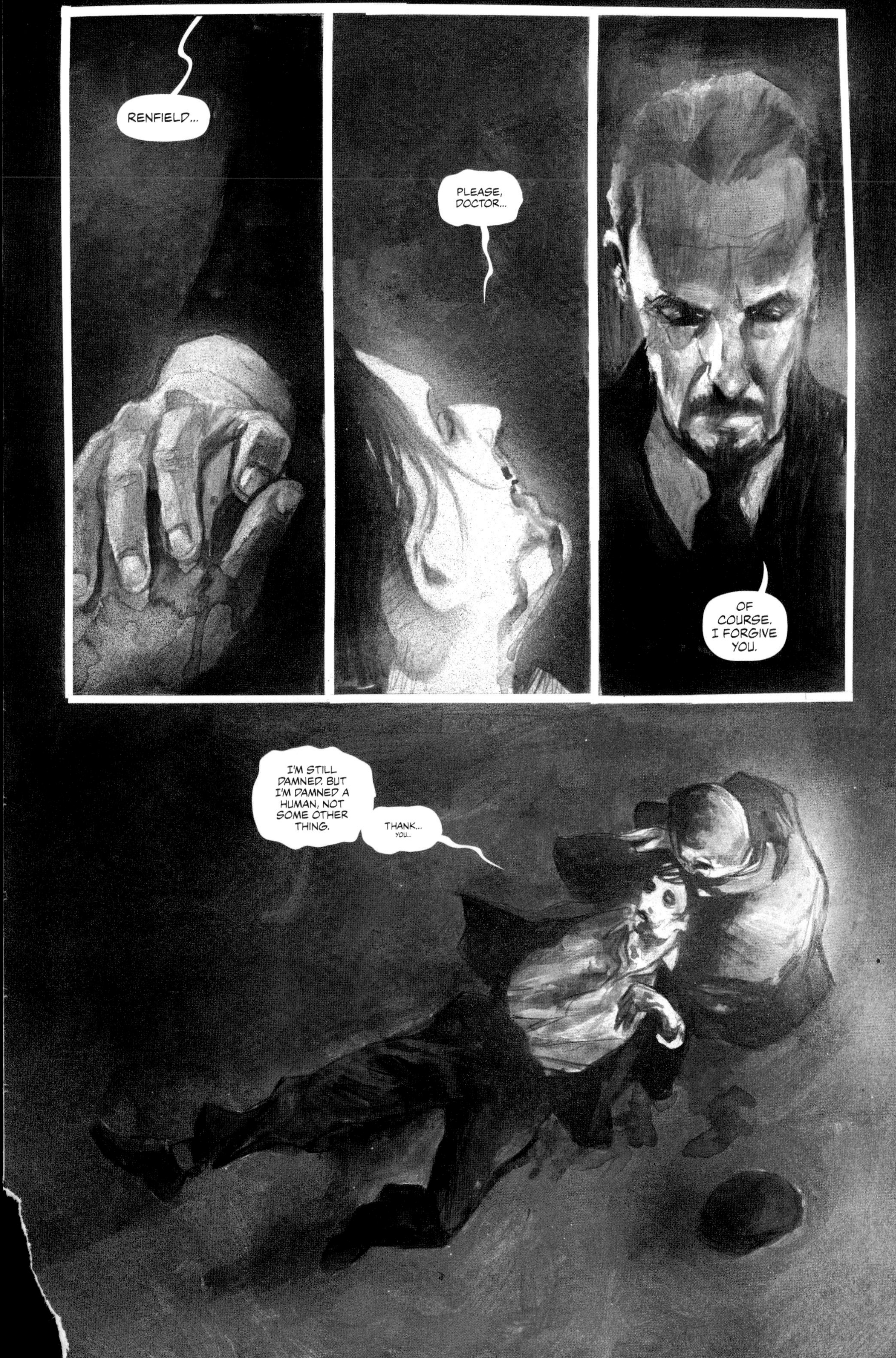
RENFIELD...
PLEASE, DOCTOR...
OF COURSE. I FORGIVE YOU.
I'M STILL DAMNED. BUT I'M DAMNED A HUMAN, NOT SOME OTHER THING.
THANK... YOU...

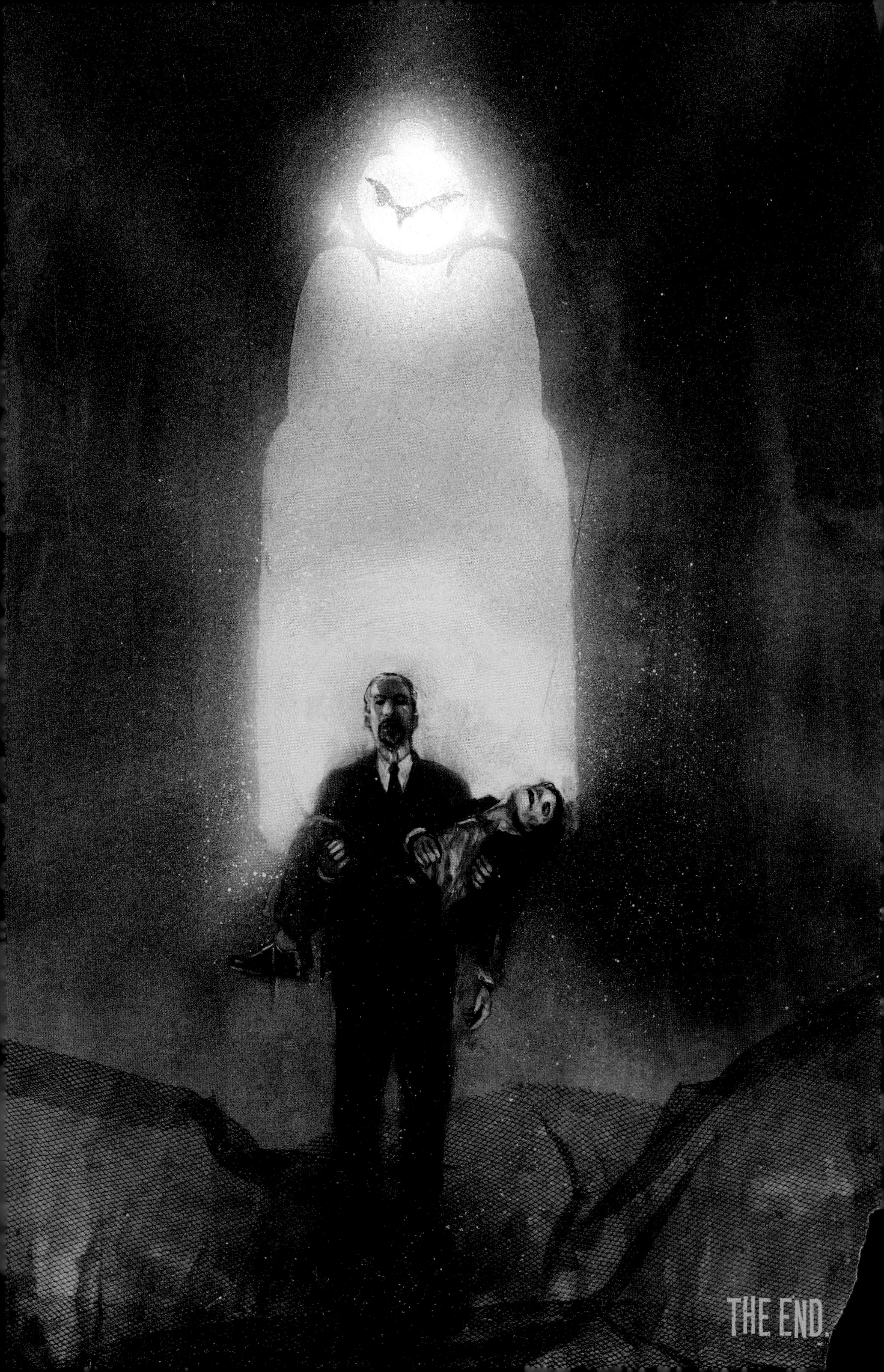
THE END.

ISSUE TWO MAIN COVER
MARTIN SIMMONDS

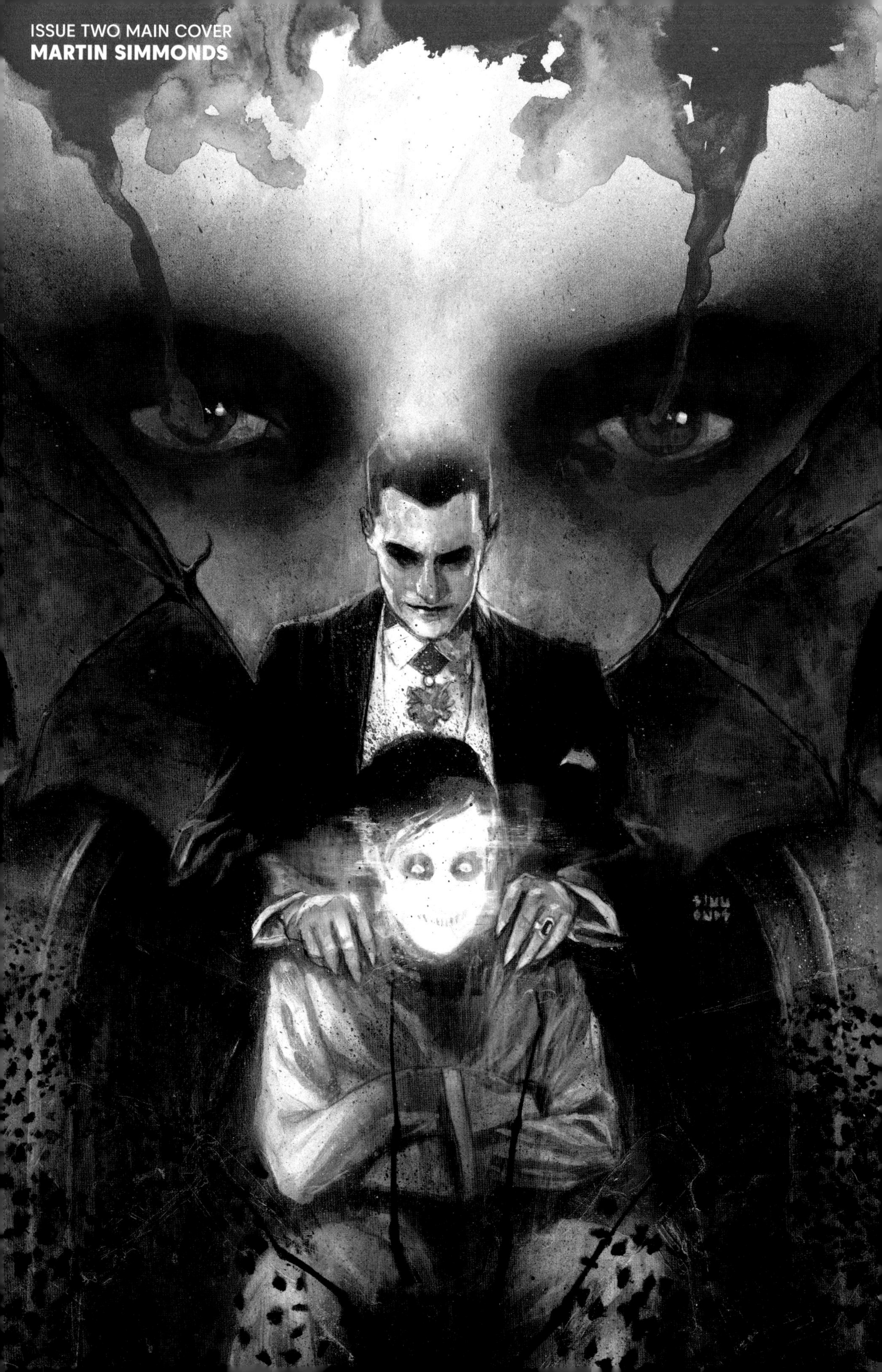

ISSUE THREE MAIN COVER
MARTIN SIMMONDS

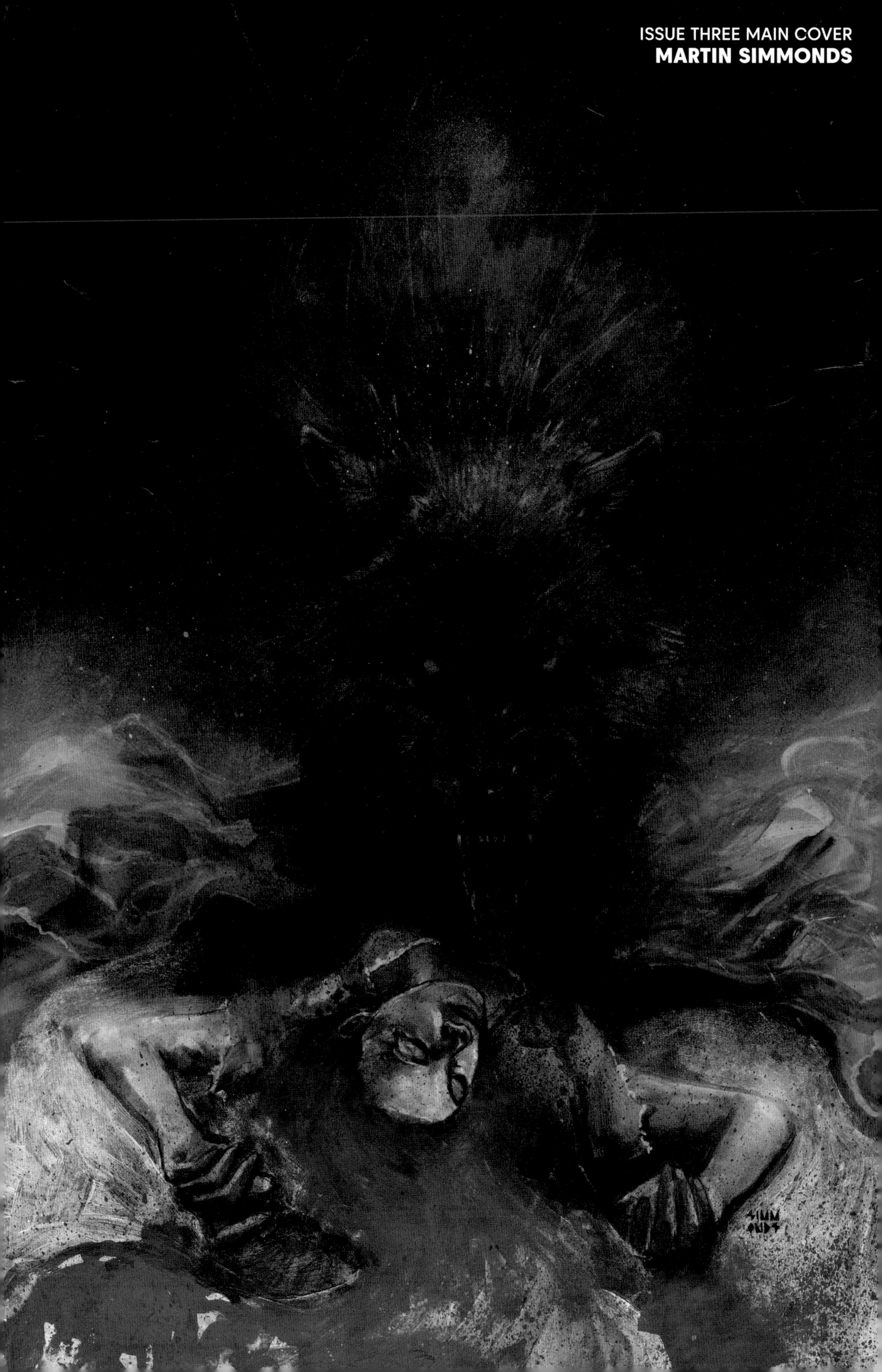

ISSUE FOUR MAIN COVER
MARTIN SIMMONDS

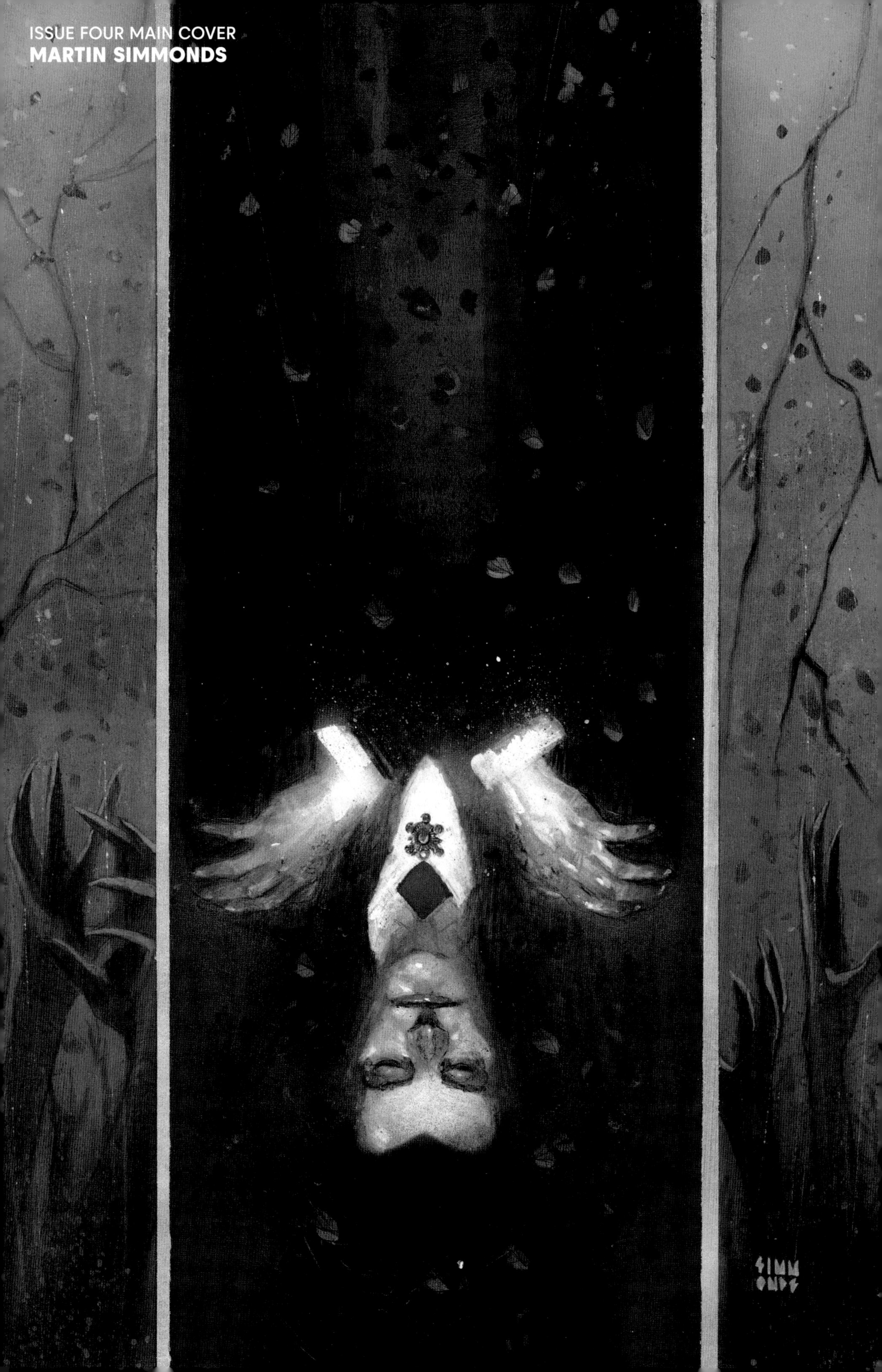
SIMMONDS

ISSUE ONE PROMOTIONAL BOOKPLATE
MARTIN SIMMONDS

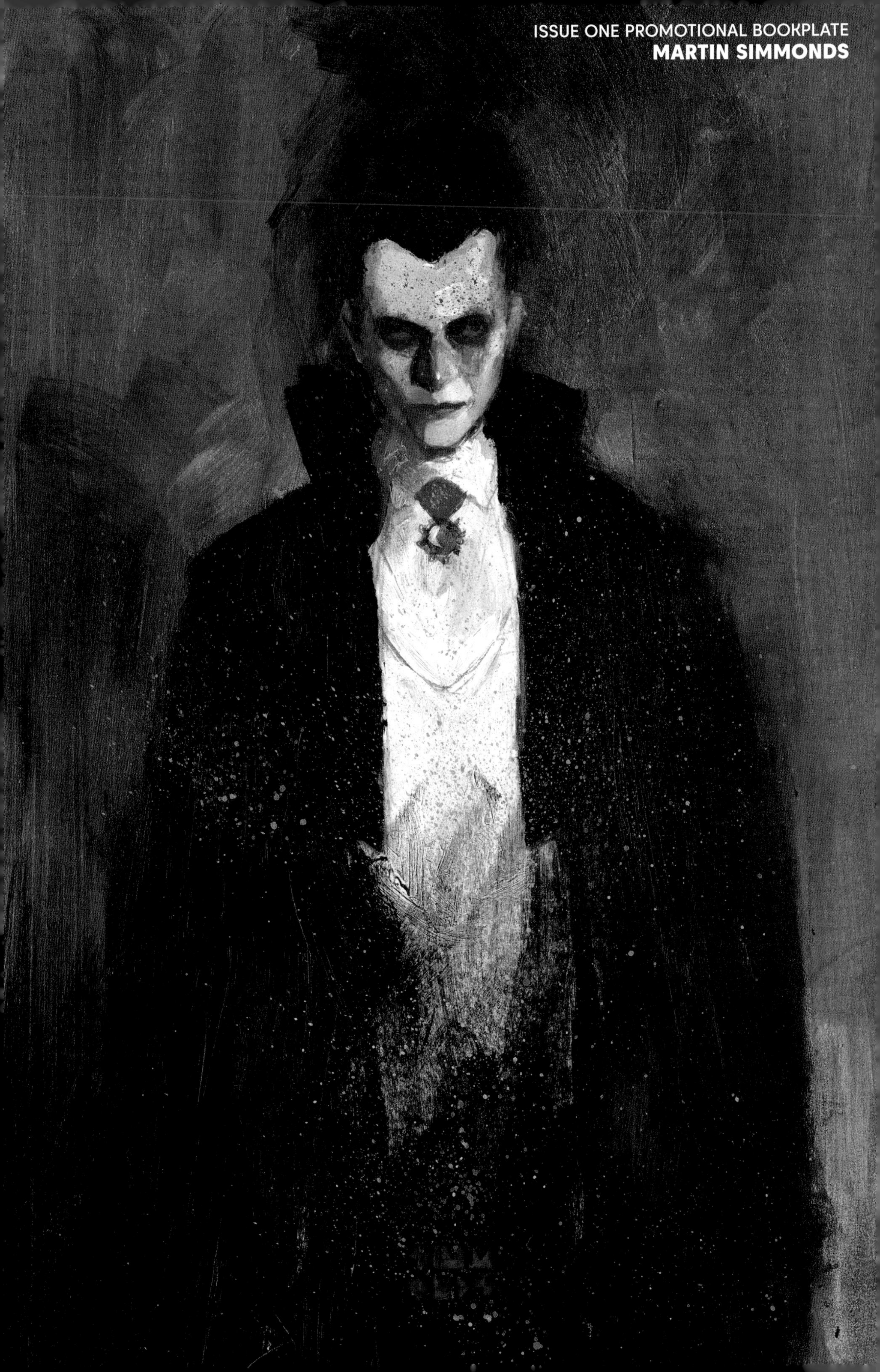

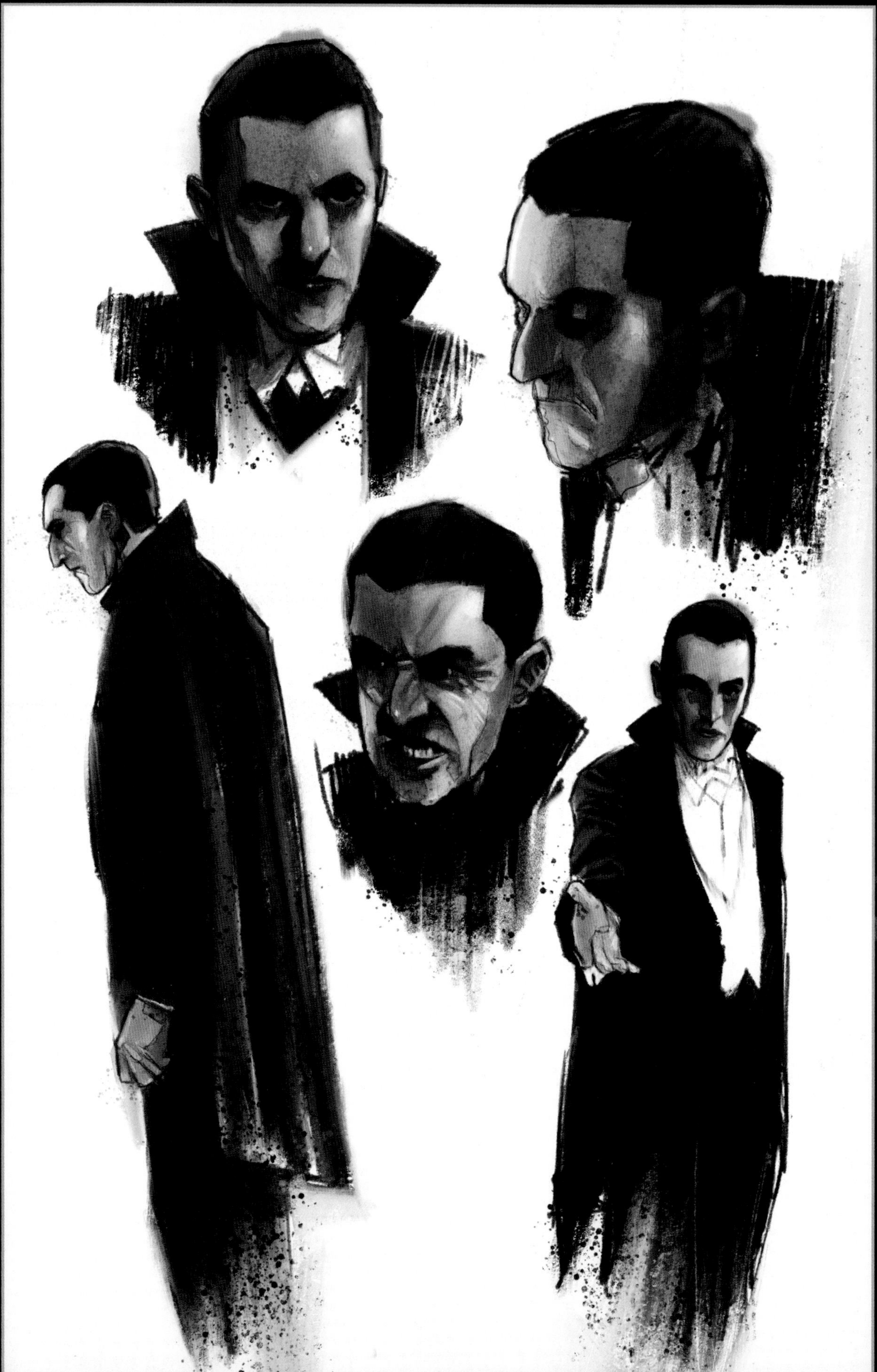

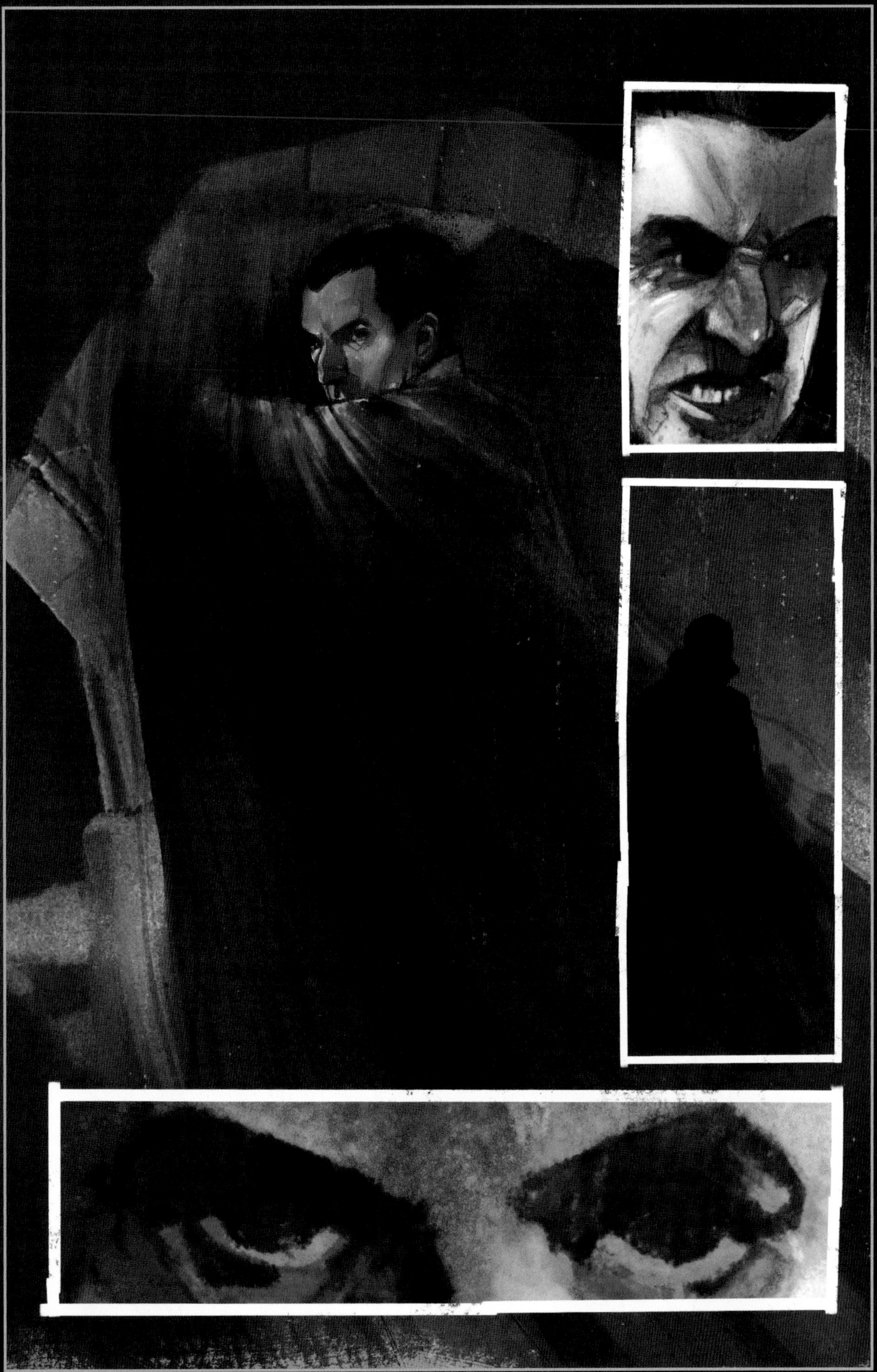

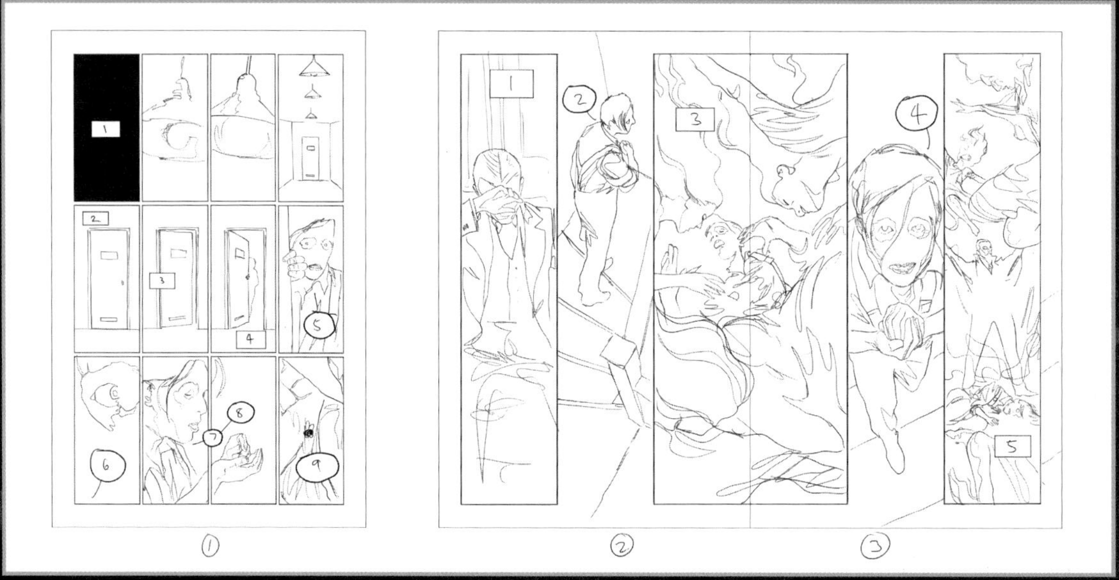

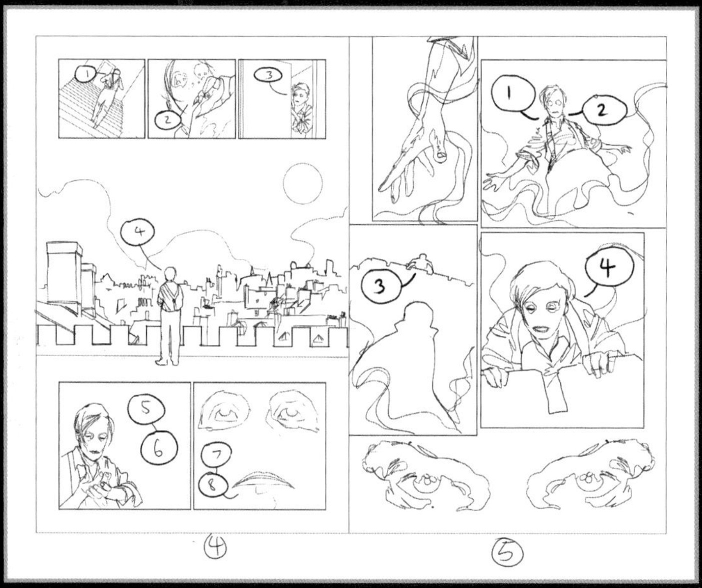

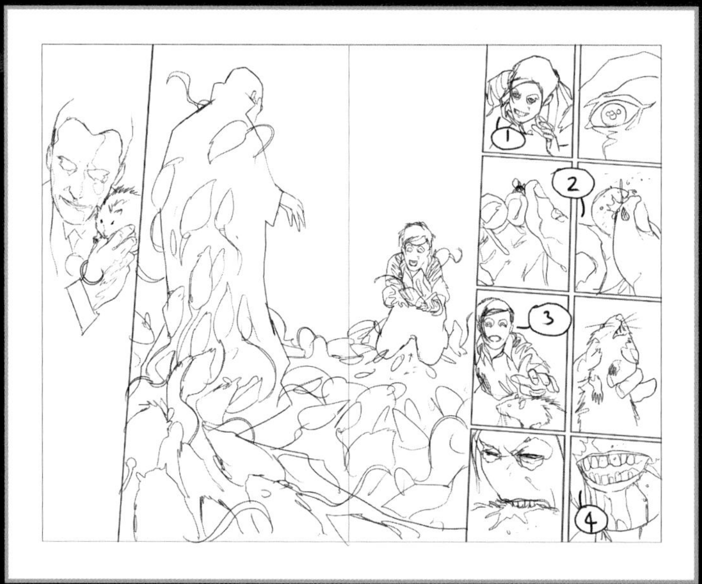

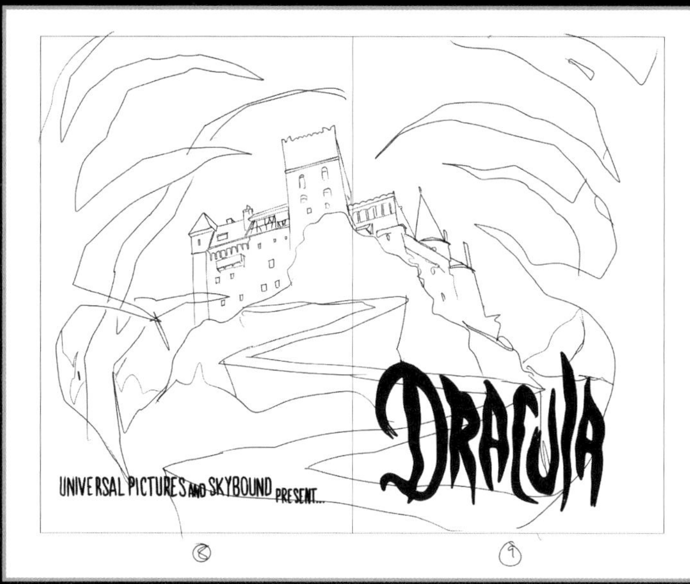
UNIVERSAL PICTURES AND SKYBOUND PRESENT...
DRACULA
8
9

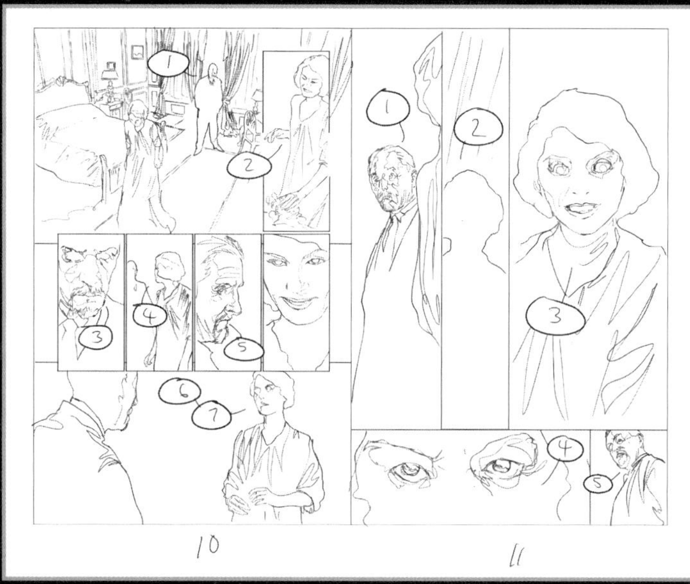
10
11

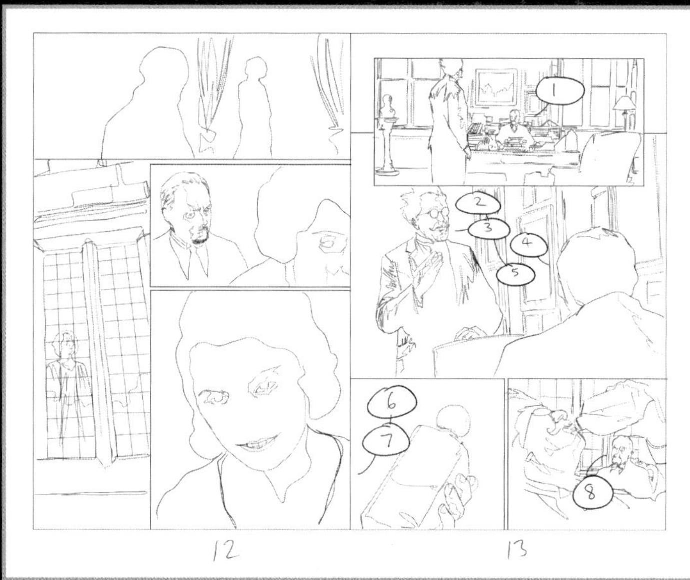
12
13

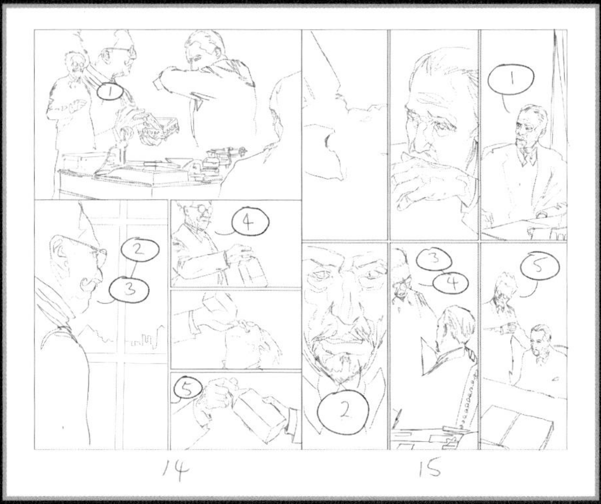
14
15

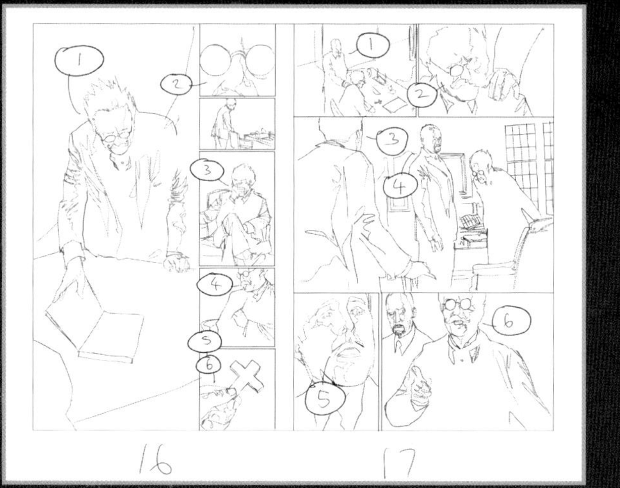
16
17

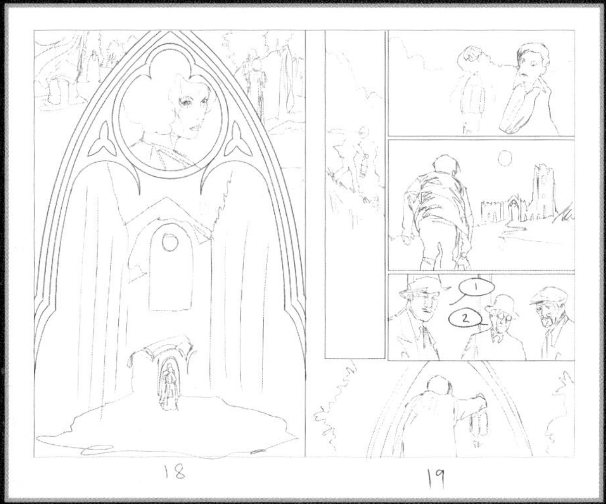
18
19

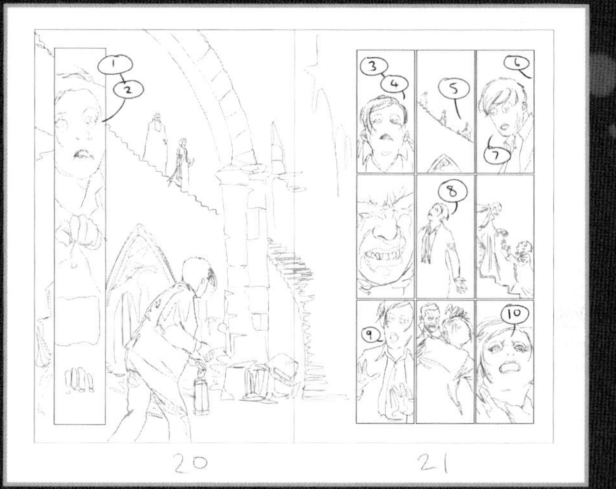
20
21

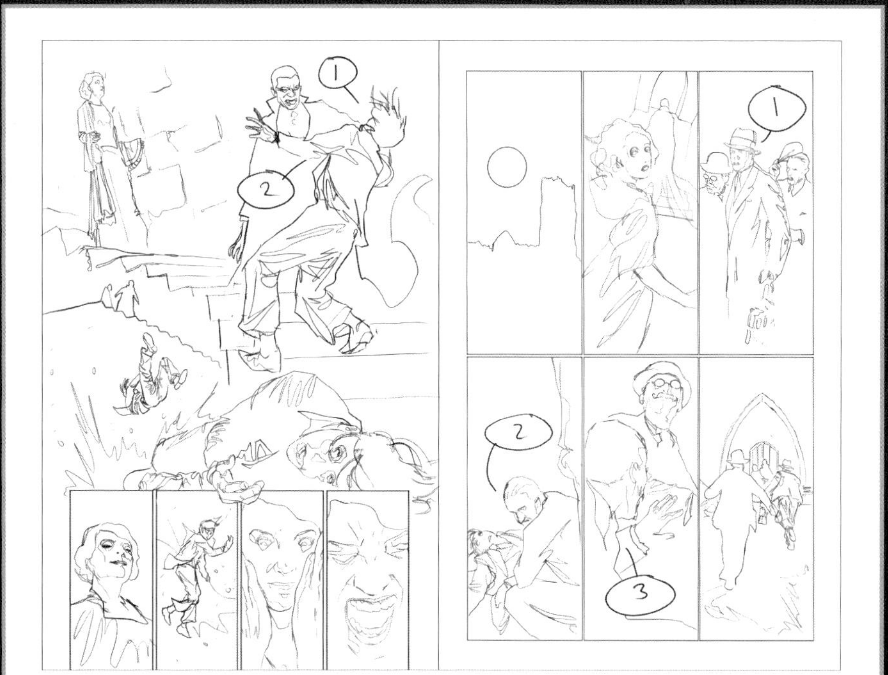
22
23

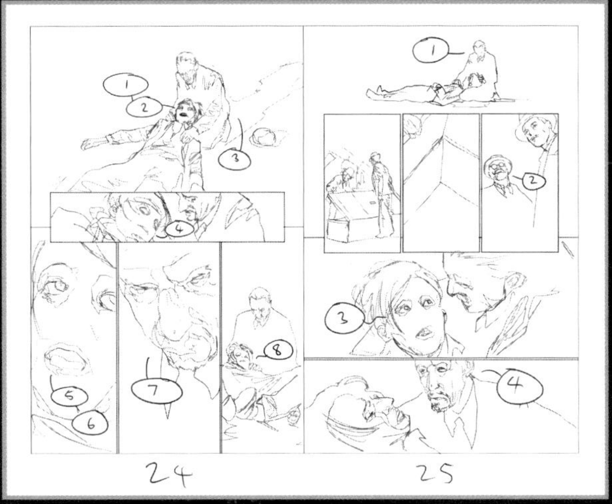
24
25

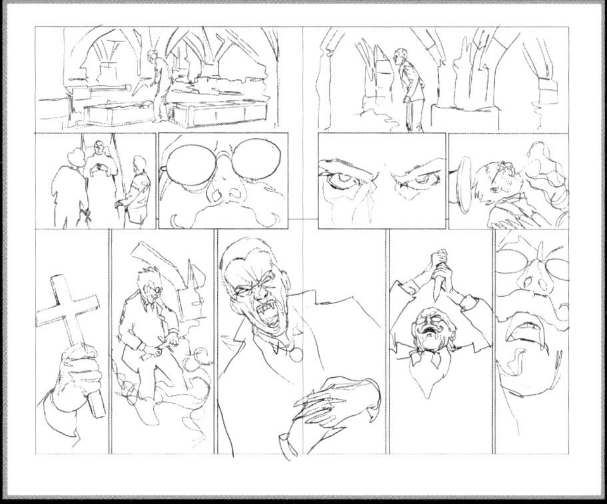

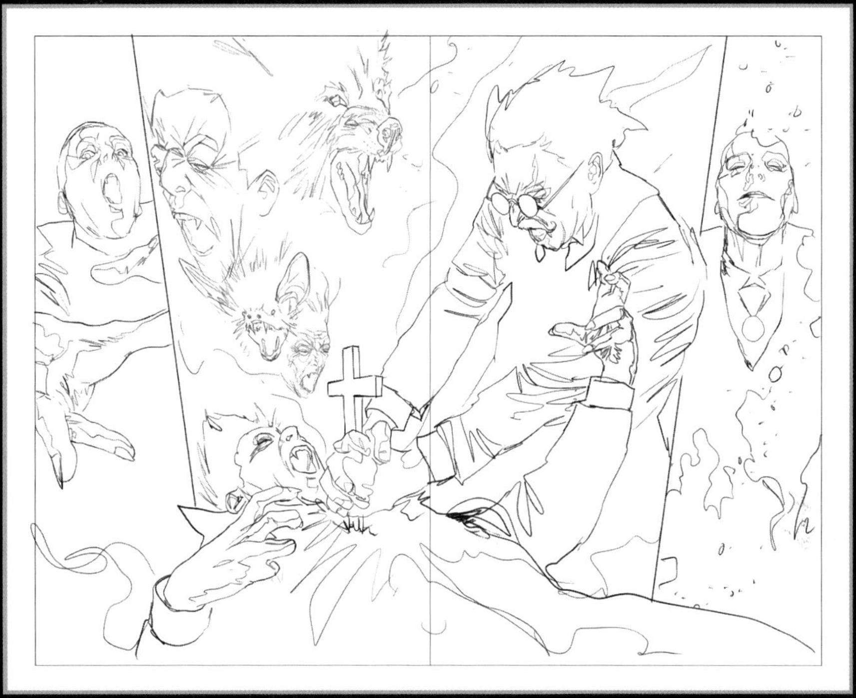

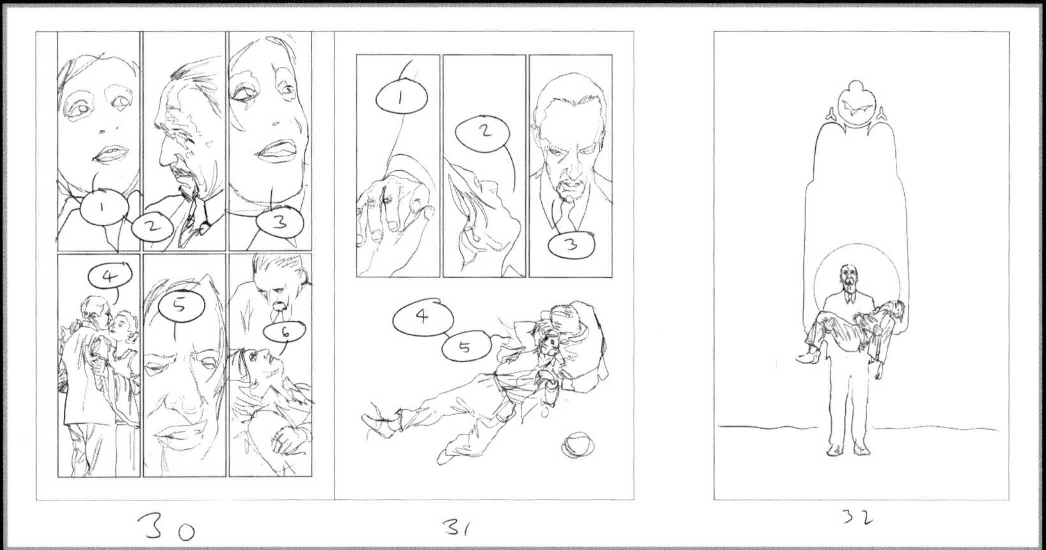
30
31
32

ABOUT THE AUTHORS

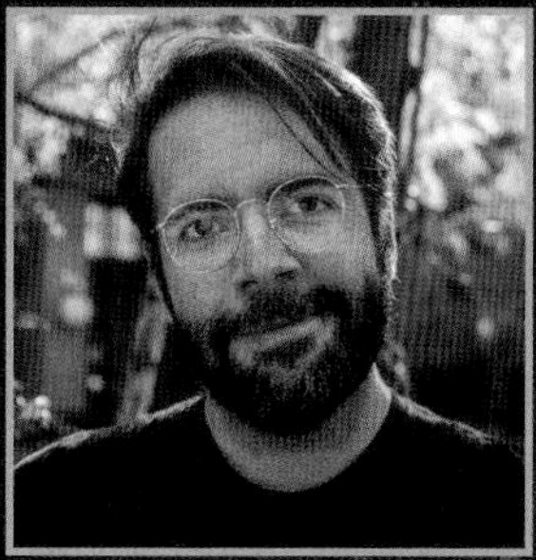

James Tynion IV is an Eisner Award winning, *New York Times* bestselling writer and publisher of comic books. He is best known for co-creating hit horror comics series like *Something is Killing the Children, The Nice House on the Lake,* and *The Department of Truth*. He is also the writer of Young Adult adventure series, including 2022 GLAAD Media Award nominated *Wynd*, and the 2017 GLAAD Media Award winner *The Woods*. He spent ten years writing various Batman titles at DC Comics, where he co-created exciting new characters like Punchline and Ghost-Maker. He lives and works in Brooklyn.

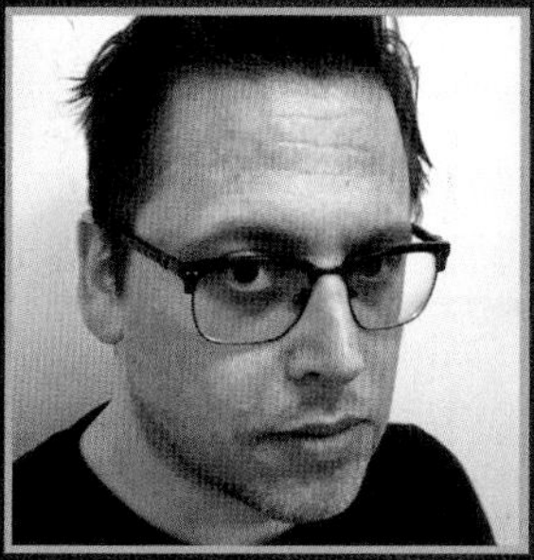

Martin Simmonds is a comic artist and co-creator of the Eisner nominated *The Department of Truth* (with James Tynion IV) for Image Comics, *Dying is Easy* (with Joe Hill) for IDW, *Punks Not Dead* (with David Barnett) for Black Crown/IDW, and *Friendo* (with Alex Paknadel) for Vault Comics. He is also one of six contributing artists on Image Comics' *Swan Songs*, an anthology series written by W Maxwell Prince. Martin is also a cover artist with his work appearing on titles from Marvel, DC, Image, Boom!, Vault, and IDW.

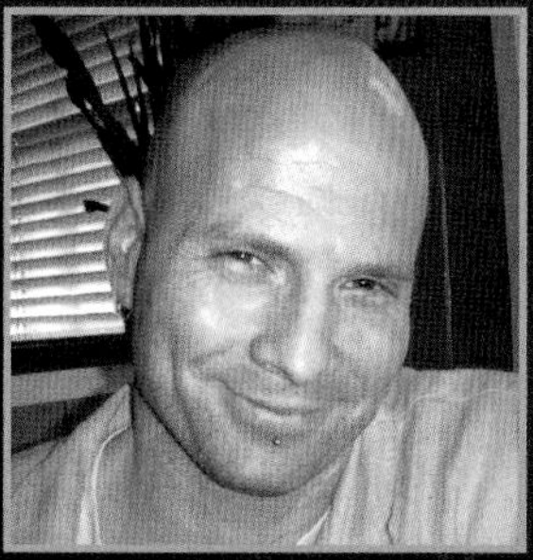

Rus Wooton is probably best known for his comic book lettering on books like *The Walking Dead, Invincible, Monstress, Deadly Class, East of West, Fantastic Four, X-Men,* and many more. Lettering full-time since 2003, drawing for as long as he can remember, and reading comics since before he could read, Rus is an artist, writer, designer, and filmmaker.